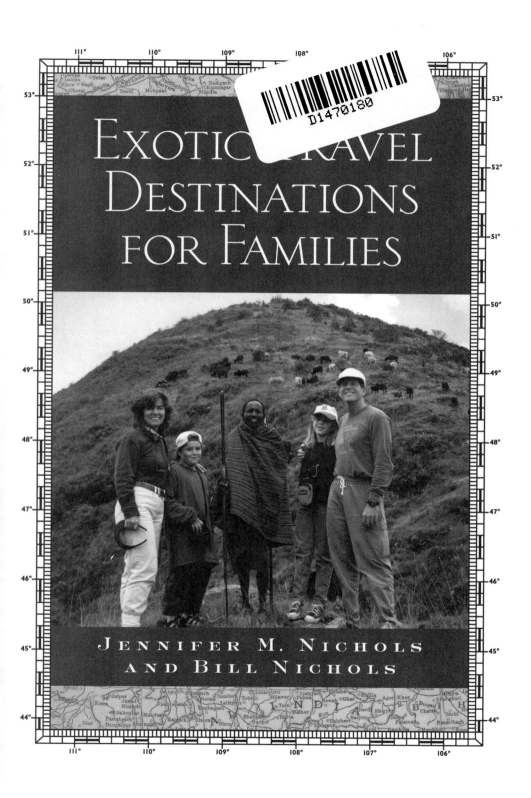

EXOTIC TRAVEL
DESTINATIONS
FOR FAMILIES

JENNIFER M. NICHOLS
AND BILL NICHOLS

Copyright ©2004 by Jennifer M. Nichols and Bill Nichols

All rights reserved. This book may not be reproduced in whole or in part or in any form or format without written permission of the publisher.

S A N T A
M O N I C A
P R E S S

Published by:
Santa Monica Press LLC
P.O. Box 1076
Santa Monica, CA 90406-1076
1-800-784-9553
www.santamonicapress.com
books@santamonicapress.com

Printed in the United States

Santa Monica Press books are available at special quantity discounts when purchased in bulk by corporations, organizations, or groups. Please call our Special Sales department at 1-800-784-9553.

This book is intended to provide general information. The publisher, author, distributor, and copyright owner are not engaged in rendering health, medical, legal, financial, or other professional advice or services, and are not liable or responsible to any person or group with respect to any loss, illness, or injury caused or alleged to be caused by the information found in this book.

Library of Congress Cataloging-in-Publication Data

Nichols, Jennifer M., 1949–2003
    Exotic travel destinations for families / by Jennifer M. Nichols and
Bill Nichols.
        p. cm.
        ISBN 1-891661-36-1
        1. Travel. 2. Children—Travel. 3. Family recreation. I. Nichols,
Bill, 1949- II. Title.
        G151.N48 2004
        910'.2'02—dc22

                                                             2003022830

Cover design by Ohmontherange Design

Interior design by Lynda "Cool Dog" Jakovich

Cover photo (left to right): Jennifer M. Nichols, Will Nichols, Maasai Tribesman, Alison Nichols, and Bill Nichols in Tanzania.

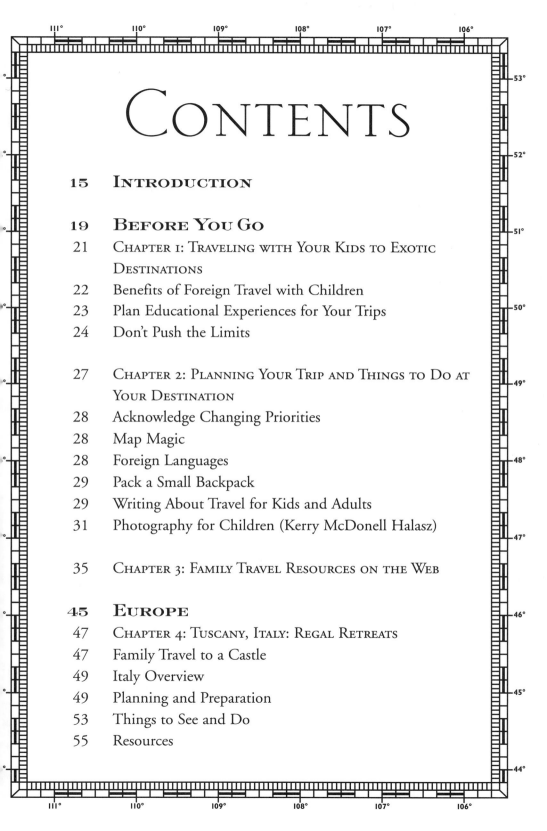

CONTENTS

DEDICATION

To our wonderful children and travel enthusiasts:
Alison and Will.

SPECIAL THANKS

To our friend and neighbor, Mary Fuller, for her thorough
and enthusiastic research on several exotic locations. Also to
our daughter, Alison McDonell Nichols, for similar fine efforts.

In Memory

Jennifer McDonell Nichols
1949–2003

This book was the inspiration of my co-author, traveling partner,
life partner, and wife. We traveled the world together.

The Nichols family at Erg Chebbi dunes, Morocco.

INTRODUCTION

MY WIFE JENNIFER was inspired to write this book. Well before we had children we lived abroad (Germany, England, and Panama) and we traveled whenever our jobs and bank account would permit. Bit by the travel bug, we couldn't stop. Fortunately, we later discovered that traveling with kids was even more fun than traveling without them. Our first trans-Atlantic flight with our daughter occurred when she was just six weeks old. (We were living in London at the time and of course we wanted to show off our first born to our relatives back in the U.S.)

Jennifer began chronicling our journeys. Eventually she was able to sell some travel articles to newspapers and magazines (an exotic trip each summer meant a fresh article to submit each autumn). However, in the autumn of 1999 we received devastating news: Jennifer was diagnosed with ALS, Lou Gehrig's disease. The disease is usually fatal. Jennifer decided that the best way to complement the excellent medical care she was receiving was to continue to live a normal life. So our travels continued, and so did Jennifer's writing. She set a goal to write this travel book, as this seemed to Jennifer an extension of normal living.

In February 2003, Jennifer and I and our two children traveled to the Alps for a ski vacation. The kids and I skied, and Jennifer—unable to safely ski by this time—worked on her book in a beautiful chalet overlooking the slopes. While there she contracted pneumonia, a common problem for those with ALS. Despite the help of doctors at a fine hospital near Zurich, she was unable to clear the pneumonia, and Jennifer died peacefully in her sleep.

Her book was about 70% complete. The remaining 30% became my goal. You are now holding the combined 100%.

We have written this book to help families enjoy their exotic travels together. The first two chapters will help you prepare for a family trip. We cover the benefits of foreign travel with children, we make suggestions about how to introduce educational experiences into your trips, and we include tips on what to do before departing. We also suggest how adults and kids can write about their trips and we give you guidance on aiding your child's photographic efforts.

Chapter three is a useful compendium of web-based travel sites to help families plan for most aspects of foreign travel, including the mundane (electricity), the unusual (eating bugs), and the unexpected (travel illnesses.)

The bulk of the book, chapters four through 27, offers travelogues of exotic destinations around the world. Supporting each travelogue is a section of travel information specific to that destination: a country overview, passport requirements, when to go, health and safety issues, and what to bring. We also suggest things to see and do for kids and adults, hotels and restaurants to consider, and we provide a list of resources for each location.

The final chapter provides suggestions for parents willing to let their teens travel abroad to study a language or perform community service. This chapter includes short reports by our two teenagers on their language and community service travels. Finally, we provide resources to use in selecting foreign travel programs for teens.

The heart of the book, the informative travelogues covering 24 exotic locations, was written by Jennifer, her sister Cindy McDonell Mitchell, my sister, Mary Nichols Sandoval, and our close friend, Sonia Ehrlich Sachs. Jennifer's other sister, Kerry McDonell Halasz, contributed the section on photography for children. My other sister Ann Nichols Plante did not contribute to this book, but she assured me that she would read it.

We chose the contributors wisely: we knew them well and we knew that they were as passionate and as adventurous as we were about traveling abroad with kids. Conveniently, they had been to several fascinating places that we had not visited.

Jennifer—if she were still with us—and I hope this book will help make your next trip truly exotic.

Happy reading and happy traveling.

Bill Nichols
January 2004

Before You Go

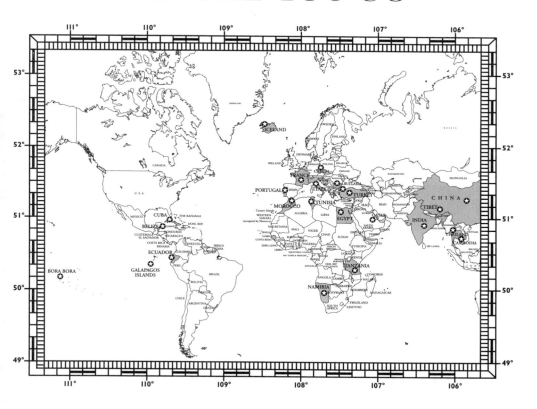

Alison, Jennifer, and Will Nichols take a break in Bangkok.

CHAPTER I

TRAVELING WITH YOUR KIDS TO EXOTIC DESTINATIONS

NO ONE CAN LABEL my two children picky eaters. After all, how many kids lick tart lemon ants off of trees in a steamy Ecuadorian rainforest? And try counting on one hand the number of young diners who lunch on sautéed bamboo worms in an exotic Bangkok restaurant. (Okay. So they didn't clean their plates . . . .)

Ah, the delectable joys of travel with the kids.

We've bumped along on camels in the Sahara, elephants in Thailand, and lawn chairs ferried on the back of a pick-up truck in Belize. We've hunkered down in an eco-tourist lodge in the Ecuadorian rainforest, luxuriated in an Italian castle, and cozied up in a dolphin reserve in Belize. We've posed with giant tortoises in the Galapagos, fed sharks in Bora Bora, and unwound snakes from our daughter's neck in Morocco. We've viewed the sole survivor of a tortoise species in the Galapagos, participated in an Islamic wedding feast in Morocco, and visited a Maasai school tucked in the hills of Tanzania. Our memories are laden with gracious people, magnificent sites, and startling customs.

Our travels with our children are not only graced with extraordinary experiences, but they have served to educate our family about culture, customs, languages, geography, architecture, history, current events, and traditional arts.

We are part of the ever-expanding segment of Americans who, each year, pocket their passports, gather their children, and head off to experience the world beyond their own backyards.

Benefits of Foreign Travel with Children

Mark Twain said, "Travel is fatal to prejudice, bigotry and narrow-mindedness." When kids travel the globe, they learn to appreciate and celebrate the many ways people all over the world conduct their lives. They observe the ways people dwell—some crammed together in mud huts, others surviving in camel hair tents in the desert, some subsisting on top of an open platform in the rainforest, and some living in mansions. They view various religions and the ways other people worship as they enter a Buddhist temple, a Moslem mosque, or watch a sacred tribal ceremony. They see extreme poverty, blatant wealth and observe the jobs people do to make a living. They realize that not everyone has a computer, a TV, a phone, electricity, or even running water. And they scrutinize the way other children live, some with no toys other than the ones they make themselves, and others working long hours for minimal wages in small stores and markets. These observations serve to make children value other cultures, lifestyles, and people. Mark Twain was right.

When viewing distinct cultures, children learn to celebrate global differences, increase their awareness of world issues, and achieve a new perspective on their own way of living. Additionally, taking your children to foreign destinations has a permanent impact on their interests, skills, and intellectual life.

For example, when my daughter Alison was five, we carted her off to Spain. While there we went to a flamenco dance and Alison drew all the elements she observed, to include the flowing dress, the dangly earrings, the pointy shoes, and even the hair combs. And she added a special element to her artwork: she insisted on labeling each item in Spanish. We queried the friendly waiters who were happy to help her. Throughout her younger travel years, she continued to draw elements that intrigued her and label her artwork in the language of the country.

This curiosity soon developed into a lifelong love for learning languages. Now 18, she is fluent in two languages and proficient in another.

Plan Educational Experiences for Your Trips

When better for our son, Will, to learn about Darwin's Theory of Evolution than in kindergarten? And where better place to learn than the Galapagos Islands—the remote, equatorial archipelago 600 miles off the coast of Ecuador. Aboard a 38-foot motorized sailboat with a crew of three, we weaved to six islands. Here animals remain just as Darwin reported in 1835, unafraid of their human interlopers. For the kids, tiptoeing over lazing sea lions, nosing up with blue-footed boobies, and peering into the eyes of giant land tortoises were the stuff of fairy tales. And evolution? By viewing species such as Darwin's finches—whose beak shapes vary from island to island depending on the vegetation—the concept was so simple, even a kindergartner could understand it.

When families travel to exotic destinations, there is great opportunity for educational adventures. Find out what's available by checking resources such as travel books, videos, *National Geographic*, the Internet, and a top-notch travel agent. Also, contact the place you are staying to find options. Inform your kids of your itinerary and the possibilities for activities and find out what interests them—animals, historical sites, traditional arts, natural wonders? Then involve your children in choosing the possibilities.

Once at your destination, you can also arrange educational intrigues. In the Galapagos, we asked our naturalist guide to point out the distinct differences in the finches and he willingly complied. Most hotels or lodges can arrange activities that range from short, simple offerings to all-day events. And don't be shy about asking individuals who work at the sites to provide additional information.

Educational experiences can also be spontaneous. While camping in the Sahara, we awakened at the crack of dawn to follow the tracks of scarab beetles across the undulating dunes. This event is seared in our children's memory. Take time for the small pleasures.

Have your children keep a travel journal. Purchase one that has lines for writing and blank pages for drawing. One activity your kids might enjoy is finding an element of the country for each letter of the alphabet, such as in Tanzania . . . Maasai for "M" and Serengeti for "S."

DON'T PUSH THE LIMITS

Sometimes, it takes a *bonk!* on the head to knock sense into travel parents. It's a 12-hour time change between Boston and Bangkok. No problem. We piled into a cab the day we arrived, sat an hour in gridlock traffic, and then dragged our groggy kids to a restaurant. Alison hit her head on a plate glass window and Will, after ordering, fell off his chair in a sleep-deprived stupor. All survived, including the glass window. Two unhappy kids. Two guilty parents. Lesson learned? The restaurant can wait. Give in to jet lag—especially with kids.

The error of our ways also came through loud and clear in Morocco when Alison suddenly shrieked, "We would have been much better off in Disney World!" Three days of driving thrust her over the edge. Although Bill and I reveled in seeing the less explored parts of this mesmerizing country, the kids had had enough. So, we paused. Two unplanned days in a cool hotel to relax, swim, and eat pizza at the hotel restaurant provided respite.

Sometimes parents need to slow the pace and give in to the kids' needs and interests. Examine your itinerary. Too much driving? Too many historical sites? Not enough time to just "chill?" If possible, revamp your schedule to slow the pace and integrate activities that appeal to the kids.

Will, Bill, and Alison Nichols act like tourists in Bangkok.

CHAPTER 2

PLANNING YOUR TRIP
AND THINGS TO DO
AT YOUR DESTINATION

EACH YEAR, as we anticipate our family sojourns to the far reaches of the world, we are tempered by the realities and demands of global travel. And we are careful not to confuse an exotic destination with a quixotic one. Our planning is thoughtful and informed. Certain countries are blatant red flags for travelers and never make our list, while others may experience short-term problems that temporarily compromise safety.

When we choose our final destination, we consider several key issues. What does this destination offer families? When the kids were young, we always made sure that animals were a part of the itinerary—the Galapagos with its people-friendly animals, a safari in Tanzania, riding elephants in Thailand, and camel trekking in Morocco. Then came a priority on activity-filled vacations. Club Med in Bora Bora and hiking in Tikal, Guatemala filled the bill. In the teen years, the interests changed drastically—the kids wanted to view unusual cultures and customs. So we journeyed back to Morocco, one of our favorite places, and this time they didn't complain about driving through the more remote regions of the country.

Acknowledge Changing Priorities

"Know why Tanzania was my favorite place, Mom?" queried Alison. The answer was obvious, coming from my animal-crazy offspring . . . or so I thought. "Because there were other kids with us, and I could escape from you guys sometimes." Escape . . . not an accurate description in the middle of the Serengeti. But the attraction of being with peers whose families were on our tour had been a significant part of her trip.

As Alison and Will have changed, so too have their travel priorities. Seven years ago in Thailand, they clung to our Bermudas as they hid from adoring women reaching out to touch their blond hair. A few years later in Bora Bora, our Bermudas were so dorky, they often didn't want to be seen with us.

So now, we dabble in a modified democratic process as we make decisions about where we will go and what we will do. After making individual lists of dream destinations, we whittle the choices, then discuss the short list to see if each destination offers something for everyone. Although Bill and I make the final decision, the kids are satisfied that their interests have been acknowledged.

Map Magic

As we discuss our itinerary, we pull out a map of our destination and identify the bordering countries and nearby bodies of water. When the kids were younger, we pointed out the continent. We trace our route of travel, then bring out a map of our home state and compare a familiar route with the one we are taking so the kids can get an idea of the distances.

Foreign Languages

Before heading to Thailand, we yearned to acquire the niceties of the language. So while devouring hot, spicy noodles at our local Thai restaurant, we booked our waiter for four language lessons; two around the table and two at our town's library. While gleaning insight about our tutor's homeland, we garnered tips on cuisine, plus learned enough words to make our way gracefully in and out of a restaurant.

Have your children try the language of any country to which you plan to travel. Before you leave, purchase small phrase books and involve yourself and your children in simple phrases. At a minimum, require your family to be fluent in the basics of the host country's language: *hello, good-bye, please, thank you, you're welcome, excuse me* AND—*where is the bathroom?*

Children might also enjoy drawing pictures of aspects that excite them and labeling them with the language of the country.

PACK A SMALL BACKPACK

It is always advantageous for children to bring along small favorite items for entertainment. Our kids bring a small camera, walkmans and headphones, drawing materials to include eight colors of magic markers, a deck of cards, journals with spaces to write and draw, paperback books and Gameboys. Also, have your kids carry one of your business cards, with the name of your hotel on the back of the card, in case they should get lost. Pack as many cards as the places your staying.

WRITING ABOUT TRAVEL FOR KIDS AND ADULTS

During our trip to the Galapagos, my daughter and I kept a detailed journal, hoping some day to write a book about our experiences. The book never came to pass, but a travel article in a major newspaper did. Travel is the ideal writing topic for adults and children. Pack a blank notebook or a specially made travel journal.

Experiencing writer's block?
- Ponder the differences between your culture and the one you are visiting.
- Record observations of people to include the ways they are dressed.
- Write your opinions on the food.
- Pick a cultural event that includes local people and take notes on the purpose, the costumes, the location, and the people observing.
- Write advice to other families traveling to this country.

Make sure you have a lead, or beginning of the article, that pulls the reader in. A lead can be an unusual quote, a startling statistic or an intriguing event. The lead for my Morocco article occurred when a surprising event happened to my daughter in the market in Marrakech. While I was gazing away from Alison, an elderly man approached me and said, "Pardon me, Madame, that snake around your daughter's neck is not poisonous." I used this quote as my lead and then described this hilarious event.

Encourage your children to submit their travel article to their school newspaper if they have one. Another place to publish is your town newspaper. There are many magazines as well that publish only articles by children. Purchase the valuable resource *Market Guide for Young Writers* by Kathy Henderson. This book lists publications that accept children's writing as well as writing contests.

My son, Will, has been a travel journal-keeper from the time he could hold a pencil. His travel talents have turned into writing about his adventures, such as this poem about world culture, written when he was 13. He published it in his school's literary magazine:

Globe Trotting
The antique wooden stand holds the weight of the world.
Floating above, a sphere balances
Two iron rings encircle the sphere and provide its axis.
My hand caresses the smooth surface, encountering years of accumulated dust.

I reach out and gently spin the globe.
Before my eyes, a million cultures fly past
Each with its own customs, traditions, legends
Some enshrouded with mystery, others swallowed up by history,
All with distinctive diversity, each with distinctive splendor

I bring my ear close to the globe's lacquered surface
I hear a thousand different tongues being spoken

Countless dialects, accents, vocabularies, lingo
The language barrier is broken and a heavenly chorus is heard.
The blending of a million tongues is oratory genius.

As I observe the world's countries, I can taste different cuisines from
across the globe.
Spicy Mexican flavors scorch my tongue,
Rich Italian dishes hint delectable Mediterranean flavors,
And tangy Indian fare provides a colorful feast.
An international smorgasbord, with delicious variety.

With my fingertips, I cross the Atlantic
I proceed east and plod through the Sahara Desert
Moving north, I trace the Silk Road,
Detouring only long enough to climb the Himalayas
I continue to the Chinese coast and sail across the Pacific Ocean
I am tempted by the Hawaiian Islands, but I continue East to the
Americas
Completing my startling trip around the world.

And if *you* want to submit an article to a newspaper or magazine, consider writing about the joys and challenges of travel with children. I always keep a small notebook with me so I can jot down quotes or intriguing events. Then, at day's end, I fill in my notes on my laptop, and often will ask my family what they enjoyed most, just in case I missed something.

PHOTOGRAPHY FOR CHILDREN
by Kerry McDonell Halasz

Encourage your children to create their own travel memories by handing them a camera before you embark on your trip! Looking through the lens of a camera will allow your children to record adventures from their own personal viewpoint and will leave them with unforgettable images and feelings of accomplishment and involvement in the journey. You don't need to spend a lot of money or worry about fidgeting with dials and controls, either. A simple point and shoot camera, digital or film, can fit the bill for the younger crowd. Children are surprisingly adept at capturing unique photographs from different perspectives and angles and need only the simplest of equipment and advice to start shooting.

Provide your young adventurer with a reliable, easy-to-use camera that is small enough to carry in a pocket or backpack. A camera with a zoom lens is ideal for getting closer to the subject without compromising safety or personal space. If you've chosen a film camera, bring along enough film to shoot one to two rolls per day. Purchase a variety of films. Point and shoot cameras typically have smaller lens openings and therefore require faster films to deal with low light and movement. Encourage your child to experiment with higher number ISO films such as 800 or 1600 and to try black and white films. The variety will stimulate creativity and make for an interesting photo album. If the camera is digital, purchase a large capacity memory card and don't forget the battery charger and/or extra batteries! Digital cameras are wonderful for kids as they can immediately view the photos and easily manipulate the images on a computer. It's also great fun, if you have access to the Internet, to send personally created postcards to family and friends at home.

There are multiple ways to photograph a subject. Putting a camera in the hands of any child from toddler to teen will open up a whole world of photographic variety and style. Are you trekking across the Sahara on camels? Encourage your young artists to shoot from every angle and perspective. Snap away at the camel's face, close up. Shoot from behind! Shoot from below. Look for interesting shadows cast by the tall behemoths. Your child will wind up with a variety of photos unique to their own perspective. Make sure your kids include family members in some of the shots. Try something fun and different! Lie down on the ground (only when safe) and shoot up to include the background and the people. Look for reflections in puddles of water.

Take a close-up shot of the intricate detail of the sculpture. Get your kids out of the habit of trying to include everything in one frame.

Don't forget to help your young one capture some images of the local residents. Most people are happy to comply when asked to pose for a picture. It's important and proper to always ask and oftentimes this will stimulate an interesting conversation about that person's culture and home. In some countries, people might ask for a small amount of money. This is acceptable; often it is a cultural norm. Ask your guide or hotel concierge how much you should pay.

When you return home, have the film developed at a reliable photo-processing lab. Spending a few extra dollars on developing is well worth the outcome. Go through all of the images with your children and help them create a photomontage of the journey while the trip is still fresh in their minds. For both the film and digital images, resist the temptation to throw away or delete images that aren't "perfect." A little blur, a bit of a tilt in the frame and even a missing head or limb can often make a mundane photo sing with creativity and style. Arrange the photos in an acid-free album, create some memory-provoking captions, add a few small mementos, and your children will have a book of their travel adventures that will last a lifetime!

The Nichols family waits for sunrise on the dunes of Erg Chebbi, Morocco.

CHAPTER 3

FAMILY TRAVEL RESOURCES ON THE WEB

ACH MONTH, 20 million globetrotters—about one-third of all American Internet users—use travel websites to plan and purchase their trips. It is no surprise that travel is the top seller on the Internet. Essential family travel topics include currency exchange, hotel booking, immunizations, maps, medical recommendations, time zones, and weather. Once parents mark these imperatives off their list, the real fun begins. Sites featuring great travel books, festivals, foreign languages, historical and cultural lures, local recipes, and writing about travel are among the many that families can access. So log on and discover a wealth of information.

ACCOMMODATIONS—www.travelweb.com

Travelweb.com (www.travelweb.com) searches for hotels in over 200 countries. You can specify price range and select from a list of 35 hotel amenities, which include babysitting and child services, fitness centers, and TV with cable. Each hotel entry includes hotel information, photos, and an option to book it online. There's even a currency converter tab if you want to calculate the cost.

ATMs—www.mastercard.com/cardholderservices/atm

Traveling to the Galapagos Islands off the coast of Ecuador and need a little money? Master Card ATM Locator (www.mastercard.com/cardholderservices/atm) lists most countries, cities, and towns in the world and specifies the location of their ATMs. By the way, the Galapagos has two ATMs—and you might even spy some giant tortoises on the way to get your cash!

BOOKS—www.bookpassage.com/travel

Name any aspect of travel . . . restaurants, history, culture . . . and you'll find a travel book devoted to it. So how do you trim your choices and select the perfect books for the entire gang? A premier book site is Book Passage (www.Bookpassage.com/travel/), which reviews travel related books on most countries in the world. Browse a wide range of reads, to include general travel guides, intriguing cultural and historical selections, cookbooks, and children's books.

CLIMATE—www.weather.yahoo.com

Can't decide whether to pack bathing suits, sweaters, or parkas for your journey? To get the weather updates for every country and most cities in the world, Yahoo! Weather (www.weather.yahoo.com) is your best bet. Click on a continent, a country, and a city, and get weekly weather reports for your destination.

CURRENCY—www.oanda.com

Whether you're pocketing Ecuadorian *Sucres*, Indian *Rupees*, or Thai *Bahts*, your conversion complications are simplified on Oanda's Currency Converter (www.oanda.com). Displaying over 160 currencies, Oanda checks current rates, and even provides a wallet size reference to take with you.

CULTURE AND TRADITIONS—www.Cultureshockconsulting.com

Information on etiquette, religious practices, and social interactions of a country helps family members appreciate and become involved in the host country. The book series, *Culture Shock!: A Guide to Customs and Etiquette*, features over 50 countries and provides practical information and advice. The series also includes a cultural quiz at the end of each book testing your newly acquired knowledge. Published by Graphic Center Publishing Company, this series can be ordered online at the major booksellers or at the Culture Shock! Website (www.cultureshock consulting.com).

DESTINATIONS—
www.cia.gov/cia/publications/factbook/; www.towd.com

To find out valuable information about every country in the world, check out The World Factbook (www.cia.gov/cia/publications/factbook/). In addition to providing a map of each country, this all-inclusive site includes information on demographics, geography, government, economy, and transportation. Got your destination nailed down? Then go to Tourism Offices Worldwide Directory (www.towd.com) which gives the official tourist website for every country in the world.

EATING BUGS—www.amazon.com

Ever wondered what it's like to eat a tarantula? How about a marinated grasshopper? And what the heck do you call bug eating? Before you head off to insect-eating destinations (and there are many of them), purchase the book *Man Eating Bugs* by Peter Menzel and Faith D'Aluisio. These world travelers have dined on meal worm spaghetti, raw scorpions, and stir fried dragonflies. With startling photography, the authors document the history and practice of bug eating around the world. This intriguing book can be ordered online through Amazon.com (www.amazon.com) and other major booksellers. By the way, the formal name for bug eating is "entomophagy."

ELECTRICITY—www.voltagevalet.com

Can your teen not travel without her beloved hair dryer? And do you cart your laptop everywhere you go? If you are traveling out of the country, you will need a transformer and/or a plug converter. Electrical appliances used in North America operate on 110–120 volts AC (Alternating Current). Going outside of our borders, however, requires conversion appliances, as most of the world operates on 220–240 volts AC. Failure to convert the voltage severely damages or destroys your appliance. Voltage Valet (www.voltagevalet.com) provides information on transformers and converters, adaptor plugs, and surge protection for your laptop. There is also a chart listing most countries in the world with the configuration of plugs and outlets, voltage, and the type of modem adaptor required. You can order all products online through Voltage Valet.

Festivals—www.festivals.com

What better way to involve your family in the culture than by attending a local festival? Festivals.com (www.festivals.com) lists thousands of world events. Pack off to Puno, Peru, and delight in decorated llamas parading through town carrying firewood. Then hang around as the wood is set alight and dancers leap through the flames.

Food and Drink—http://www.cdc.gov/travel/foodwatr.htm

Sampling local food is part of the travel experience. But adhere to the most important and easily followed health rule: take care in what you eat and drink. The best advice for developing nations is "Cook it, boil it, peel it...or forget it." And if you're not certain if the water is safe, don't drink it. Hotel food is generally safe, as are busy restaurants that look clean and well run. The authoritative site for comprehensive information on global food issues and warnings is the Center for Disease Control site (http://www.cdc.gov/travel/foodwater.htm)

Foreign Languages—www.travlang.com

If you are unable to book a language lesson at your ethnic restaurant of choice in your home city, try an Internet resource. Travlang Foreign Languages (www.travlang.com) presents over 85 languages for reading and listening so that you can bone up on useful words and phrases before you head off. There's even a quick quiz to test your knowledge. With Travlang, you can have a word a day sent to your email in your language of choice. Travlang also offers language translators, audio language CD's, and Harry Potter . . . in 24 languages.

FOREIGN TRAVEL—www.travel.state.gov/yourtripabroad.html

The best way to insure a happy and healthy trip out of the country is to plan ahead. Traveling families should learn about travel basics, to include passports, visas, customs, immunization, and culture. Your Trip Abroad (www.travel.state.gov/yourtripabroad.html) presents accessible, important information on significant aspects of foreign travel. The site also provides links to other sources of travel information.

HEALTH ISSUES—www.cdc.gov/travel/index.htm

For official information on all travel health questions, go to the Center for Disease Control's comprehensive site, (www.cdc.gov/travel/index.htm). Specifics on traveling with children, safe food and water, outbreaks, vaccinations, and special needs travelers are available for every country in the world.

HISTORICAL INFORMATION—
http://fp.thesalmons.org/lynn/world.heritage.html

The UNESCO World Heritage List (http://fp.thesalmons.org/lynn/world.heritage.html) features over 690 different sites around the world selected by the World Heritage Committee. Some might be immediately recognizable, such as the Great Wall of China, the Galapagos Islands, and ancient Thebes in Egypt. But other worthy sites might remain obscure, and unvisited, if not for this informative resource. Each site leads to related links covering historical and cultural information, along with personal travel narratives, and even multimedia experiences. Click on the Moroccan city of Marrakech, for example, to listen to traditional Moroccan music, view slide shows of the city, and even learn a bit of Arabic.

Immunizations—www.cdc.gov/travel/vaccinat.htm

The most reliable authority on country specific vaccinations for children and adults is the Center for Diseases Control's website, Travelers' Health (www.cdc.gov/travel/vaccinat.htm). This site provides information on required and suggested vaccines for all countries and gives an overall immunization schedule for children.

Jet Lag—www.doctor-travel.com/jetlag.html

Jet lag occurs when you travel by air across more than three time zones. Fatigue, insomnia, lack of concentration, loss of appetite, and disorientation are common effects. It may take children longer than adults to adjust, but there are ways of minimizing the impact.

On the plane, set your watch to your destination's time. When flying during your destination's bedtime, sleep. If it's daytime at your locale? Stay awake. Don't think what time it is back home, and also avoid taking a nap once you arrive; it impedes adjustment to your new time zone. If you feel you have to, make it brief.

And if you are an active person exercise. A German study concluded that sedentary travelers experienced more jet lag than those who remained active. Physical activity, on the plane and once you arrive, circulates the blood and helps you feel re-energized. Some think that dehydration causes jet lag, so drink two glasses of water before boarding the plane and at least four cups in flight.

For advice on how to handle jet lag, log on to Doctor Travel. (www.doctor-travel.com/jetlag.html).

Over-the-Counter Kits—
www.drwisetravel.com/firstaid.html

"Remember when you took enough Pepto-Bismol to supply the entire city of Quito?" my husband persistently taunts, harkening back to our trip to Ecuador. I have now refined my first aid kit, and take only enough Pepto Bismol for the family (and a few extras, just in case). My recent addition is lice shampoo, following an outbreak in my daughter's hair in Morocco. Unbeknownst to us, the itchy critters had hijacked her locks at a Vermont camp and hitched a free ride to Marrakech.

Although tailored to your family's needs, recommended first aid kits include many of the medications and supplies families use regularly and stock in their medicine cabinets. Don't forget to pack Tylenol or aspirin, Band-Aids, tweezers, tape and gauze, antiseptic cream and most importantly, any prescription drugs the family is taking. Among the sites containing recommendations for over-the-counter kits is The Travel Clinic (www.drwisetravel.com/firstaid.html).

PASSPORTS AND VISAS—
www.travel.state.gov/download_applications.html;
www.travel.state.gov/links

If you don't own a passport, there are multiple ways to get one. Aside from official passport agencies located in 13 major U.S. cities, most county or municipal offices and post offices can provide the DS-11 application form. You can also download your own form at (www.travel.state.gov/download_applications.html). A 25-business day turnaround is standard. However, unplanned and emergency travel, with proof of departure within the next 10 days, can speed the process overnight. Don't forget two colored or black and white 2"x 2" photos, taken within the last six months. The best place to get a photo taken is at a professional photo shop that knows the requirements for size and type of paper. Passport fees are $40.00 for children under 16 and $60.00 for those over 16.

Children under 14 must obtain a passport, and must submit proof of U.S. citizenship in the form of a birth certificate, Unless requested, children under 14 need not appear, however children 14–17 must appear.

The official government website contains an easy-to-use locator to find the nearest passport office to your home town.

European countries do not require visas from Americans, however many other countries do. It is advisable to determine before you leave if your destination requires visas. Internet links to United States Embassies and Consulates Worldwide (www.travel.state.gov/links.htm) provide this information. Visas can be obtained through Embassies or consulates of the country you are planning to visit. For additional information on visas, call the Visa Services' Public Inquiries Branch at 202-663-1225.

SAFETY ABROAD—

www.state.gov/www/regions_missions.html

Following common sense rules of safety in developing countries is not dissimilar from what you would adhere to in America. Don't leave luggage unattended in public areas . . . don't accept packages from strangers . . . avoid being a target with flashy clothing and expensive jewelry . . . and don't carry large amounts of money or extra credit cards. If you get into trouble, contact the U.S. State Department (www.state.gov/www/regions_missions.html) to locate the American embassy. Consular Information Sheets and Travel Warnings can be obtained 24 hours a day by calling (202) 647-5225 from a touch-tone phone.

TRAVEL ILLNESSES—

www.my.webmd.com/content/dmk/dmk_article_40084;
www.istm.org; www.cdc.gov/travel/index.htm

When traveling to a foreign country, families need to know what health precautions to take. Log on to WebMD Health (www.my.webmd.com/content/dmk/dmk_article_40084). This informative site includes information on motion sickness, traveler's diarrhea, and altitude sickness, among others. There is also a valuable chart that lists diseases such as malaria, yellow fever, and cholera and tells how they are transmitted, what countries harbor them, the common symptoms, prevention, and treatment. The site also gives recommendations for travelers with special health problems such as diabetes, heart and lung problems, and pregnancy.

The International Society of Travel Medicine (www.istm.org) provides information on travel clinics in over 40 countries. Most are in major cities and all speak English. So before you head off, check this site for a nearby clinic, just in case.

For official information on all travel health questions, go to the Center for Disease Control's comprehensive site, (www.cdc.gov/travel/index.htm). Specifics on traveling with children, safe food and water, outbreaks, vaccinations, and special needs travelers are available for every country in the world. And if you think you might require a doctor during your travels, sign up before you go for the free services of The International Association for Medical Assistance to Travelers (IAMAT) (www.iamat.org/). This non-profit group can connect travelers with English speaking, western-trained doctors in over 300 cities.

U.S. Embassies and Consulates—www.travel.state.gov/links

Links to United States Embassies and Consulates Worldwide (www.travel.state.gov/links) is an all-inclusive site that lists every American Embassy and Consulate in the world. Most pages contain comprehensive information regarding services offered to American travelers, to include passport replacement, help in getting funds, and emergency situations.

World Clock—www.timeanddate.com/worldclock

Need to know what time it is in your destination—let's say Sofia, Bulgaria? World Clock (www.timeanddate.com/worldclock) shows what time it is in your city of choice. It also lets you know what time the sun rises and sets, provides the international dialing code, and as an extra bonus, lists travel books on the destination.

WRITING ABOUT TRAVEL—
www.absolute-sway.com/winthrop/advice.html;
www.writersdigest.com/guidelines/index.html

For children who want to try their hand at writing and submitting a travel article or related piece, author Elizabeth Winthrop (www.absolute-sway.com/winthrop/advice.html) offers writing advice and links to markets that accept young writers' works.

WritersDigest.com (www.writersdigest.com/guidelines/index.htm) is a leading source for adult travel magazine markets.

YOU'VE GOT MAIL—www.cybercafes.com

"Aw, mom, can't I just check my email?" Not in the middle of the Sahara, dear! But venture into most any city and log on at the friendly cybercafe to reconnect with the world. Cybercafes.com (www.cybercafes.com) lists 4,208 Internet cafes in 140 countries. In Caye Caulker, Belize, you can sip your espresso and have your hair braided while you surf the web at the Netto's Cybercafe.

Europe

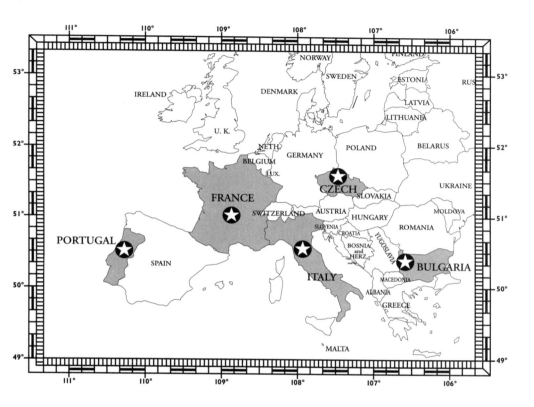

Kerry Halasz, Jennifer Nichols, and Cindy Mitchell above
Castello di Pergolato, near Florence.

CHAPTER 4

TUSCANY, ITALY: REGAL RETREATS

FAMILY TRAVEL TO A CASTLE

Luxuriating in a castle fulfills dreams . . . dreams conjured up as children while reading those unforgettable tales about Sleeping Beauty, Cinderella, and Beauty and the Beast. Now, those childhood dreams can come true. Castles around the world are available for family rental, and you don't need access to the royal treasury to claim your occupation. Castle prices are affordable, especially if you gather your extended family and split the cost. And unlike the castle life that Cinderella and her cohorts experienced—freezing in winter, shivering in cold baths and using a toilet cut in stone—castle life in our times has been upgraded to the highest standard, while keeping in tact the history and charm of these royal properties.

Given the availability of these regal retreats, a castle that fits your family's needs—from toddlers to teens—can also address your clan's interests and budget priorities. After all, your wish is your castle's command.

For one idyllic week, my two sisters and I united our husbands and teens in *Castello di Pergolato*, a medieval castle straddling a verdant hill eight miles south of Florence. *Pergolato*, built by an influential Florentine family in the year 1000, is now owned and has been refurbished by one of the few remaining Italian counts. *Pergolato* was purchased in the 1970s by Count Cesare Poccianti, who lavished it with a spectacular collection of furniture, artwork, antiques, and family memorabilia. Our castle layout included a great hall, two living rooms, a formal dining room, two elegant master bedrooms, six double suites, and six single rooms, many with en suite bathrooms. A swimming pool completed the castle design.

Split among our three families, the cost of this Tuscan jewel equaled what we would have spent for a week at a family resort . . . but we got more for our money. Never has our resort invoice included a personal staff of two gourmet cooks, two housekeepers, and an administrator who honored requests ranging from booking restaurants to organizing private museum tours.

These royal properties, increasingly available worldwide for private rental, combine the best of resort offerings with the unique benefits of castle life: total privacy, unlimited space, and complete freedom of choice regarding what you do and when you do it. After all, when you rent a castle, you rule.

Castello di Pergolato was ideal for our five teens who were granted their very own wing of the castle with a spacious game room, a private loggia, and beautifully appointed individual bedrooms. Our kids delighted in choreographing a synchronized diving show in the pool, playing card games on the loggia, and luxuriating in their private bedrooms with startling views of the lush Tuscan countryside.

They explored every aspect of their regal surroundings. They descended into the dark depths of a dungeon that sent shivers down their spines as they gazed into the seemingly bottomless well, once a repository for medieval murder victims. They tried on a chain mail arm covering that once belonged to a medieval soldier found plastered inside the wall. And to travel into modern times, they danced to blaring music in their own game room.

While the kids occupied themselves with castle activities, the adults sipped wine on the castle loggia while watching the sun set on the distant hills; basked in sublime serenity *sans* the usual intrusions of TV, Internet, and cell phones; and even booked an acupuncturist for a relaxing family needling session around the swimming pool.

Venturing outside the castle walls, adults and kids experienced the culture and rhythm of the local area—yet another benefit to castle occupation. We explored the day-to-day life and history of the community surrounding the castle; strolled the lush Tuscan countryside admiring the views of our imposing home away from home; and even wandered to nearby villages to buy truffles and wine for inclusion in our evening dinners—a six course Tuscan feast prepared by our two superb, in-castle chefs.

Traveling outside our domain, we enjoyed day trips to Florence, Sienna, and Pisa. Here, our teens learned the history of these ancient wonders by climbing towers, exploring the old town squares, and visiting museums.

Castello di Pergolato gives castles a good name. In the confines of its elegant yet welcoming surroundings, our 11 clan members felt pampered, entertained, and even slightly regal.

So gather your family and secure your castle keys. Your rights to a royal vacation await.

ITALY OVERVIEW

- Italy: Slightly larger than Arizona
- Population: 57.7 million
- Capital: Rome (Population: 3 million)
- Ethnicity: Predominantly Italian
- Religious Affiliation: Predominantly Roman Catholic
- Language: Italian
- Currency: Euro
- Tuscany: One of Italy's 20 regions

PLANNING AND PREPARATION

Passports

Italy requires American citizens to have a valid passport.

When to Go

Tourists arrive in droves during the summer months, so expect crowds then. Spring and autumn tend to have pleasant temperatures and fewer crowds. In southern Italy and Sicily the weather can even be hot during these times of year. Winter requires warm clothing and an umbrella to protect against the occasional cold rains. In the north, especially in the Alps, snowfall can be heavy—to the enjoyment of skiers.

Health Issues

There are no inoculations required for Italy. The standard of medical care is high.

Safety

Families should take normal travel precautions to guard against pickpockets and burglars.

What to Bring

Comfortable walking shoes are a necessity, as most visitors to Tuscany walk substantial distances visiting the classic towns and the pleasant countryside. A guidebook to Tuscany's art treasures will heighten one's appreciation of the many museums there.

Castle Locations

Most royal properties are scattered throughout Western Europe, with a heavy concentration in England, Ireland, Scotland, Italy, and France. Spain, Portugal, Austria, and Germany also have a selection of properties. Among other alluring global locations are Morocco and South Africa, as well as the Eastern European countries of Hungary, Czech Republic, and Poland.

Castle Prices

Rental prices of castles vary greatly. Location, size, level of refurbishment, services, and amenities are among the determining factors, with weekly costs ranging from approximately $4,000 to up to $50,000, while the number of guests can span from four to 40. Before securing your castle keys, however, shop around for the best deal.

The most common way to arrange rental is through a U.S. or European broker (see Resources). With the availability of the Internet, castle shoppers can also conduct their own searches to get a broad overview of available properties and variation in pricing. Additionally, portal sites, such as Castle Directory.com (www.castledirectory.com), are yet another Internet option with their direct connection and listing of the email addresses of individual property owners.

Castle Considerations

Families should consider castle amenities before booking a particular property. Castle activities range from those aimed at the most active of residents to those intended for guests who just want to relax. "Some clients just want to slip away and do a bit of fishing, riding, antiquing. . . or just plain nothing," says Suzanne Cohen of Suzanne B. Cohen and Associates, a rental agency located in Augusta, Maine. "Others require house staff, cooks, drivers and even fireworks at the end of a medieval ball." Cohen's clients have also requested photographers and private musical performances.

Peruse castle offerings and you'll find a wide array of amenities. . . billiard rooms, cellar bars, small discotheques, personal gyms, game rooms in a converted dungeon, chapels, swimming pools, stables, fishing, and private putting greens. Many have updated their features and boast entertainment centers and Internet connections.

Sample Properties

One property flush with amenities is *Chateau de Tourreau* in Provence, France. Accommodating 32 people, this property includes a tennis court, basketball court, croquet lawn, swimming pool with adjoining children's pool, water-polo facilities, and a home cinema.

But there are also properties where you can experience a more tranquil lifestyle. *Quinta dos Loridos* is a 16th century palace in central Portugal, near the village of Bombarral. Built around a courtyard garden, this property produces sparkling wine and features an extensive wine cellar. Or perhaps castle occupants desire aromatic scents to calm them. Castle Forbes in Aberdeenshire, Scotland, which accommodates ten people, boasts the world's smallest private perfumery.

Many castle properties lay claim to famous residents; yet another lure to some castle renters. *Chateau Colle Noir* in the Var region of the south of France was once owned and renovated by Christian Dior. Accommodating 24 guests, this chateau is close to the village in Montaroux, near the western end of the Riviera. Another property where you can rub imaginary elbows with previous famous occupants is Knappogue Castle in County Clare, Ireland. Accommodating 10 guests, this property was once home to the warrior clan The McNamara's, and was also occupied by Oliver Cromwell's troops. It has been host to many heads of states, including Charles de Gaulle of France.

Before booking, families should check to see if a particular castle is appropriate for young children. Families with little ones should inquire about castle size and layout, artifacts, furnishings, and amenities.

Questions to Ask Booking Agents
- What is the off-season and high season rental cost?
- What is the initial deposit, and the damage deposit?
- What are the extra costs? (Heating, linens, laundry, meals, etc.)
- What is suggested tipping?
- If there are in-castle chefs, what is the approximate weekly cost of food?
- What amenities are available free of charge?
- What is the cancellation policy?
- Can the agency provide references from families who have stayed in the castle?
- What is the minimum age recommended for children, given the amenities, layout, and level of formality in the castle?
- What historical information is available about the castle? (Websites, brochures, books, videos, etc.)

Castle Rental Companies and Information
Each company rents other properties in addition to castles. Our bill for a one-week stay for 11 people was $10,000. This price included cooking and housecleaning services. Extra costs included food (we

paid $300 per family for one week of breakfast and dinner), laundry, final cleaning fee, and gratuities. *Castello di Pergolato* is located in San Casciano Val di Pesa, Italy, 10 miles south of Florence. Manageable day trips are to Florence, Sienna, Lucca, Pisa, and Chianti wine country. Booking agent: Dr. B. Luise Schnabel. 50026 San Casciano Val di Pesa, Italy. Tel/fax: 39-55-8249331.

- **The Best in Italy** www.thebestinitaly.com. Tel: 30-055-223064 in Florence, Italy.
- **Castle Directory.com** www.castledirectory.com. Portal site lists individual castles for rent in Czechoslovakia, South Africa, France, Ireland, Scotland, and others. Clients deal directly with each castle owner.
- **European Escapes** www.europeanescapes.com. Tel: 888-387-6589. Rents castles in Ireland, France, Portugal.
- **International Chapters of St. John's Wood, London.** Tel: 44-020-7722-0722. www.villa-rentals.com. Rents castles in Austria, France, Ireland, Portugal, Scotland.
- **The Parker Company** www.theparkercompany.com. Tel: 800-280-2811. Rents castles in Italy.
- **Suzanne B. Cohen and Associates** www.villaeurope.com. Tel: 207-622-0743. Rents castles in Ireland and Italy.
- **Villas International** www.villasintl.com. Tel: 800-221-2260. Rents castles throughout Europe.
- **Castles on the Web** www.castlesontheweb.com. General information about castle history for families.

THINGS TO SEE AND DO

Activities for Kids

- Have your children read about the original occupants of the castle, information that is generally available through the rental agency. Have them imagine what life was like back then, how the furniture was different and how the facilities were changed.
- Encourage your kids to draw a floor plan of the castle.

• See the area surrounding the castle and imagine what life was like for the first owners.

Day trips in Tuscany

Florence—Often regarded as the most beautiful city in Italy, Florence offers a host of activities for families. In one day, your kids can go eye to eye with Michelangelo's "David" at the Galleria Dell' Accademia, strike a heavenly gaze at Botticelli's "The Birth of Venus" at the famous Uffizi Gallery, and drop a few Euros at the shop-lined bridge, the Ponte Vecchio. Save time for imbibing in delicious Tuscan cuisine, then top your meal off with gelato.

Sienna—Sienna is a city that has seen little change since medieval times. The family lure is the fan-shaped, *Piazza Il Campo*, a town square lined with restaurants and small shops. This square plays host to *Palio*, a bareback horse race which dates back to the 1400s and takes place on July 2nd and August 16th each year. From the Piazza del Campo, walk the narrow winding streets to explore this city's history and culture. A few blocks west of the square is the Duomo, purported to be the most magnificent Gothic cathedral in Italy. Have your kids look at the marble floors and ask them how long it took to complete it. Five years? A decade? Try 200!

Pisa—The Leaning Tower of Pisa is stable at last. Closed from 1990–2001 for repair, this 750-year-old tower welcomes families who want to climb its spiraling 293 steps. Climbing up you will view the interior of the Tower which forms a sort of cylindrical well. Once at the top, families can view the splendid Italian countryside. The tower stands in Campo dei Miracoli (the field of miracles), and includes the Duomo and the Baptistery, both open to the public.

Lucca—This walled town has a claim to fame: it's where Caesar, Pompey, and Crassus agreed to rule Rome as a triumvirate in 56 B.C. The center of this picturesque town, with its narrow shop-lined streets, can be explored by foot. And families will enjoy trekking along Lucca's 16th century ramparts which encircles the town and is shaded by stately trees. Then take a hike up the tree-topped tower of the medieval Palazio Guinigi.

RESOURCES

Official Websites

Italian Government Tourist Board—www.italiantourism.com
Tourism in Tuscany—www.turismo.toscana.it/

Books for Adults

Castles and Fortresses by Robin S. Oggins
Country Series: Castles of England, Scotland and Wales by Paul Johnson
Italian Country Hideaways: Vacationing in Tuscany and Umbria's Private Villas, Castles and Estates by Kelley F. Hurst
Dream Sleeps: Castles and Palace Hotels of Europe by Pamela L. Barrus
Culture Shock! Italy by Raymond Flower

Books for Children

Cross Sections Castle by Stephen Biesty
A Medieval Castle (Inside Story) by Fiona McDonald
Knights and Castles: 50 Hands-On Activities to Experience the Middle Ages by Avery Hart
Days of Knights and Damsels: An Activity Guide by Laurie Carlson

Videos and DVDs

Great Castles of Europe: Fortress to Fairy Tale

Will Nichols takes a break in Beynac, France.

CHAPTER 5

LES EYZIES, FRANCE: EXPLORING CRO-MAGNON ART CAVES

FAMILY TRAVEL TO LES EYZIES, FRANCE

"Our guide is so bossy and impatient, Mom," my critical, 14-year-old daughter whispered. Alison discreetly eyed the tall, dominant archeologist we had hired to take us to Cro-Magnon art caves in Les Eyzies, France. Truth be told, I had to agree with her teenage assessment. After all, how many guides follow their clients into the pharmacy, then cut ten customers to earn the first place in line . . . or stand askance, tapping a foot impatiently while we rushed to the bank to get money (to pay her, no less).

And how many guides start their tour by saying, "If you have the image of Cro-Magnons as ape-like people running around grunting," seemingly reading our minds, "then there's no point of me even taking you down to the caves." But she did escort us to the caves—in spite of our misconceptions—and we experienced an artistic extravaganza of a lifetime.

These caves are underfoot in Les Eyzies-de-Tayac, nestled in the Dordogne region of southwestern France. Les Eyzies, referred to as "the world capital of prehistory," is a one street village of 900 inhabitants. The Vezere and Beune Rivers meet in this village, and it here that the first bones of *Homo Sapiens Sapiens* were unearthed. Attracting between 800,000 and one million visitors each year, Les

Eyzies is devoted to tourism with a broad range of hotels and restaurants. Besides viewing the amazing art caves, families touring this region are in for a historical jaunt, as the region is rife with castles, fortified towns, and museums.

We explored three of the more than 200 caves in this region: *Font-de-Gaume, Grotte des Combarelles,* and *Abri du Cap Blanc.* The limestone walls of these subterranean chambers were painted, etched, and carved with a bevy of prehistoric animals and humans—images so realistic that their likes would not be seen again in European art until the Renaissance.

As we made our way to the first cave, *Font-de-Gaume,* our guide issued another brazen verbal order, this time to Alison and Will. "Don't believe what your teachers have taught you about prehistoric times," she said, as they waited to enter the cave. "Most of the time, they are wrong." This comment settled well with my offspring, as they shot a squinty-eyed "we told you so," look at me.

Entering this cave, we were struck by the beauty and accuracy of the artwork. As we walked the narrow, twisting path, we viewed over 200 figures seared into the limestone walls, dominated by bisons and intermingled with mammoths, reindeer, and horses. "Why did they paint these animals?" Will asked as he viewed the images circling around him.

"So they could have power over them," our guide replied.

Even by today's standards this artwork is astounding; so too is the process by which it was created. These ancient artists built scaffolding to access unreachable areas, created dimension by using the relief of their limestone canvases to highlight anatomical details, and even invented spray painting. Mixing ochre, soot, and blood with their saliva, they blew the mixture through a hollowed bone and onto their rock canvas.

Our next cave, *Grotte des Combarelles,* fell prey to a flood shortly after the Ice Age. Created over a period of 2,000 years, the etchings of human figures and animals survived. The kids studied the human figures—all female—and asked if they really looked like that. One theory is that these figures may have been part of a fertility cult, with their hanging breasts and large rumps. Another is that these females served to educate the young about the history of their people.

Our last cave, *Abri du Cap Blanc,* was nestled in a wooded hillside. This cave contains a frieze of horses and bison. The work was carefully polished and graced a pock-marked background. It's theorized that people actually lived in this cave, as evidenced by the light that filtered in and by a female skeleton found in this shelter.

As we bid *au revoir* to our officious guide, we did have to give her credit. She had indeed educated us with her explanation of the Cro-Magnon way of life. Any misconceptions my family might have *ever* harbored about our ancient relatives dissipated as she took us deep into the earth to view the startling, 14,000-year-old artwork. "Cro Magnons are us," she stated as she said good-bye. We wholeheartedly agreed.

At day's end we went back to our hotel, Les Glycines, for dinner. This three star accommodation prides itself on its cuisine. Alison and Will couldn't stop talking about what they had seen in the caves . . . until I ordered the coveted delicacy of the region: foie gras. "How is it made?" Will asked.

"By forcing food down the necks of geese, and then extracting its liver," we explained.

The kids were outraged "How could you eat that when it's pure torture for those poor birds?" Alison asked.

"I have to support the local economy," I replied.

"Yes, but you are adding to the death of geese," she said.

My enthusiasm for this delicacy suddenly disappeared . . . besides, I did not want the kids shooting barbs at me while I ate. So I passed on the politically incorrect appetizer.

The next day we made our way to the National Museum of Prehistory in Les Eyzies, occupying a renovated 16th century chateau. It features stone and bone tools and the world's foremost grouping of Paleolithic engravings and sculpture. To the delight of the kids, it also exhibited animals from the cavemen's time: skulls of large bears and alligators and, astonishingly, a prehistoric rhinoceros with its skin preserved after being pulled from the tar pit where it died.

Sarlat was our next destination—a half hour drive from Les Eyzies. Here, most of the buildings were constructed between 1450 and 1500, creating an architectural unity with its stone buildings, steep roofs, and towering steeples. We were lucky it was Wednesday, as it was market day in this Renaissance town . . . and we reaped one more benefit as it was the day of a 99% solar eclipse. The kids went into the tourist office and emerged with four pairs of sun viewing glasses. We had just enough time to see the town before we donned our glasses. Lining the narrow footpaths were hundreds of vendors selling pastries, cheeses, spice, nuts, fish, arts and crafts, jewelry, and wine. Interspersed with the vendors were cafes and restaurants, which emanated the smell of crepes and baked goods. Finally, the sun entertained us as we gathered in the courtyard of a church with 50 other observers who donned their glasses and even gazed through CD's to shade their view of this solar event.

The next day we continued our historical wanderings by visiting Beynac—a castle extraordinaire dating from the 12th century. Soaring high on a cliff, 500 feet above the Dordogne River, families can tour Beynac and view grand rooms, drawbridges, armor, tapestries, and second floor toilets carved in stone with the dropping on the first floor outside the castle. "Yech, gross," the kids said as they sat on the stone holes. Outside this imposing fortress was a medieval village with steep winding stone walkways. Restaurants and small shops graced the village. My son's favorite was a shop featuring armor reproductions. "Can I have a full armor suit or even a chain mail suit?" Will asked. "We can mail it to our house." Ah . . . no, I thought, but after he scoped out the prices, he settled for several miniature knights in shining armor.

Our trip to the world's capital of prehistory was a roaring success. We had dispelled our preconceived notions about Cro-Magnons, viewed ancient artwork, visited magnificent castles, and soaked up the astounding history of the region.

FRANCE OVERVIEW

- France: Approximately twice the size of Colorado
- Population: 60 million
- Capital: Paris (Population: 14 million)
- Ethnicity: 92% French, 3% North African, and 5% other

- Religious affiliation: 90% Roman Catholic, 2% Protestant, 1% Muslim, 1% Jewish, 6% unaffiliated
- Official language: French
- Currency: Euro

PLANNING AND PREPARATION

Passports

Americans are required to have a valid passport to enter France.

When to Go

Springtime in Paris is not just a cliché, it really is a wonderful season to visit the city. Spring is also a wonderful time to visit the area around Les Eyzies. As well, summer is beautiful as the temperature there tends to be warm but seldom oppressively hot. Often in the summer visitors must reserve an entry time for some of the caves. During late autumn and winter colder weather and shorter days restrict the amount of outdoor time one can spend in what is essentially an outdoor (and an inside-a-cave) destination.

Health Issues

Medical facilities in France are comparable to those in the U.S. and have broad availability. There are no immunizations required. The water is safe to drink from the tap.

Safety

Violent crime is low in France, however tourists should be aware of pickpockets at major tourist sites and on public transportation. The French government has an anti-terrorist program in place.

What to Bring

Hiking the caves in Les Eyzies requires sturdy hiking boots. No photos are allowed to be taken in the caves, however, snapping pictures at the historical sites is an opportunity not to be missed.

THINGS TO SEE AND DO

Activities for Kids

- Familiarize your children with the artwork and art process before you enter the caves. Ask them to brainstorm how these ancient relatives made spray paint. (Answer: They mixed ochre, soot, and blood with their saliva, then blew the mixture through a hollowed bone and onto their rock canvas.)
- Encourage your kids to draw their favorite animals from each cave and label them in French.
- After you visit the National Museum of Prehistory, ask your children to note the similarities between Cro-Magnons and modern society.

Les Eyzies and the Surrounding Area

National Museum of Prehistory—This museum, in the heart of Les Eyzies, features the most significant collection of Paleolithic items, including bone and stone tools and the world's foremost display of Paleolithic engravings and sculpture. The museum is open year round and guided tours are available. Fees: Children under 18 are free; 18–25 $3.00; adults $5.00.

Caves—Note: Only 200 visitors a day are allowed in the many of the caves. Tours start every 30 minutes. Families can reserve a spot by contacting the Service de Reservation. Tel: (33) 5-53-06-90-80. A few caves are available off-season if families call the reservation service.

 Font-de-Gaume—This cave has the reputation for having the best polychrome prehistoric paintings open to the public. Here the guides adjust the lighting so visitors can observe the fullness and depth of the paintings. Open April to September, every day except Tuesday.

 Grotte des Combarelles—This cave features 800 engravings, including startling reindeers. Closed Wednesdays.

Abri du Cap Blanc—This cave features a 42-foot-high frieze of horses, adapting to the contours of the limestone rock. Open daily April–October.

Grotte deBernifal—This cave touts 100 paintings and engravings with the dominant animal being the mammoth. Open June–September.

Villages

Sarlat—Be sure to go to Sarlat on market days, Wednesday and Saturday. This town of magnificent architectural unity has many sites for families to explore including Cathedral St. Sacerdos, a blue-topped steeple church built in the 6th century and dedicated to a leper-curing bishop. Don't forget to go to the tourist center, formerly the Hotel de Malville, for a bevy of information on Sarlat.

Northeast of Sarlat—Moulin de las Tour is a facility which produces walnut, hazelnut, and almond oils in a process done hundreds of years ago. You can observe the oil making process on Fridays (Monday and Wednesdays in July and August).

Castles in the Areas

Beynac—Situated on a rock, this castle overlooks the Dordogne River. Taken over by Richard the Lionhearted in the 100 Years War, it is one of the most beautiful castles and villages in France.

Castelnaud—Poised on a rock above the village, this castle changed hands nine times between English and French during the 100 Years War. A museum with objects of war from the Middle Ages is on the grounds.

Marqueyssac—This castle offers a unique panorama of the most beautiful castles and villages of the valley. Although closed to visitors, families can spend time walking the amazing gardens of this property.

Hotels in Les Eyzies

Hotel Centenaire—Cost: Double room $100–$175. 20 Units. Great cuisine in the restaurant. Website: www.hotelducentenaire.fr. Tel: (33) 5 53 06 68 68. Fax: (33) 5 53 06 92 41.

Hotel Du Passeur—Cost: Double room $40–$65. 20 Units. Tel: (33) 5-53-06-97-13. Fax: (33) 5-53-06-91-63.

Hotel Glycines: Cost: Double room $75–$180. Fine cuisine, spectacular grounds. Tel.: (33) 5 53 06 97 07. Fax: (33) 5 53 06 92 19. Email: hotel@les-glycines-dordogne.com. Website: www.cote.azur.fr/hotel-auberge-les-glycines-hyeres_1001.htm.

Restaurants

Laugerie-Basse Restaurant (Les-Eyzies)—Tel: (33) 553-06-97-91. Serves authentic Périgord specialties.

La Sarladerie (Sarlat)—1 Côte de Toulouse, Sarlat, Tel: (33) 553-59-06-77. Specializes in salads for vegetarians and non-vegetarians. (Try the foie gras salad.) Located in the heart of Sarlat's ancient quarter. Open only July 1–September 30.

Le Sénéchal (Beynac)—Le Château Féodal de Beynac, Beynac. Tel: (33) 553-29-50-40. Gourmet cuisine and an incredible panorama across from the Beynac castle.

RESOURCES

Official Website

Website of the Les Eyzies Tourist Office: www.leseyzies.com

Books for Adults

The Rough Guide Dordogne and the Lot by Jan Dodd
The Mind in the Cave: Consciousness and the Origins of Art by David
Lewis-Williams
The Most Beautiful Villages of the Dordogne by James Bentley

Books for Children

First Painter by Kathryn Lasky
Painters of the Caves by Patricia Lauber
Prehistoric Rock Art by Marinella Terzi
Boy of the Painted Cave by Justin Denzel

Videos and DVDs

France: the Dordogne Region, the French Riviera

Alison Nichols on the steps of the Rila Monastery, Bulgaria.

CHAPTER 6

SOFIA, BULGARIA: ON THE CUSP—CAPITALISM OVERCOMING COMMUNISM

FAMILY TRAVEL TO SOFIA, BULGARIA

Since the 7th century B.C., Bulgaria has been on the itinerary for any-one passing through Europe: the Romans, Greeks, Huns, Crusaders, Magyars, Serbs, Byzantines, Slavs, Turks, Russians, Germans . . . and the Nichols family. We didn't leave Bulgaria in a disarray as those that preceded us. But I must confess that our original plan was to use this Eastern European country merely as a stepping stone to hop on a train in Sofia, Bulgaria's capital, and ride the rails to Istanbul, Turkey.

Our stepping stone plans were fortuitous, as spending four days in Bulgaria offered surprising intrigue, captivating activities, and a window of opportunity for our two teens, Alison and Will, to observe a country and its people working its way up from four decades of Communism.

Bulgaria is bordered by Romania, Yugoslavia, Macedonia, Greece, Turkey, and the Black Sea. This Balkan country is still struggling to evolve from life behind the iron curtain which weighed heavily from 1946 to 1989. As a Soviet satellite, Bulgaria has been afflicted with paralyzing inflation and unstable government. Now this country is beginning to find its economic footing, and since the exit of Communism, is bolstering itself from the bottom of the heap of the eastern bloc countries. The 2001 election of Prime Minister Simeon Saxe-Coburg-Gotha—who was actually the country's previous monarch (at the tender age of 6) before escaping with his royal family to Egypt and then to Spain—has given new hope to the population, 70% who live below the poverty line.

But in spite of past struggles, Bulgaria offers much to families. Here, Old World charm and architecture intermingle with historical sites, modern facilities, and a broad offering of hotels and restaurants.

Arriving at the Sofia airport, our family was immediately surrounded by hoards of men trying to sell taxi rides and offering discounts to hotels. "I can make discount for you," they claimed. We had already booked a hotel, so we hopped in a cab and began our journey. Our driver was behind the wheel of a Lada, a Russian-made car resembling a flattened VW bug, or as my husband Bill described, "A finely tuned racing machine made from tinker toys and tin can parts." The roads in the center of Sofia were potholed and many had no lines marking the lanes. Cab drivers veered in and out as if steering bumper cars.

We gazed out the windows, startled by the immense differences from other European capitals. "Look at all those rundown buildings and the wild weeds," Alison said. Vast numbers of unattractive Soviet-era cement high rise apartment buildings and shocks of overgrown weeds punctuated the landscape. There was one familiar site along the way: *Makgohange* . . . or McDonald's.

Within 20 minutes we were in the countryside at the base of Mt. Vitosha, with its gently rolling hills, well-kept houses and the 7-year-old Castle Hotel Hrankov, where we had booked two rooms. This Best Western affiliate is set in a wealthy section of Sofia, surrounded by attractive, newly constructed homes selling for extremely high prices. Hrankov offers two pools, a gym, massage, acupressure, tennis, squash, and a casino.

After checking in, the clerk asked, "Do you have any weapons?" Ah . . . no. But if we had, we were told that we were required to check them at the desk before entering the casino. Room assignments came next. The kids had never seen this type of décor. "It looks like what you would see in a western movie," Will said. He was right, the furnishings smacked of cowboy days with a heavy dose of ranch style furnishings, but with psychedelic, red and white carpeting . . . from the '70s.

Our first full day was spent in Sofia, a city of 1.2 million people that is a blend of many cultures as evidenced by its orthodox churches, grand cathedrals, towering minarets, impressive synagogues and Roman ruins. There was yet another culture in Sofia—gypsies who begged on the streets for money.

Our first stop was St. Alexander Nevsky Patriarchel Cathedral, perhaps the most beautiful Russian Orthodox church in Europe. Almost 85% of the Bulgarain population is Bulgarian Orthodox. This imposing cathedral was built to commemorate 200,000 Russian soldiers who gave their lives in the 1877–78 war for Bulgarian liberation from the Ottoman yoke. In the crypt of the cathedral is a small icon store, which sells 18th and 19th century icons, and even a few medieval pieces. These images of saints and martyrs are one of the world's oldest artistic endeavors. While purchasing an icon, the kids spied several modern images, including photos of Bill and Chelsea Clinton on their visit to this crypt when Clinton was president.

Exiting the crypt, we spied across the street a cartoon scene: a huge dancing bear tethered to a long chain that was secured on a ring in his nose. His gypsy owner leaned against a tree, waiting for tourists to snap photos so he could collect a fee. As I aimed my camera, Alison called out, "Don't take a picture, mom. Once you pay him, it means he can keep the bear longer." She was right. Although dancing bears used to be popular across Europe hundreds of years ago, today, only a few Eastern bloc countries still flaunt them. Bulgaria, at last count, had ten legally registered bears. But a Vienna based animal rights group, called Four Paws, is seeking them out and paying the owners to send the animals to a bear reserve park in southwest Bulgaria.

Continuing our tour of the town we happened upon a street market with a wide array of art, icons, antiques, and jewelry. This market is open daily from 9:00 A.M. to, according to one vendor, "time there's no sun."

We worked our way along cobblestone streets, to Vitosha Boulevard, Sofia's premier shopping street. Shops, cafes, and restaurants lined this pedestrian walkway which ran many blocks. The city center was in a state of refurbishment—peeling paint combined with newly renovated buildings. A huge sombrero caught the kids' eyes; a hat that served as a roof for a Mexican restaurant, El Sombrero. The food was not as spicy as the Mexican dishes we are used to, but delicious nonetheless. There's a broad selection of ethic restaurants in Sofia, to include Japanese, French, Chinese, Lebanese, Indian, Turkish, Italian, and, of course, traditional Bulgarian. And dining is generally inexpensive—our Mexican meal for four was only $20.00.

We wound up our day by shopping at the craft shop part of the National Art Gallery, where we viewed such Bulgarian crafts as rugs, costumes, pottery, weavings, carved wood, and dolls.

Our second day was spent in the area of Mt. Vishova, walking the countryside and enjoying the activities of our hotel. Will challenged my husband Bill to a race in the indoor pool while Alison and I lifted weights. Then we all played squash and returned to our ranch style psychedelic rooms to freshen up and prepare for the final activity of the day—food! Walking the area and gazing at the attractive homes, we happened upon Perla Restaurant, which offers attractive indoor and outdoor dining and an exotic menu. Kangaroo cutlet, ostrich filet, breaded tongue and brain (it didn't specify of what), and parson's nose in butter topped the list while this extensive menu also included goulash soup, vegetable stuffed peppers, and 32 kinds of chicken dishes. Our tab was $40 for four, which included dessert.

On our third day, we went south from Sofia to the Rila Monastery, now a UNESCO World Heritage Site, and the most significant of Bulgaria's scores of monasteries. These imposing structures capture the history of the country and are closely related to the political, spiritual, and cultural progress of the Bulgarian people.

We booked a cab for $50, and began our five-hour round-trip journey. Our driver, Sasha, was a middle-aged man who spoke English. As we left Sofia and drove through fertile fields in the gently rolling Bulgarian landscape, Sasha entertained us . . . rather the kids . . . with CDs of American rap music.

"How was your life under Communist rule?" I asked.

"I made only $20 a month, and I was always hungry," he said as he recalled his life behind the iron curtain. While steering his slick, black Mercedes taxi along winding roads, he continued his lament. "It was horrible. I had to get tickets for food."

"Since the fall of Communism, my life improves every day," he said. "I now make $300 a month. And this is good."

Sasha's story jolted the kids, and as we stopped for a snack they inquired how he managed on that small amount. "I get $40 a month for allowance," said Will. "How was he able to live on $20?" This example on life under Communist rule fostered a rash of questions from the kids. "How did people live?" "What did they make?" "Did people visit Bulgaria then?" My husband and I explained precepts of Communism and told of our trip to Russia before they were born.

Getting back in the car, we drove through a narrow, winding valley which led to the Rila Monastery, founded in the 10th century by a Bulgarian hermit, Ivan Rilski, or St. John of Rila. He chose this location because of its astonishing beauty. The monastery has been beautifully maintained and includes a magnificent three-domed church with 1,200 religious frescoes rimming its walls, a medieval tower and a courtyard. Families can explore the monastery, which is still occupied by monks and has 300 rooms for its occupants. Many of the rooms were decorated in the fashion of various Bulgarian towns, thus creating an architectural geography of Bulgaria.

On our fourth day, we packed our bags and went back into Sofia to buy train tickets for the ride to Istanbul. We were sorry to leave Bulgaria, but Turkey was beckoning. We boarded our train and observed the splendid sights and magnificent countryside of this nation on the cusp of success. "Can we come back to Bulgaria and see the whole country?" Will asked.

"You bet we will," I said.

BULGARIA OVERVIEW

- Bulgaria: The size of Tennessee
- Population: 7.5 million

- Capital: Sofia (Population: 1.2 million)
- Ethnicity: 86% Bulgarian, 9% Turks, and 5% Roma (gypsy) and Macedonians
- Religious Affiliation: 85% Bulgarian Orthodox and 13% Muslim
- Official Language: Bulgarian
- Currency: Bulgarian Leva
- Alphabet: Cyrillic

Planning and Preparation

Passports

U.S. citizens must have a valid passport, and if staying for over 30 days, a visa is required.

When to Go

Bulgaria's climate is temperate with hot dry summers and cold damp winters. Spring and summer are ideal times to visit (April—September). However, if your family is made up of ski bums, you might want to consider going in winter, as there are several ski areas throughout the country.

Health Issues

There are no inoculations required in Bulgaria, as there are no health risks. However, if families require medical care, private clinics are advised. Tap water is safe to drink in all parts of the country.

Safety

Travelers should be aware of pickpockets and petty crime in cities and tourist areas, otherwise Bulgaria is a safe destination.

What to Bring

Low light film is quite useful when taking photographs in Bulgaria's churches and monasteries. Many have beautiful murals, but are a poorly lit.

Money

While credit cards may be used to pay for services in major cities—such as car rental, classy hotels and restaurants—they are useless throughout the rest of Bulgaria. The same goes for traveler's checks. There are ATMs in the major cities, so if you're traveling into rural areas, load up on cash.

THINGS TO SEE AND DO

Activities for Kids

• Have your children note the differences between their society and Bulgaria's. The most obvious difference is the use of the Cyrillic alphabet. But they will notice much more—large cement buildings, roads with no lines, different cars, gypsies . . . .

• Ask someone what life was like under Communism.

• If you see tethered bears, ask you kids what ideas they have to free the bears.

In Sofia

The National History Museum—Boulevard Vitosha. Open Tuesday–Sunday. Located in the former Palace of Justice, this museum houses a wide array of objects from ancient artifacts to nineteenth century folk costumes.

Halite—Browse the market hall, or Halite, for a broad range of objects, to include special Bulgarian food items. Open daily from 7 am to midnight, this market was recently refurbished, and contains two floors of stalls.

Outside Sofia

Rila Monastery—Founded in the 10th century, this famous monastery is 60 miles south of Sofia. In addition to viewing many of the historical parts of the monastery, families can go into several buildings.

Koprivshtitsa—This enchanting town, 65 miles east of Sofia, has 383 houses and monuments restored to their original appearance. Koprivshtitsa, nestled in a lush valley, has a legendary history, which is shown, in the historical homes which families can visit. Also have a look at this town's cache of treasures, which include embroidered items, old weapons, ceramics, costumes, and jewelry. With its white ivy covered walls, yellow and red houses, and iron-studded gates, this town transports families back to the 19th century. Koprivshtitsa has a claim to fame—here the first bullet was fired in 1876 in the April uprising against the Ottoman regime. A regional festival with folk groups is held annually on or around August 15th.

Hotels in Sofia

Castle Hrankov Hotel—Rates start at $120 for a double room. Large modern hotel built to look like a castle—sort of. Squash and tennis courts, outdoor and indoor pool, casino. Located in Sofia suburb in foothills of Vitosha Mountains. 53 "Krusheva Gradina" St., Dragalevtzi, Sofia. www.hrankov-bg.com. Tel: (359) 2 967 2929. Fax (359) 2 294 5967.

Hilton Sofia—Rates start at $155 for a double room. Located in the heart of the city. Swimming pool, sauna, steam room. 1 Boulevard Bulgaria, Sofia, Bulgaria. www.hilton.com.

Radisson SAS Grand Hotel Sofia—Rates start at $140 for a double room. Opposite the Parliament building and the Alexander Nevski Cathedral. Situated in the city center, walking distance from many cultural and tourist sites. The surrounding streets offer nice boutiques, cafes, discotheques, and clubs with live music and entertainment. 4 Narodno Sabranie Square, Sofia, Bulgaria. www.radisson.com.

Traditional Food Items

Special food items include *shopska* salad, a combination of brined sheep's cheese, sunflower oil, and other ingredients; *tarator,* a soup with yogurt, walnuts, dill, and sunflower oil; *shoppe* style cheese which is baked until a crust is formed, then garnished with sliced tomatoes, parsley, and chili.

Restaurants in Sofia

El Sombrero—16 Sveta Nedelia Square, Sofia. Mexican cuisine

Restaurant Amber—Burel Street. No. 70, Sofia. Bulgarian and International cuisine.

33 Chairs—Asen Zlatarov 14. Bulgarian and International cuisine.

Biad—General Gurko 16. This folk club serves Barbecue, Bulgarian, Greek, Serbian, and Turkish food, and has live, folk-pop performers.

Asia—Chiprovtsi 4. A premier Chinese restaurant, providing substantial servings.

Baalbek—Vasil Levski 4. Serving top quality Lebanese food.

Pizza Palace—bul. Vitosha 34. Sofia's best pizza place, also serving Italian cuisine.

Perla—19 Lyubotrun Str. A wide, exotic array of international offerings.

RESOURCES

Official Website
www.bulgariatravel.org

Books for Adults
The Rough Guide to Bulgaria
A Concise History of Bulgaria by R.J. Crampton

Voices from the Gulag: Life and Death in Communist Bulgaria by Tzvetan Todorov

Bulgaria: Enchantment of the World by Abraham Resnick

Books for Children

Bulgaria…in Pictures (Visual Geography) by Mary M. Rodgers (Editor)

Videos and DVDs

Rick Steves' Europe: Bulgaria, Eastern Turkey, Slovenia, and Croatia by Rick Steves

Hannah going for a ride with Jeff Sachs in Prague.

CHAPTER 7

PRAGUE, CZECH REPUBLIC: MEMORIES FROM A MOM'S ESCAPE

BY SONIA EHRLICH SACHS

FAMILY TRAVEL TO PRAGUE, CZECH REPUBLIC

"If we go there, will they let us escape again?" asked my seven-year-old daughter, Hannah, when I told her that we were going to visit my native city, Prague, in the Czech Republic. I did not realize that she appropriated some overheard fragments of my personal history of escaping from communist Czechoslovakia as a teenager in the late sixties. Postponing for another seven years the explanation of the "velvet revolution" which brought democracy and market economy to the Czech people, I merely reassured my daughter that this time, we would be guests of the government, and that they would take good care of us and then let us come home to Boston again.

Prague, smack in the heart of Europe, is one of its most beautiful cities with a rich display of preserved architectural history from Romanesque churches, Gothic Cathedrals, Renaissance townhouses, and splendid Baroque palaces and churches, all blending naturally with charming art nouveau and playful cubism. The "Golden City" or the "City of a Hundred Spires" lies on both sides of the Vltava River (the Moldau), which is spanned by picturesque bridges. One such bridge, the Charles Bridge, and its bridge towers, were built in the High Gothic style of the 14th century and adorned in the 17th century with graceful baroque statues of historical figures and saints, making this bridge a striking structure has become a main tourist attraction. On a hill overlooking the whole city and its environs is the majestic, thousand-year-old Prague Castle, Hradèany.

The usual access to the castle is from the main castle square, through a majestic gate guarded by giant statues of battling Titans, via a series of courtyards with water fountains flanked by the Royal Palace, the Romanesque Basilica of St. George and the exquisite St. Vitus cathedral, the site of coronations and burials of Czech kings. However, my Prague classmate from kindergarten showed us a picturesque back way to the castle, approaching it from the river, going up the hill which has been built up over the centuries by nobility whose Baroque palaces and mansions encircled the castle. One such mansion and gardens are the Ledebour gardens, which is a series of ornamental terraces embellished by attractive plants and a few sculptures, climbing up the hill and linking up ultimately to the Royal gardens which then lead one to the castle. The views of the city from this spot are magnificent.

The kids' favorite tourist spot is the renowned Golden Lane, a street of miniature houses built 400 years ago into the arches of the castle wall. Formerly for the gatekeepers, these miniature houses were subsequently inhabited by craftsmen and the king's alchemists. During the last century Franz Kafka and the Czech Nobel laureate, Joseph Seifert, lived in these diminutive, one-room houses. These miniature houses brought out some instinctive glee in Hannah who reveled in the childish dimensions of the little doorways, windows, and doll-like furniture.

Strolling through the narrow cobblestone streets of Prague with my daughter in hand, I self-consciously felt the irony of the situation. I remember the feel of my mother's hand as she held the grocery bag in the other hand, walking down these streets, looking for stores that were not yet sold out. She often put me in a long line of people waiting for hours for bread in front of the bakery shop, while depositing my brother and sister in other lines outside of the butcher and vegetable stores while she went to look for available items in a different part of town. I tried to explain what a food shortage was to Hannah, but it seemed so theoretical to this American-made girl as we sat in an expensive pastry shop in the "The Old Town Square" which is now filled with boutiques and goods from all over the world. She uttered her own version of Queen Antoinette's "let them eat cake" by asking why, if stores were empty, didn't my parents take us out to restaurants.

The "Lesser Quarter Square" is a beautiful square that has been the stage of tumultuous events including the playing out of the violent conflicts between the Catholic Habsburg rulers and the Hussites, the Czech Protestant reformers. However the centerpiece is the Old Town Hall with a huge, beautiful astronomical clock built in 1490, showing, with remarkable precision, the time, the phases of the moon and the equinoxes. Wherever we happened to be, like clockwork, Hannah wanted us to return to this clock for the hourly spectacle where figurines of Christ and his twelve apostles appear in a window. Flanking the horologe are four moving specters. One is a skeleton shaking a bell in one hand and an hourglass in the other, to remind us, hourly, of our mortality. The other moving figurines are a Turk (representing the threat of the encroaching Ottoman Empire), a miser shaking a bag of coins, and a narcissist looking in a mirror. The apocryphal story has it that the Master Astronomer who built this complex machine was blinded by the councilmen so that he would not build a rival instrument for anyone else. For revenge he destroyed the mechanism which made the clock non-functional for many years. The sobering effect of this display was lost on Hannah who was dazzled by the performance as is the ever present, large crowd of tourists.

When I was growing up in Prague, my totally assimilated Jewish parents did not speak much of our Jewish origin given the openly anti-Semitic sentiment of the communist regime. I vaguely knew that many of my relatives died in concentration camps; I vaguely knew that my father and older sister were denied academic privileges because of being Jewish. I heard boys call my brother a Jew when they were fighting so for a long time I associated the word with an insult.

Now, 35 years later, I was taking my youngest child and my husband to the section of Prague where Jews thrived and suffered for centuries, leaving behind a rich legacy in architecture, artifacts, and lore. Unlike me, my husband grew up in an openly Jewish community of Detroit, observing many of the Jewish holidays and rituals like his bar mitzvah. However, it was me, with my new-found pride in my new-found heritage that was showing him and our child the remnants of the Jewish ghetto, consisting at this point of a couple of synagogues, a town hall, and a cemetery.

Hannah was just learning how to tell time so she was mesmerized by the Jewish Town Hall, an elegant Rococo edifice, which has a clock with Hebrew script, going in reverse order, and a dial going "anti-clockwise." (This engendered a discussion whether time could go backwards.) Next to it is a synagogue that houses the Jewish Museum which has many objects from all over Central Europe. Hitler set this up intending for it to be the collection of items used in religious customs and in everyday life of the eradicated people. It was called "An Exotic Museum of an Extinct Race." One of the most remarkable buildings is the "Old-New Synagogue" which was built in the year 1270, making it the oldest in Europe. Built in the Early Gothic style of its contemporaneous churches, it has flying buttresses, but contrary to the architectural norm, it has a non-functional fifth rib in its vaulting in order for it not to appear as a shape of a cross. One enters the synagogue by going down the stairs, which, we were told, is so that the synagogue could be tall and yet not surpass the height of the surrounding churches.

We took Hannah to the Old Jewish Cemetery, which is 500 years old. Because Jews were not allowed to expand out of the ghetto, there are 12 layers of burials on top of each other. The gravestones, therefore, are crammed next to each other jutting out at uneven angles. The tombstones have epitaphs often describing bits of the person's life and profession. At the end of the cemetery is Pinkas Synagogue, a late-

Gothic structure from the 15th century, which has become a memorial to Czech Jews murdered in concentration camps, with the 77,297 names inscribed on its walls. We showed Hannah the names of our family members high up on the wall; it was a very poignant moment for us. On a previous trip, we took our older children to Terezin, the deportation camp used for sorting Jewish families like mine to the different concentration camps. It was almost impossible for us and for the children to view it. It had a profound impression on them about man's inhumanity to man.

I showed Hannah my elementary school, my apartment building, my playground and park, and we visited with the people I grew up with and their children. Sitting in their tiny apartments, we reminisced how different even such a meeting is from what it was when we were growing up under communism. Under the threat of imprisonment, one could not be seen talking to a foreigner, much less have him in one's apartment. My father used to meet and talk with certain friends only while walking in the park, because we knew our apartment had listening devices implanted. Back then, we received letters from our relatives and friends in the "west," already opened and with the emblem of the police censor brazenly stamped on them. I remember the pained face of my father when I asked him about something from my school history lesson, not understanding until much later that the schools taught history heavily twisted by communist ideology; but if he told me the truth then, being a naïve child I could have told the teacher and that could have—and has for other families—ended tragically.

I showed Hannah and my husband the Charles University that has two major distinctions. One is that having been founded in 1348, it is the oldest university in Central Europe, and the other is that two of its graduates are my father and my sister. I delight in telling the story that in the mid-seventeenth century, one of Charles University's pre-eminent philosophers and pedagogues, Jan Comenius, was offered to be the first president of Harvard University, my and my husband's alma mater. Comenius turned down the offer since Prague was a major intellectual center, while Harvard at that time was a fledgling and inauspicious school in Cambridge, Massachusetts.

Since I cannot infuse my family with enthusiasm for the rich literature and theater of this country, I indulge them in the many arts of universal language. Prague is always pulsating with music, especially in the spring. There are concerts in many of its churches and music halls, often classical but sometimes very adventurous. We go to the Tyl Theater that boasted the world premier of Don Giovanni in 1787, which Mozart composed in and for Prague. A hit with us and the kids and throngs of tourists is the Mime Theater in Prague, "Laterna Magica," which has brought the art of black theater and mime to a very sophisticated level.

When we leave the Czech Republic by car across the border to one of its neighboring countries, I predictably have a nauseating feeling and palpitations. The transaction is straightforward. We approach the border, we slow down, we wave our U.S. passport out of the car window, we get waved on by the guard who lackadaisically peers at us while talking to the other guards. In that one minute, I invariably relive the somewhat different scenario of 36 years ago. Approaching the border with my parents and siblings in a tiny Fiat, we were immediately surrounded by soldiers shouting and pointing their guns at us but mercifully leaving us alive to try our luck at a different border. We eventually did get through a border to the Yugoslavian shore where, in the middle of the night, a small smugglers' boat took us to our freedom in the west.

CZECH REPUBLIC OVERVIEW

- Czech Republic: Slightly smaller than South Carolina
- Population: 10.3 million
- Capital: Prague (Population: 1.2 million)
- Ethnicity: 81% Czech, 14% Moravian, 3% Slovak, 2% other
- Religious Affiliation: 40% Atheist, 39% Roman Catholic, 5% Protestant, 3% Eastern Orthodox, 13% other
- Official Language: Czech
- Currency: Czech Koruna

PLANNING AND PREPARATION

Passports

A valid passport is required for entry into the Czech Republic. Visas are only required for stays longer than 90 days.

When to Go

Spring and autumn are hardly evident in Prague. Summers are long with an average temperature of 63 degrees in July and August, while winters are cool and wet with an average temperature of 29 degrees in January.

Health Issues

No immunizations are recommended. Medical facilities are available but may be limited in rural areas. Often, doctors and hospitals require payment in cash for health services.

Safety

Violent crime is very low in the Czech Republic. However, with the substantial increase in tourism, there has been an increase in such street crime as pick-pocketing, mainly in the most frequented areas of tourism in Prague and on public transportation. Also, there has been significant overcharging by taxis, particularly in areas frequented by tourists. Agree on the price before your family hops into the cab.

What to Bring

Even in the summer, central Europe can have spells of cool rain. Bring a light water resistant jacket.

THINGS TO SEE AND DO

Activities for Kids

- Read the sections of this chapter which tell of the author's Jewish life in Prague— and her escape—to your children. Discuss with your kids life under Nazi and communist rule.

- Take your children across the Charles Bridge and have them pick their favorite sculpture among the 30 that line both sides of the bridge. Have them draw their favorite sculpture.

In Prague

Old Town—The Old Town is the heart Prague, with the best shops, markets, restaurants, and cafes. The Old Town Square is gorgeous with its bevy of buildings from Medieval and Baroque times. The centerpiece of the square is the modern art statue of Jan Hus, a priest who was excommunicated and burned in 1415 for his radical views. The 18th century Goltz-Kinsky Palace stands on the eastern side of the square, with the Tyn Church behind it. This church is one of most outstanding religious buildings in Prague.

The Old Town Hall dominates the southeastern corner of the square. The Astronomical Clock sets in the highest tower of the Old Town Hall. Constructed in 1410, its purpose was to show the movement of the sun and moon to reveal the months of the year.

Charles Bridge—The bridge is a work of art. Built in 1357, this bridge has sculptures lining its sides.

Prague Castle—The Prague Castle, separated from the Old Town by the Moldau River, regally towers over the city. The Castle is not a single building but rather a village—initiated between the 9th and 16th centuries—that drapes down a hill

Golden Lane—This collection of tiny houses was built in the 16th century as homes for King Rudolf II's guards, craftsmen, and servants.

Jewish Quarter—At the northern edge of the Old Town lies the Jewish Quarter, known as Josefov. From 1939–1945 occupation, the growing Jewish community was almost destroyed. Currently, a small community of Orthodox Jews live here.

Outside Prague

Terezin—Terezin came under the authority of the German military during World War II. Jews from Prague were sent to Terezin in 1941, followed by other Jews from the Czech Republic and Jews from other countries as well. Over 30,000 people perished here. Families can visit the underground corridors and cells as well as book guided tours. Open April–October, daily from 9:00 A.M.–Noon and 1:00 P.M.–5:00 P.M.

Kutna Hora—Kutna Hora is medieval town 44 miles east of Prague. Recognized by UNESCO as a World Heritage Site, this picturesque town owes its fame to silver mines. During the 14th and 15th centuries, Kutna Hora was one the wealthiest places in Europe, and was also the cultural and economic apex of Bohemia, competing with Prague. The dominant feature of this town is St. Barbara's Cathedral. Families will enjoy Hradek (the Little Castle), which is now a museum displaying the history of silver mining. You may also visit one of the medieval silver mines.

Hotels in Prague

Movenpick Hotel—Cost: Double room $98–$165. Actually consists of two separate hotels connected by a cable car with a beautiful view of Prague. Central location adjacent to city center Mozartova 261. Tel: (420) 2 57-15-1111. Fax: (420) 2 57-15-3131.

Hotel Le Palais—Cost: Double room $235–$295. One of the most beautiful examples of Belle Époque architecture in Central Europe The hotel is a delightful gem of 19th century architecture with its peaceful yet central location. U Zvonaøky 1. Tel: (420) 2 22-56-3356. Fax: (420) 2 22-56-3350. E-mail: lepalais@abaka.com.

Hotel U Krize—Cost: Double room $100–$140. Situated in the very center of Prague, in one of the most historical parts of the city called Mala Strana. The hotel has been reconstructed from a 16th century building. Accommodation in 16 rooms and 6 suites. Ujezd 20.

Restaurants
Czech Cuisine
U Fleku—Kremecova 11. Tel: (420) 2 49 15 5118. A traditional pub, restaurant, and brewery located in central Prague. Serves traditional Czech cuisine. A brewery museum is located on premises.

Restaurant Pod Vezi—Mostecka 2. Tel: (420) 2 57 53 2041. Located in a hotel of the same name, this beautiful restaurant has high arched ceilings. Serves Czech and international cuisine.

Restaurant Pelikan—Na Prikope 7. Tel: (420) 2 24 21 0697. Relatively upscale Art Deco style décor. Diners are treated to 1930's–era music.

Italian Cuisine
Casa Mia Pizzeria—Vodickova 17. Tel: (420) 2-96 23 8201. In a courtyard that has been transformed into an Italian piazza, this atmospheric restaurant serves pizza and sophisticated Mediterranean seafood dishes.

Don Giovanni—Karolinv Svetle 34. Tel: (420) 2 22 22 2060. Seats 80. Located very near the Charles Bridge. Specialty is Italian cuisine.

RESOURCES
Official Websites
www.visitczech.cz
www.czechcenter.com

Books for Adults
Czech Republic (Culture Shock!) by Tim Nollen

Frommer's Prague & the Best of the Czech Republic by Hana Mastrini
I Never Saw Another Butterfly: Children's Drawings and Poems from Terezin Concentration Camp 1942–1944 by Hana Volavkova
Knopf Guide Prague

Books for Children

The Three Golden Keys by Peter Sis
Czech Republic (Cultures of the World) by Efstathia Sioras
Eva's Summer Vacation: A Story of the Czech Republic by Jan Machalek
Czech Republic (Country Insights, City and Village Life) by Rob Humphreys

Videos and DVDs

Eastern Cities: Prague, Budapest and Istanbul

The cousins visit Monsanto, Portugal. Will Nichols, Patrick Sandoval, Alison Nichols, and Amalia Sandoval.

CHAPTER 8

PORTUGAL:
HISTORY, BEACHES,
AND GRILLED SARDINES

BY MARY NICHOLS SANDOVAL

FAMILY TRAVEL TO PORTUGAL

"Mommmmm!!!" cried my pre-teen daughter when the family was discussing plans for our summer holiday. "Why do we always have to end up going to some weird place like North Yemen or Libya? I'm just soooo embarrassed at school in September when the kids ask me where I went for the summer. Why can't we just go to some *normal* place like everyone else? You know, like a beach or something."

Our son, who was already a teenager, but just barely, said, "But I really like the places we go. Everybody else does such dumb stuff in the summer and we do cool stuff and then I always have a lot of good material to write reports for social studies."

"Who cares about stupid social studies reports? I just want a normal vacation!" and out of the room she stomped.

I began to think that maybe we should keep her hormonal and emotional needs in mind when planning this year's family trip. At the same time I just couldn't bear the idea of spending two weeks on a beach literally carpeted in beach towels with block upon block of high rise buildings in the background and sunburned flesh at every turn. Where to go to keep all of us happy? We needed a beach area with potential for several social studies reports and interesting places near by.

"What about southern Portugal?" asked my husband later that evening when the kids were not around. "The beaches are supposed to be nice and not too crowded and we could still find a lot to do. The grilled sardines are famous all over Europe." (I'd forgotten to include the culinary status of the place along with the sand, sights, and social studies.)

The next day I began my research on beaches in southern Portugal and began to feel more optimistic. We made the children promise, however, that we would visit Lisbon and Evora on our way to the south.

We decided to try a small fishing village called Alvor, in the coastal area known as the Algarve. From our reading we discovered that the area was "beach-like" enough to satisfy our daughter, but that small whitewashed villages still remained and there would be plenty of grilled sardines. We decided to spend the last part of our vacation time there, so our daughter would be sure to have the beach fresh in her mind when she returned to school in September. First we would visit Lisbon, then drive south.

Lisbon never fails to enchant me, despite many visits spread over various decades. The best part of this visit, however, was seeing how the children were also enchanted. We knew better than to try to interest the children in churches and museums, with the exception of the Gulbenkian Museum, and so this visit was dedicated to spending time in the streets and parks, riding the cable cars, taking a boat across the bay, shopping at the flea market, and taking some short side trips to Belem and Sintra.

Though the entire city still looks to me as though it could use a good face lift and all of the façades are blackened by that mixture of mold and saline so typical of port cities, a lot has been done to clean up the city since the early seventies and the end of the Portuguese colonial empire in Africa when every inch of brick or stone in Lisbon was covered with graffiti and thousands upon thousands of displaced Angolans and Mozambicans slept in every park and plaza. On our first day in

Lisbon we rode the cable car from the Baixa, or lower and more modern part of the city, to the Alfama, the old area of Lisbon that stretches below the Castle of São Jorge (St. George), where we wandered through the winding streets, some so narrow we had to press up against the walls as the cable car went by. We were lucky to be there on a Tuesday and visited the flea market, where my daughter was in her element. As long as there is something, anything at all, to buy, she is almost blissful.

Many shoppers were buying Portuguese towels and sheets, which are supposedly of good quality and reasonably priced, but I had purchased some on a previous visit and was not especially impressed. We all enjoyed looking at the Portuguese ceramics and bought several unusual pieces. Our son later wandered around the walls and ramparts of the Saint George Castle, looking for inspiration for a social studies report (which actually did not come till several days later when we were on our way to Evora). Later that morning we tried three other interesting modes of transportation which go from the Baixa neighborhood to the Chiado neighborhood on top of another hill across from the Alfama. One is the Santa Justa elevator. I suffer just a bit from claustrophobia, but the ride was fortunately short. Elevators that are nearly a hundred years old are not usually my first choice for going up a mountain, but the kids thought this was great fun. We then used the escalator inside the subway station to go back down to the bottom of the hill and came up yet again on the funicular tram which seems to go straight up the side of the mountain. Lisbon has always reminded me of a medieval San Francisco with its hills, bridges, cable cars, and the rides up and down were inexpensive ways to entertain the kids.

Another short but successful excursion with the children was a boat trip across the Tagus River to the southern bank, an area of Lisbon called Almada. A landmark of this sector of the city is the huge statue of Christ which overlooks the mouth of the river. The riverfront is lined with small and very typical fish restaurants specializing in grilled cod. Fishing boats sail in and out of the small port area and there is a good view of the April 25th Bridge, which is very similar to the Golden Gate Bridge of San Francisco.

The only museum "required" during our stay in Lisbon was the Gulbenkian Museum, named after its owner and built on beautiful grounds to house his personal collection of all sorts of paintings, jewelry, and furniture. This visit was a concession to Mom who needed a little bit of culture before we hit the beach.

In the evening, after a delicious fish dinner, we went to the port area where old warehouses have been turned into trendy bars and discotheques. Taking your teenagers to a bar in Europe does not have quite the same connotation as it would in the United States, and it is not uncommon to see families in such places if it's still early. The kids thought this was great, though they probably wished they didn't have to be seen in such a place with their parents. We're always interested to see how older, rundown areas of a city can be reconverted.

The kids weren't too excited about the visit to Belem, an area on the outskirts of the city where the beautiful Jeronimos Monastery is located, but even they agreed that the 16th century architecture was spectacular.

The visit to Sintra, a Renaissance village that had been the summer home of the royal families for centuries, was almost vetoed by our daughter, who had begun to wonder if we would ever get to the beach. We finally agreed to look at the monuments and palaces from the *outside*, visit the botanical gardens, and continue to Evora.

The drive to Evora through the Alentejo province was lovely: slightly rolling hills, fields of wheat undulating in the breeze, and gnarled old cork trees dotting the landscape. Our son showed special interest in the cork trees and I could imagine his first social studies report in September: "Portugal is the world's number one producer of cork, which comes from the bark of the cork oak tree (*quercos suber*). A cork tree can produce cork for about 150 years. The bark is stripped from the tree every nine years and the planks of cork are cut by hand, using small axes." We didn't get to see the cork being harvested, but we did stop the car to examine the trees which had most recently been stripped. The kids were fascinated by some bits of bark they picked up. They were nearly two inches thick and the layer beneath the outer bark looked just like the cork in a wine bottle. I was sure the pieces of cork would become part of the social studies presentation.

We arrived in Evora in the evening when the biggest full moon I had ever seen was just rising on the eastern horizon. I've seen many full moons in many parts of the world, but this one, hovering above the hillside, setting off the outline of the town with the medieval steeple of the cathedral in the center, is the one that still stands out in my mind. Evora turned out to be a magical town in other respects as well. That night, with the moon now high in the sky, we walked through the town to the Roman ruins of the temple to Diana, dating from the third century. My daughter and I were too mesmerized by the moonlight and the ancient columns to think of historical details, but my son was, I'm sure, pondering over another social studies report. "Evora was an important Roman settlement in the Alentejo region, which was a cereal producing area. The Roman name for Evora was *Ebora Cerelis*. There were copper and iron mines near Evora and a marble quarry. After the Roman period, the town was ruled by the Moors until . . . ." The windows of our small hotel in the center of the town looked out over the cobblestone streets and the tiled roofs, with their myriad television antennas forming a virtual forest silhouetted against the moon-lit sky.

We slept with the windows wide open and were awakened in the early morning by the church bells of every church in the town, calling the worshipers to mass. The bells were ringing simultaneously, but at the same time never exactly at the same moment, so it was like a concert of chimes, some deep and brassy and somber, others lighter and tinkly, which seemed to go on and on. Everyone uses the cliché about "stepping back in time," but at that moment I felt that feeling I get only in Europe, of history, tradition, architecture, and culture, all blended together, which makes a lasting impression upon the senses.

Back to the present, though, as we finally headed for the beach and our pre-teen daughter's dream vacation. We drove south through more cork forests, mixed with olive and Mediterranean oak, to reach the Algarve, the southern Atlantic coastal region. Alvor, where we stayed, has a very developed coastal area with modern hotels and self-catering apartments, but the original village retains its charm with narrow streets, whitewashed houses, and many small and typical restaurants (for the grilled sardines, of course!). There is a long, sandy beach in Alvor, which was a short walk from our apartment, but there are also little coves under the cliffs with rock arches and other rock formations in the water quite close to the shore, and these were the beaches that the children really enjoyed. There were other children at the apartment complex, and our kids soon had a group of peers to spend time with.

A short drive from Alvor is Praia da Rocha, famous for its huge rock arch, but this beach is much more crowded than the smaller beaches at Alvor. The larger town of Portimão is a big tourist shopping area, modern and rather uninteresting in my opinion, but our daughter enjoyed looking at the tourist junk. We spent one day at one of the numerous water parks along the coast; I know that's something you can do anywhere (no social studies report there!), but the kids had such a good time that we did, too. In the evenings after the sun went down, we drove to other towns along the coast to sample the grilled sardines (not much difference, if you ask me) and other fresh fish, and my husband decided that some we had in the port at Armação de Pêra were the best. As we saw the other coastal tourist towns, many of them blocks of high buildings on a beach front, we were glad to have chosen Alvor.

September was a good month for all concerned. Our daughter was able to prove that she had actually been to a beach by the tan she brought back, and I overheard phone conversations telling her girlfriends about this really cool guy she had talked to in Portugal. Patrick got an A+ on the oral report about the cork industry, and was already thinking of the Evora report for the unit on the Romans. My husband and I decided that beach towns aren't so bad, after all, if you just choose the right beach.

PORTUGAL OVERVIEW

- Portugal: Slightly smaller than Indiana
- Population: 10.6 million

- Capital: Lisbon (Population 2.6 million)
- Ethnicity: 99% Portuguese, Cape Verdean, Brazilian, Spanish
- Religious Affiliation: 92% Roman Catholic, 5% Protestant, 3% other
- Language: Portuguese (official)
- Currency: Euro

PLANNING AND PREPARATION

Passports

Americans are required to have a valid passport to enter Portugal.

When to Go

Summer is hot and sunny, but the coastal areas are kept cooler by the Portuguese trade winds. The interior, away from the sea, can get very hot in summer. The Algarve coast is sheltered from the north wind and has the higher summer temperatures. Spring and fall are quite pleasant. Winters are mild in Portugal, being south of most of the other European countries. At this time of year you need a sweater and an umbrella.

Health Issues

Medical facilities in Portugal are comparable to those in the U.S. and have broad availability. There are no immunizations required. The water is safe to drink from the tap.

Safety

Violent crime is low in Portugal, however tourists should be aware of pickpockets at major tourist sites and on public transportation.

What to Bring

At some point, after too much sun you will still want to be outdoors. Bring a light, long sleeve cotton shirt to protect yourself from the rays.

THINGS TO SEE AND DO

Activities for Kids

- When driving past a cork forest, let the kids collect some cork bark scraps. Have them compare the bark to a finished cork stopper.
- Have the kids learn a few basic phrases in Portuguese and in Spanish and note the similarities. (Good day: *Bom dia*—Portuguese, *Buenos dias*—Spanish; yes: *sim*—Portuguese, *sí*—Spanish)
- In Lisbon, ride the elevator, escalator, and funicular—all three—from Baixa to Chiado. Have the kids compare and contrast each ride, e.g. speed, capacity, age of transport, etc.

Lisbon and nearby

Castle of São Jorge (St. George)—The castle sits on one of Lisbon's highest hills and offers excellent vistas of the city. Likely the original site of an iron age fortress, followed by a Roman fort, the current castle was begun in the 1100s and has been added onto many times since. Within the walls are attractive gardens.

Alfama—This is the old quarter of Lisbon, nestled downhill from St. George's Castle. A maze of narrow cobbled streets makes this section a wonderful walking destination. Attractive during the day because of open markets and the general street scene, Alfama comes alive at night. It is filled with restaurants and taverns.

Jeronimos Monastery—The *Mosteiro dos Jerónimos* and the *Torre de Belém,* on the outskirts of Lisbon, are striking architectural relics from the period of Portuguese exploration. Construction began in 1502. They are situated in Belém, the sixteenth-century port from which the Portuguese caravels set sail on voyages of discovery and trade. Although the port no longer exists, the site has become a pleasant leisure area. The decorative features carved out of the monastery's stone will entice your children. Encourage them to find symbols inspired by the sea (such as ropes, fish, and conches).

Sintra—Located 18 miles west of Lisbon, Sintra contains a fabulous collection of monuments from a whole host of different epochs, ranging from prehistoric times to the present day. The visitor can choose among the Neolithic, *Tholos do Monge*; the eighth-century Moorish fortification, *Castelo dos Mouros*; or the Franciscan monastery, *Convento dos Capuchos*. The town of Sintra still retains its essentially mediaeval layout, with narrow and labyrinthine streets, steps, and arcades. Thanks to its unique microclimate, Sintra has some of the most beautiful parks in Portugal. The town is dominated by its multi-style, multi-era, National Palace. This spectacular site is a UNESCO World Heritage site. While in Sintra do not miss The Toy Museum, over 20,000 pieces from the 16th to the 20th-century. In the suburbs lies the *Cabo da Roca*—the westernmost point in continental Europe.

Evora—This beautiful town of Roman origins lies 81 miles east of Lisbon. Its historic center is a UNESCO World Heritage site. Its unique quality stems from the whitewashed houses decorated with wrought-iron balconies dating from the 16th to the 18th century. The town's Roman temple is not to be missed. The convent of Lóios has been turned into a *pousada*—a government owned inn in an historic building (similar to Spain's popular *Paradores*).

In the South

Alvor—Located on Portugal's Algarve coast, Alvor has been a fishing village since Roman times. Although this ancient coastal village is now a very popular holiday location, the enclosed narrow streets have kept development to a minimum. Many of these streets now boast bars with live music and different types of restaurants, but leading off from these there are still memories of the older fishing village. Be sure to sample the grilled sardines while visiting. The village faces a natural lagoon opening onto the sea. There is a choice of a long open sandy beach or a number of small coves tucked under the cliffs. Nearby is *Praia da Rocha* with its huge rock arch.

Hotels in Lisbon

D. Maria Pousada—Cost: Double room $189–$199. Located in the building formerly used by the Royal Guard of the Court in the Palace of Queluz, known as the "Portuguese Versailles." 8 miles from Lisbon center. www.pousadas.pt/01pousadas/30ctlisboa/033maria1/index.html. Tel: (351) 21 435 61 58. Fax: (351) 21 435 61 89.

Le Méridien Park Atlantic Lisboa—Cost: Double room $146–$186. Five-star hotel situated in the center of Lisbon, facing the Eduardo VII Park. Rua Castilho 149, Lisbon 1099-034. www.lemeridien.com/portugal/lisbon/hotel_pt1604.shtml. Tel: 1 800 543 4300.

As Janelas Verdes—Cost: Double room $161. The Hotel is adjacent to the National Ancient Art Museum and close to the Tagus River. Rua Das Janelas Verdes 47, Lisbon 1200-690. Tel: 21 396 81 44. Fax: 21 396 81 44.

Hotels in Evora

Hotel Pousada Loios—Cost: Double room $204–$224. Originally a 15th century convent, this hotel is situated in the heart of historic Evora, a UNESCO World Heritage Site. www.pousadas.pt/01pousadas/40planicies/044loios/index.html#salta. Tel: (351) 218 442 001. Fax: (351) 218 442 085

Hotels in Alvor

Pestana Delfim Hotel—Cost: Double room $189–$237. Praia Dos Tres Irmaos, Alvor 8501 904. Tel: (351) 282 40 08 00. Fax (351) 282 40 08 99.

Restaurants in Lisbon

Algures Na Mouraria—Rua das Farinhas 1, Lisbon. Portuguese and Angolan food. Chicken cooked with ginger, or stewed in palm nut oil, and spicy beef.

Gambrinus—Rua Portas de S. Antão 23-25, Lisbon. Situated on a busy street full of fish restaurants. Seafood.

RESOURCES

Official Website

www.portugal.org/travelAndTourism

Books for Adults

Lonely Planet Portugal by Julia Wilkinson, John King
Walking in Portugal by Bethan Davies, Ben Cole
The Portuguese Empire, 1415–1808: A World on the Move by A. J. R. Russell-Wood

Books for Children

Prince Henry the Navigator by Leonard Everett Fisher
Portugal in Pictures by James Nach (Editor)

Videos and DVDs

Portugal: Southern Coast & Lisbon
Portugal—Land of Discoveries
Portugal—The Algarve

SOUTH AND CENTRAL AMERICA

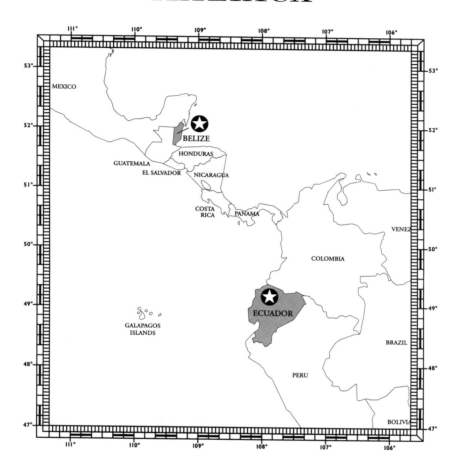

Shower time for Bill and Will Nichols near Chaa Creek, Belize.

CHAPTER 9

BELIZE: ESCAPADES ON LAND AND SEA

FAMILY TRAVEL TO BELIZE

Screaming isn't a travel behavior we relish, however in the Central American country of Belize, my family of four shrieked . . . for joy, exuberance, and laughter. After all, how else would families respond to bobbing along in lawn chairs ferried on the back of a pick-up truck, snorkeling with silky skinned sting rays or riding on the side of a horse?

Belize is nestled on the Caribbean coast between Mexico and Guatemala. This Central American country has set aside 40% of its land for parks and natural reserves, which includes a captivating mix of tropical forests rich with wildlife, magnificent mountains and mysterious Mayan temples. This ethnically diverse country's primary language is English, however Spanish is spoken widely. And best of all, Belize is just a hop, skip, and a jump from its nearby neighbor—the United States.

We began our adventure at Chaa Creek, an award-winning resort set in the foothills of the Maya Mountains above the Macal River. This ecotourist lodge offers 21 airy cottages, including three luxury suites, each replete with Central American furnishings. Chaa Creek provides environmental, cultural, and archeological activities appealing to kids and adults. Encompassing 330 acres, this lodge possesses over 70 Maya sites on its property—three of which have been excavated and whose artifacts are on display in the main center. We booked two cabins, each with a full bathroom with hot water, spacious living space, and decks with comfy chairs for imbibing in the natural wonders of the area.

Our first screaming jaunt was renting a canoe for a row down the Macal River. We packed our boat with dry clothing for our destination: San Ignacio, where we would lunch before being driven back to the lodge. As we rowed, Belizean women waved at us as they washed their clothes in the river. Mistakenly paddling our canoe into shallow water, my husband Bill climbed out, using his leg to conceivably put us back on course. But land-locked guy that he is, he tipped the canoe and all of our clothes rushed down the fast flowing river. After much effort and complaining by the kids, we were able to right our transport and rowed to San Ignacio where we crept into the restaurant in our bathing suits. Thankfully no one stared—at least obviously.

Walking through this town, we were met by the driver who would transport us back to the lodge. "How are we all going to fit in that small pick up truck?" Will asked. Before we could answer, the driver showed us to our seats: four lawn chairs ferried on the back of the truck. It was the jumpiest ride we ever had—save a roller coaster. The kids loved it and asked if we could do it again. Ah . . . no, I don't think so, unless we have seat belts, bike helmets, and full body suits.

Returning to Chaa Creek, we dined in the open-air restaurant on scrumptious cuisine—fresh tropical fruits, local freshwater fish, home baked cookies—then made our way back to our cabins where we were lured to sleep by the divine sounds of some of the 250 bird species that grace this area.

The next day, we rented horses to tour the area around Chaa Creek. Led by two guides, we explored the tropical rainforest examining insects, observing wildlife, and viewing the thick, lush foliage that encased us. Finishing up the ride, I noticed Will's horse racing off to the corral. "He's riding on the side of the horse, Mom," Alison yelled out. Indeed, Will was almost parallel to the ground. I called out to the guides to stop him and they chased after him, stopped him, then righted this wayward boy. This was my one shriek of angst.

On our third day, we drove to Chumpiate Pottery Cave, located in the back of a farmhouse and set amid a lush forest. We were greeted by a man carrying four helmets with headlights. Following this man on a winding trail we entered a dark, deep cave to view large Mayan pots set up on a ledge. The man shown a light on a minute Mayan figure drawn on one of the pots, as the kids climbed a ladder to examine it with their headlights, and then examined everything in sight with their new-found toy. Then, we went deeper into the cave. He asked to turn off our headlights and we experienced a blackness never before seen.

Following our cave experience, we went back to Chaa Creek to participate in the remaining activities: visiting the butterfly farm, viewing medicinal plants, then trekking to a cabin where we observed and held snakes—not my favorite activity.

Reluctantly bidding farewell to Chaa Creek, we drove to Belize City, boarded a motorboat, and headed to Blackbird Caye, a lodge located on a small island, one hour off the coast of Belize. Checking into our spacious cabin, we were lured outside by the startling nature that surrounded us. The kids chased sea crabs and followed their paths as they criss-crossed in the golden sand. Then sitting in lawn chairs (this time, they didn't bounce) on the beach, we observed hundreds of birds as they swooped down to the ocean hunting for fish.

Our first day at Blackbird Caye, we hopped on a boat, accompanied by 10 scuba divers. Our destination? The famous Blue Hole. In the beginning, this natural wonder was a cave, then 10,000 years ago, the roof fell in as the land subsided into the sea. It is almost a perfect dark blue circular hole, 1,000 feet in diameter, and 412 feet deep. Once arriving at this famed water spot, the divers donned their equipment and disappeared into the deep blue. The four of us intended to snorkel, however the captain would not allow Will to snorkel over such a deep abyss because of his age. He pouted as he leaned over the side of the boat observing his family snorkeling below.

Following our water adventure, we motored to an island: Half Moon Caye Natural Monument, surrounded by four sunken ships. This island earned its reputation as a monument because of its clownlike inhabitants: 4,000 red footed boobies, one of 98 species of winged wonders on this caye. Walking into a thick forest we spied hundreds of these birds with long blue beaks, white bodies, and their trademark, bright red feet. "Are these related to the blue footed boobies we saw in the Galapagos?" Will asked. Indeed they were. After lunch we followed the kids to the beach, where we sat in the smooth sand and let the waves tickle our feet.

Our last destination was the town of San Pedro, located on the southern tip of Ambergris Caye, near the Barrier Reef. This Caye is a flat island, 25 miles long, formed of limestone. San Pedro does not allow cars, so visitors maneuver golf carts on the white sand streets.

We checked into our hotel, Victoria House, and the first thing Alison and Will wanted to do was hop in the golf cart and drive to town. "Please let us drive," they whined. We complied. Showing them how to take turns, make arm signals, drive straight and stop, they got behind the wheel, and made their way into town. As they happily careened through the town, we were waved down by a local man." You have to be 18 to drive," he said politely. Alison was nine and Will, six ... Oops! We quickly shifted drivers before anyone else told us—like a policeman.

The next day, we boarded a glass bottom boat and went to Ambergis Caye, where we snorkeled with stingrays. Descending into the water we were met by two dozen of these graceful creatures. "You can touch the gray ones," the captain said, "but don't step on the tan ones—or they will live up to their names!" The kids reached out and felt the gray, silken skin. It was an experience of a lifetime.

Our last visit was Caye Caulker, an island near San Pedro and known for its shipbuilding—small wooden crafts. Caye Caulker attributes its tourism to the arrival of hippies in the late sixties and early seventies. We arrived on a day that the residents were participating in a bike race. Bikes ranging from fifties' style contraptions to chic racing bikes were lined up at the starting line for a race through the village. After waiting for the winner, we walked through a field with small, brightly painted cottages on stilts, then lunched at one of the village's 25 restaurants and ordered fresh fish cooked to perfection.

Then we boarded the boat for our final night in Belize—a country that had entertained, educated, and filled us with enjoyable shrieks.

BELIZE OVERVIEW

- Belize: Slightly smaller than Massachusetts.
- Population: 263,000
- Capital: Belmopan (Population: 5,100)
- Ethnicity: 49% Mestizo, 25% Creole, 11% Maya, 6% Garifuna, 9% other
- Religious Affiliation: 50% Roman Catholic, 27% Protestant, 9% none, 14% other
- Official Language: English. Other languages include Spanish, Mayan, Garifuna, and Creole
- Currency: Belizean Dollar
- Chief of State: Queen Elizabeth II

PLANNING AND PREPARATION

Passports

U.S. citizens are required to have a valid passport.

When to Go

Anytime! Belize's climate is subtropical, and the country's annual mean temperature is 79 degrees Fahrenheit. The humidity is tempered by the sea breezes. The rainy season is usually between June and August and the dry season is between February and May. However, the busiest tourist time is November to May.

Health Issues

Check with your health clinic regarding yellow fever vaccine and malaria pills. Medical facilities in urban areas are limited, and in rural areas extremely limited.

Safety

Tourists should exercise caution and good judgment when visiting Belize, as with most countries. Muggings, robbery, and violent crime has risen in the last few years. Common sense tells visitors to not wear expensive jewelry and to keep valuables out of sight.

What to Bring

Belize, a country with a very casual life-style, doesn't require dressy clothing. Shorts, T-shirts, and bathing suits are the order of the day, as well as comfortable sneakers. It is advisable to bring a hat, sunglasses, and sunscreen, as the tropical sun can be intense. If your family is trekking in the jungle or visiting the Mayan ruins, then pack loose fitting, light colored cotton pants and shirts, along with comfortable hiking shoes. Consider a wide brimmed hat to protect you from the sun and rain—and don't forget the insect repellent. A water bottle is recommended along with camera and binoculars.

THINGS TO SEE AND DO

Activities for Kids

- Families will view a number of Mayan ruins, so inform your children about the history of these people in Belize. The Maya civilization lived in Belize from 1000 BC to 1500 AD, and at its population peak, the Mayas numbered one to two million. No one knows why the civilization fell apart and vanished, but several theories include famine, war, and natural disasters.
- Encourage your kids to draw a Mayan ruin, and animals they observe, such as the red-footed booby and stingray.

Belize City—This capital city, lying in the heart of the country, is an easy jaunt from any destination. While there, visit the Museum of Belize with Mayan artifacts and the Maritime Museum where the history of fishing and shipbuilding is displayed.

Mayan Archeological Temples and Palaces—The Belize Department of Archeology maintains six ancient Mayan sites that are easily accessible to tourists. They are:

- **Altun Ha**—Located near Rockstone Pond Village, this is the most extensively excavated ruin in Belize.
- **Caracol**—Located in the Chiquibul Rain Forest, the drive to this ruin is spectacular.
- **Cerros**—Located south of Corozal Town, this site was a key trading center.
- **Lamanai**—Located on the banks of the New River Lagoon in North Central Belize, this ruin was a large ceremonial center.
- **Lubaantun**—Located near San Pedro in the Toledo District, this site is a large ceremonial center and contains 11 major structures, grouped around five main plazas.
- **Xunantunich**—Located eight miles west of San Ignacio, this site was a ceremonial center and consists of six major plazas and is surrounded by more than 25 temples and palaces

The Blue Hole—The Blue Hole is located in the center of Lighthouse Reef Atoll, approximately 50 miles east of Belize City. Jacques Cousteau popularized this wonder, which is the favorite dive site in Belize. Viewed from the air, it looks like a dark blue ball floating in the water.

Half Moon Caye—Set at the southeast corner of Lighthouse Reef Atoll, Half Moon Caye was the first reserve to be named by the Natural Parks System. The reason? To protect the Red-footed Booby— a bird that is found elsewhere only in the Galapagos Islands. Families touring Half Moon Caye will view hundreds of these unusual birds, as well as some of the other 98 bird species found on this island, which include Ospreys, Mangrove Warblers, and White-Crowned Pigeons. This Caye is a superb snorkeling adventure.

Ambergis Caye—This Caye is 20 miles long and two miles wide. The island is shaded by coconut and mangrove trees, and shielded by one of the world's longest barrier reefs. San Pedro, the caye's only town, includes offerings of small shops, inexpensive accommodations, a range of restaurants, and many recreational activities.

Hotels

Chaa Creek—Rates: Double rooms range between $150–$165. Children under 18 sharing their parent's room are free. Breakfast—$10. Packed lunch—$8. Dinner—$26. Children 1–5 years—free meals. 6–11 years—half price. Located on the banks of the Macal River, a few miles from San Ignacio. Cabins: 21, including three luxury suites. Activities: horseback riding, mountain biking, canoeing, hiking, bird watching, and visiting Mayan sites. Facilities: Natural History Center, Butterfly Farm, and a Spa. The restaurant features a mix of Caribbean, Mexican and Belizean cuisine. Address: P.O. Box 53, San Ignacio, Cayo District, Belize, Central America. Tel: (501) 824-2037. Fax: (501) 824-2501. www.chaacreek.com. Email: reservations@chaacreek.com.

Blackbird Caye Resort—Activities: Diving, snorkeling, fishing, windsurfing, canoeing and kayaking. This resort only offers multiple nights. Go to their website for prices: www.blackbirdresort.com.

Victoria House—Rates: $155–$195 for a double room—low to high season. Rates vary depending on type of accommodation. Meal Plan: Breakfast/Dinner—$40. Breakfast/Lunch/Dinner—$55. Children under 12: One free per adult if occupying same room, otherwise Breakfast/Dinner—$20. Breakfast/Lunch/Dinner—$25. San Pedro, Ambergis Caye. Activities: Diving, snorkeling, fishing, mainland tours, sailing, and birding. Reservations: Tel: (800) 247-5159. Website: www.victoria-house.com. Email: info@victoria-house.com.

Restaurants

The Smokey Mermaid Restaurant (Belize City)—13 Cork Street, Belize City. Tel: (501) 2-34759. The restaurant is housed in the inner courtyard of the grand, colonial-style Great House Inn. The menu is an eclectic blend of "pub grub," local seafood, and gooey desserts.

Cocina Caramba (Ambergis Caye)—Pescador Drive, San Pedro. Caribbean and Mexican food served al fresco in this quaint, family-owned restaurant.

RESOURCES
Official Websites
www.travelbelize.org
www.belizetourism.org

Books for Adults
Lonely Planet Belize by Carolyn Miller Carlstroem
Fodor's Belize and Guatemala by Melisse Gelula
Belize: Land of the Free by the Carib Sea by Thor Janson
The Maya of Belize John Eric Sidney Thompson
Time Among the Maya by Ronald Wright

Books for Children
Hands of the Maya by Rachel Crandell
The Maya: Journey into Civilization by Robert Nicholson

Videos and DVDs
Belize: A Tropical Kingdom

Alison, Will, and Jennifer Nichols deep in the jungle near La Selva Lodge, Ecuador.

CHAPTER 10

ECUADOR: RAINFOREST RETREAT

FAMILY TRAVEL TO THE ECUADORIAN RAINFOREST

The tarzan cry was unmistakable. "Ah . . . ah-ah-ah . . . ah-ah-ah . . . ,"
my son Will sang out as he clutched tightly to his dad's back. These
two wild males had hitched a ride on a dangling vine and swung
across a small valley in the middle of the Ecuadorian rainforest.
Although this bold endeavor smacked of the famous jungle man, no
Tarzan movie could have prepared my family of four for the experiences we would have in this lush ecosystem. We visited an indigenous
family, fished for piranhas, decorated our faces with red goop from a
plant, and ate delectable, tangy bugs.

These intriguing family adventures occurred at La Selva Jungle
Lodge, situated on a rise overlooking Lake Garzachocha and lying deep
in the Ecuadorian Amazon region. Winner of the coveted Ecotourism
Award, granted by the World Congress on Tourism and the Environment,
La Selva is a family destination that delights, educates, and entertains
moms, dads, and especially . . . children.

La Selva is located in the Amazon region of South America; a
green girdle, encompassing the Equator that cuts a swath through the
countries of Columbia, Peru, Brazil, Bolivia, Venezuela, and, of course,
Ecuador. As the world's largest rainforest, it blankets two million

square miles of territory. Although occupying only 6% of the world's space, the rainforest shelters 50% of the planet's wildlife species.

Ecuador, approximately the size of Colorado, touts one the highest levels of bio-diversity in the world. For example, in its 30,000 square miles of rainforest, one hectare harbors as many frog species as in all of North America, while one tree embodies more ant species than in all of the British Isles combined. And of the world's 9,000 known bird species, Ecuador is home to over 1,500.

To get to La Selva, we experienced a transportation extravaganza. First, we hopped on a windowless, jittery military transport plane in Quito and flew to Coca, a somewhat chaotic oil boomtown. Next, we jumped on an open-sided bus, rode to the river, then boarded a motorized canoe which shuttled us for two hours down the Rio Napo, a tributary of the Amazon. Once stepping onto land, our journey continued with a 45-minute trek through the rainforest. We had one more mode of transportation—two dugout canoes for the ride across Lake Garzachocha to La Selva.

We arrived at the lodge midday, and were shown to our two rustically charming cabanas built of bamboo strips, with peaked roofs made of straw, and resting on stilts. Each cabin had two beds draped by mosquito netting, a kerosene lantern, and a bathroom with running (luke warm) water. The twenty cabins at La Selva were each connected by a raised, bamboo walkway.

After the kids claimed their cabin, our daughter Alison came into our cabin with a worried look on her face "Mom, what if I have to go to the bathroom in the middle of the night," she said, "and something jumps at me?" This fear solidified after she eavesdropped on a woman who told a story about going into the bathroom in the dark and suddenly felt a big *SPLAT* on her neck. As she tried to remove it, she realized it was a small frog whose feet had suction cup toe pads. Each time the woman levered one foot off, it stuck again. This woman appropriately named the creature the "cardiac arrest" frog. This story had indeed affected Alison, so for the first evening, each kid had a parent as a roommate. Fortunately, no frogs appeared.

La Selva offers over a dozen diverse tours in the morning and the afternoon, and for the brave of heart there is also a night expedition to view nocturnal animals such as caiman, monkeys, insects, and owls.

For our first afternoon outing, we donned knee high rubber boots, lathered ourselves with insect repellent, then met our two machete-laden naturalist guides and off we went for our first adventure in the rainforest. We hiked close to home on the Mandicoccha Trial. One guide cut the foliage with his machete as we followed behind, while the other guide pointed to and explained every living object. Life flourished everywhere we looked. Insects prospered on bushes and trees, birds soared above us, and we even spied a few screeching monkeys jumping from tree to tree. Alison and Will searched high and low, taking in all that our lush surroundings had to offer. All of a sudden, it started to pour down rain. No problem. Our guides hacked at giant leaves, then handed us four, which we held over our heads as we made our way back to our cabins. "Nature's umbrella," Alison said.

La Selva prides itself on its meals. French, North American and traditional Ecuadorian food provides a rich mix of cuisines. A variety of local fruits, including granadillas—a delicious golden passion fruit—graced each meal. The kids' favorite was a deep-dish pizza that far exceeded in taste anything they had chomped down on in the U.S. My favorite was the fresh fish, and my husband's most delectable fare? A sautéed beetle grub that he munched down on one evening after dinner. "Gross," the kids cried and covered their eyes as he brought the bug to his front teeth, then smiled widely.

Speaking of bugs, our second day brought delectable joys to Alison and Will, as our guide led us to a site where thousands of small ants caked a trunk of a tree. "Go ahead, lick them," he said.

"No way," Alison said.

"What do they taste like?" Will queried, as he approached the tree trunk and examined the minute critters.

"Well, if you get enough in your mouth, they taste like lemon. In fact, we call them lemon ants."

Now Alison joined Will at the tree, and within seconds, she stuck out her tongue and sopped up the ants. Facing the group, she scrunched her eyes shut, then swallowed. I anticipated a rash of vomit, but to my surprise, she said, "They're not too bad, Mom. Try them." I took a pass, claiming I was allergic to bugs, but Will and Bill imbibed, licking their index fingers, then swallowing the ants that had adhered to it. Now my family only needed to eat 1,999 more species of bugs—the estimated number of critters around the globe that provide substantial protein, fat, minerals, vitamins, and . . . delectable tastes.

Our afternoon trek featured the Tarzan experience. Our guides led us to a small valley where they collected a number of long, snaking rope-like liana vines. We thought these vines grew from a tree, but our guide explained that they climb up tree trunks to reach the sunlight, and when they reach the canopy, they attach to other vines forming a powerful, maze-like network. Some grow to be 800 feet long. All of a sudden, our guide grabbed a vine, pulled on it, then, *whoosh* . . . across the valley he flew. "Now you do it," he hollered from the other side. Before Bill had time to think, the kids were jumping around him in excited ecstasy. So he grabbed the vine, held by the other guide and Will jumped on his back and away they flew. Then Alison hitched a ride with the remaining guide and within seconds the entire group was on the other side. "Come on, Mom," Will yelled. "Don't be a chicken!"

Looking down at the valley and viewing sharp rocks sticking up among the ground covering, I couldn't believe I had let my family do this, but it happened so quickly, I did not have time to react. Never again, I thought. "No," I shouted to them, "I'm allergic to vines!"

On the way back to the cabins, our guide hacked off some chest-nut-like seeds from a plant. After slicing each, he handed us these round objects, called *achiotes,* and told us to decorate our faces with the liquid inside each seed. Alison stuck her finger in the seed and the red goop stuck to it. It was like Halloween fun as she carefully applied two lines on her cheeks, and one each on her nose and chin. Then before Will had a chance to apply his makeup, Alison rushed over and did the same to him, this time using a small twig to delicately paint his face. Fully decorated, we returned to our cabanas.

For our third day, we went outside the La Selva area to go fishing in a motorized dug out canoe. The kids had never fished before, so this expedition generated great excitement. All eyes were on our guide as he passed out a piece of rough wood with a fishing line wrapped around the length of it to each fisherman. Attached to the end of each line was a hook on which we were instructed to secure the bait: cut up pieces of fish. "What are we fishing for, anyway?" asked Bill.

"Piranhas," our guide casually replied.

Both kids look startled and Will whispered, "Mom, don't piranhas eat people?"

After allaying Will's fears by telling him they were indeed carnivorous, but only ate small animals—never humans—we threw our lines in the water. We fished for a half-hour before hitting pay dirt. Suddenly, Alison felt a pull on her line. She instantly handed it to our guide, who pulled the fluttering piranha out of the water, grabbed its yellow-tan, six-inch-long body, then quickly set it on the bottom of the boat. Once this creature stopped moving, he removed the hook, then levered its mouth open, revealing its serrated teeth, which gave us all shivers. "Are you sure they don't eat people?" Will asked again. Looking at the teeth, which resembled a disfigured saw blade, well . . . I couldn't be sure.

In the afternoon, we again stepped into the dugout canoe and went up the Rio Napo River for an hour ride. Our destination was the home of an indigenous family who lived high up on a cliff adjacent to the river. Ecuador is home to over forty indigenous "nations" or groups, the majority of which live in the rainforest. Banking the canoe, we waded in knee deep water to a sheer cliff, which had a tree trunk up the side with notches cut out of it for climbing. Cautiously making our way to the top we were met by a young man holding a small monkey. "Hola," he said as he extended his hand to each of us, helping us the last few steps of the way.

The family spoke Quichua, the most prevalent native tongue in the country. However, the young man also spoke Spanish, as did our bilingual guide, so we didn't miss any information. There were 11 members in this family—three generations of babies to grandparents. They lived on an open platform, resting on stilts with a thatched roof. There were no beds, no furniture, no toilet, and no toys. Grouped around the center post were several old appliances, including an old, hand-cranked, wringer washing machine, and an icebox.

As Alison and Will looked at this platform house and observed the family, they were all questions. "Where do they sleep? What do the kids play with? Where do they bathe and go to the bathroom? How do they cook? How do they get to school?" As they surveyed the surroundings, they came up with the answers . . . they slept on woven mats; the kids made their own toys, or played with the monkey; they bathed in the river and went to the bathroom in an outhouse on the grounds; they cooked in two dugout holes for fire; and the kids got to school the same way we had come to their home—climbing down the cliff and then taking a boat.

The young man followed us around and showed us his array of animals: several colorful parrots and the small monkey he continued to hold. He explained to our guide that they had killed the monkey's mother for food, then kept her baby as a pet. As we were getting ready to leave, the grandfather offered us a white frothy drink called *chi-cha*. Bill and I were on the same wave length, recalling drinking the same beverage in Peru—pre-kids—and learning after we drank it that it had been mixed in someone's mouth. We weren't sure about this one, but politely declined anyway.

Our guide motioned for us to leave, so we waved good-bye to the family and journeyed back to La Selva. On the way back, Bill and I decided it was time to explain to the kids about the destruction of the rainforest caused by ranching, logging, and gas and oil endeavors. To bring the annihilation to a kid's level, Bill quoted a figure that he read about in a book. "Did you know that every *second,* the space equal to the size of two football fields, is destroyed in the rainforest?" he said. This startling figure had indeed sunk in, as the kids repeated it time and time again when people asked about their trip.

Our final day in the rainforest we termed as kids' day. Bill and I told Alison and Will they could each pick an activity that interested them. There was only one rule, however . . . no Tarzan vine swinging. Alison chose the butterfly farm, a five-minute walk from our cabin. This farm, one of the few in the world, breeds 35,000 butterflies a year for exportation. The kids were able to observe all stages of development: egg, caterpillar, pupa, and, of course, the brilliantly colored butterflies which fluttered around us and even landed on our shoulders.

For his activity, Will chose a 135-foot observation tower that was constructed in a giant kapok tree. Stairs wrapped around the trunk built in an ecologically sound fashion with no nails. Once entering the tower, we gained a new perspective on the rainforest—a bird's eye view of the highest canopy. Here, hundreds of feathered friends flew by, providing yet another perspective on the magnificent environment.

Our rainforest adventure came to a close all too soon. We had learned about this extraordinary ecosystem, experienced its diverse pleasures, overcome scary and distasteful moments, observed animal and plant species we would never see again . . . and had experienced nature's most remarkable orchestration of life.

Would we take the kids back to La Selva? You bet we would.

ECUADOR OVERVIEW

- Ecuador: Approximately the size of Colorado
- Population: 13.5 million
- Capital: Quito (Population: 1.2 million)
- Ethnicity: 65% Mestizo (mixed Amerindian and white), 25% Amerindian, 7% Spanish and others, 3% black
- Religious Affiliation: 95% Catholic (many combine their Catholicism with traditional beliefs), 5% other
- Official Language: Spanish; Native Language: Quichua is widely spoken
- Currency: U.S. Dollar
- Ecuador: Straddles the Equator, in Northern and Southern Hemispheres

- Ecuadorian Regions: the Amazon, the Pacific Coast, the high-lands, and the Galapagos Islands

Planning and Preparation

Passports

Each visitor to Ecuador is required to have a valid passport and proof of a return ticket. There is no visa requirement for stays of under 90 days. An airport exit fee of $25 per person is required upon leaving the country.

When to Go

The dry season in the rainforest is late August through February, although throughout the year the climate is warm (72 to 80 degrees), humid, and may feature driving rainstorms.

Health Issues

Yellow fever vaccinations as well as cholera are recommended for Ecuador. As of February 2000, the yellow fever vaccine was not required to enter Ecuador unless travelers are entering from a country that is considered a yellow fever risk area. Requirements can change, however, so check with the Ecuadorian Embassy (www.usembassy.org.ec) before departing. Also, the Hepatitis A vaccine or immune globulin (IG) is recommended for all South American travelers. Another vaccination to consider is an anti-tetanus booster. A reputable travel clinic can advise families of all suggested vaccinations.

There is malaria risk in the Amazon jungle lowlands, therefore antimalarial medications, taken before, during, and after travel are advisable, at the discretion of your physician. Mosquitoes are the primary carriers of malaria, so any precaution you can take against mosquito and other insect bites are advisable. Use an effective insect repellent (DEET is advisable), wear protective clothing, and make sure your lodge has mosquito netting.

Safety

The rainforest is relatively safe as long as one follows the instructions of the guides. Encounters with jungle animals (e.g. snakes, crocodiles in the rivers, etc.) are rare. You are unlikely to run into problems as long as you keep alert, stick to clearly worn paths, and stay out of lakes and rivers unless your guide tells you they are safe.

What to Bring

Clothing is a key element for protection and comfort in the rainforest. Light weight cotton, long sleeve shirts and pants are advisable to keep insects from biting. Experts recommend nylon belts as opposed to leather, as they are prone to collect green moss almost overnight. Do not take open-toed shoes, but rather hiking boots that provide protection against wet, slippery conditions. La Selva provides knee-length boots with textured bottoms. Be sure to take an extra pair of shoes for when your jungle walkers get wet. A waterproof daypack is advisable to carry a water bottle and to keep your camera dry.

Ecuadorian Rainforest

Labeled as "the lungs of the planet," the world's rainforest releases oxygen and moisture to approximately one billion people who live in the tropics. Americans and other people of temperate lands also feel the benefit because the rainforest helps regulate global climate. The rain forest also plays a major role in the health of our planet, as 25% of drugs sold in pharmacies (approximate 7,000) contain rainforest ingredients. Quinine for malaria; curare for multiple sclerosis and Parkinson's disease are gathered from the rainforest, as well as many industrial products, including latex, resins, and minerals.

Sadly, cattle ranching, mineral and oil explorations, and logging are taking a profound toll on the rainforest. Experts claim this significant ecosystem could be destroyed by the year 2030, particularly at the current rate of destruction that occurs each day and is equal in size to New York City. Fortunately, international environmental and human rights organizations monitor, protest, and take action against those who jeopardize the rainforest.

Ecuador's rainforest, located in the eastern sector of the country, is known as *El Oriente*. This lush ecosystem boasts some of the Amazon's most biologically diverse and pristine areas.

THINGS TO SEE AND DO

Activities for Kids

- Have your children draw their favorite animal, insect and plant. Ask your guide to tell them how label them in Spanish.
- Inform your kids why rainforests are called rainforests. Because they're so wet. Each year, tropical rainforests receive 160 to 400 inches of rain. Los Angeles receives 10 to 20 inches of rain yearly! Also because rainforests lie in close proximity to the equator, temperatures average 75 to 80 degrees all year. Have your kids brainstorm what this climate does to animals, plants, and insects. To confirm your answers ask your guide.
- A tropical rainforest has four layers: the emergent trees, canopy, the understory, and the forest floor. The emergent and canopy layers are the top of the rainforest, where a few trees, called emergents, grow out above the green growth to catch the sun. Most of the plant growth seeks the sun, so the largest number of animals, including monkeys, birds, and tree frogs, live in the canopy. The understory is below the canopy where young trees and shrubs grow. The forest floor is almost bare because only a small amount of light can seep through the canopy and understory to the ground. Fallen leaves and branches rot quickly to release nutrients for other plants to grow. Point out to your kids these four levels and have them identify plants and animals typical to each level.

There are innumerable options for tours at La Selva, only limited by the family's and naturalist guide's imagination. Here are 11 of the many excursions:

1. Walk by a native's house—This three hour walk takes families through the primary forest as well as past the huts of indige-

nous neighbors along the Napo river. There is some physical challenge to this hike.

2. Mandicocha trail—This is an easy trail close to the hotel which is usually replete with wildlife any time of day. This excursion can last as long as families want.

3. Mandicocha-Mandiyacu—This 3- to 4-hour excursion follows the Mandicocha trail until families reach Mandicocha lake, which has a completely different ecosystem than Lake Garzacocha (where the hotel is located). Families board paddle canoes for a one and half hour glide down Mandiyacu stream, where myriad wildlife can be seen along the shores of the stream. Once reaching the Napo river, families board a motorized canoe for the trip back to La Selva.

4. El Salado—This two-hour excursion combines a picnic lunch with a trip across the Napo River (see following). Here families will delight in viewing parrots, parakeets and thousands of macaws.

5. High forest trail—The duration of this excursion varies between three to five hours. Families cross the Napo River and then hike a challenging mountain trail which offers yet another ecosystem with a variety of birds and other wildlife unique to this area. Hungry after all this activity? This trail provides the opportunity to lick lemon ants off a tree.

6. Challuacocha lake—Families take a motorized canoe trip down the Napo River, then walk and take a paddle canoe trip to Challuacocha lake. Picnic at a shelter overlooking the lake, then it's your choice: go for a relaxing canoeing jaunt, fish for piranhas, or hike for two-hours through yet another unique forest.

7. Pilche trail—Cross Garzacocha lake then walk one hour to view an enormous colony of leafcutter ants and amazing wildlife.

8. Ruth's trail—This trail, named after the owner's mother, is a good place to keep an eye out for jaguars.

9. Night excursions—Sample the La Selva nightlife by canoeing or walking after dark to view nocturnal creatures such as caiman, monkeys, insects, and owls.

10. 135-foot observation tower—Not far from the lodge you can walk up a tower to get a bird's eye view of the highest canopy.
11. Butterfly farm—Available every afternoon and on the grounds of the lodge, families can photograph butterflies at close range and, with luck, witness the miracle of metamorphosis.

Jungle Lodges

La Selva Jungle Lodge—Price: 3 nights/4 days: $547. 4 nights/5 days: $684. Price includes three meals a day and all tours. La Selva offers 20 cabins; 13 cabins are double occupancy, one cabin sleeps three, one sleeps four and one sleeps up to seven and has two full baths. Each room has a bathroom and showers. Tel: (593) 2 550 995 or 554 686. Fax: (593) 2 567 297. Email: laselva@uio.satnet.net. Website: www.laselvajunglelodge.com/.

Yachana Lodge—Cost: High season (July, August, December) 3 nights/4 days—Adults: $320; Children under 12: $160. 4 nights/5 days—Adults: $400; Children: $200. Price includes three meals and excursions. Yachana, which means "a place of learning," is located on the Rio Napo. Yachana provides a range of hikes led by local, bilingual guides. There are also opportunities to visit a local tribal healer, participate in a cleansing ceremony, try out a blowpipe, and learn about the uses of medicinal plants. Accommodations include 11 cabins, which sleep two or three guests, and three family cabins for up to five guests. All rooms have a private bathroom with warm water. Tel: (593) 2 2566-035. Fax: (593) 2 2523-777. Email: infor@yachana.com. Website: www.yachana.com.

Kapawi Lodge—Located in one of the most remote areas of the Ecuadorian Amazon, Kapawi Lodge rests on the Pastaza River and is accessible only by small aircraft. The lodge was created in partnership with the Achuar—a local tribe of Amazonian Indians. Kapawi has 20 double rooms, each with private bathroom, sun-heated showers, and electricity provided by a solar power system. Completed in 1996,

Kapawi adheres to the Achuar concept of architecture; it is built without a single metal nail. Tours, conducted by a naturalist guide and an Achuar guide, include visits to Achuar communities, rainforest hikes, river canoeing, and bird-watching. Cost: 3 nights/4 days: $600 per person. 4 nights/5 days: $720 per person. Children under seven pay half price. Three meals a day are included in the price as well as tours. Kapawi does not have contact information. Contact Amazon Adventures located in Austin, Texas. Tel: 800-232-5658. Email: jmc12@amazonadventures.com. Website: www.amazonadventures.com/kapawi.htm.

RESOURCES

Official Websites
Official Ecuador Website:
www.vivecuador.com

Other Useful Websites:
www.ecuaworld.com
www.rainforestweb.org
www.rain-tree.com

Websites for the Kids:
www.eduweb.com/amazon.html
www.ran.org/kids_action/index.html

Books for Adults
Portraits of the Rainforest by Adrian Forsyth
Stinging Trees and Wait-A-Whiles: Confessions of a Rainforest Biologist by William F. Laurance
The Birds of Ecuador by Robert S. Ridgely
Rough Guide to Ecuador by Harry Ades

Books for Children
Look Closer: Rain Forest by Barbara Taylor and Frank Greenaway

Here is the Tropical Rainforest by Madeleine Dunphy
Nature's Green Umbrella: Tropical Rainforests by Gail Gibbons
The Great Kapok Tree: A Tale of the Amazon Rainforest by Lynne Cherry
At Home in the Rainforest by Diane Willow
A Walk in the Rainforest by Kristen Joy Pratt
The Remarkable Rainforest: An Active Learning Book for Kids by Toni Albert
One Day in the Tropical Rainforest by Jean Craighead George
Exploring the Rainforest: Science Activities for Kids by Anthony D. Fredericks
How Monkeys Make Chocolate: Food and Medicines from the Rainforest by Adrain Forsyth

Family Books
Man Eating Bugs by Peter Menzel
Draw Rainforest Animals by D.C. Dubosque

Videos and DVDs
National Geographic Really Wild Animals: Totally Tropical Rainforest
Amazing Animals Video: Rainforest Animals
National Geographic's Rainforest

AFRICA

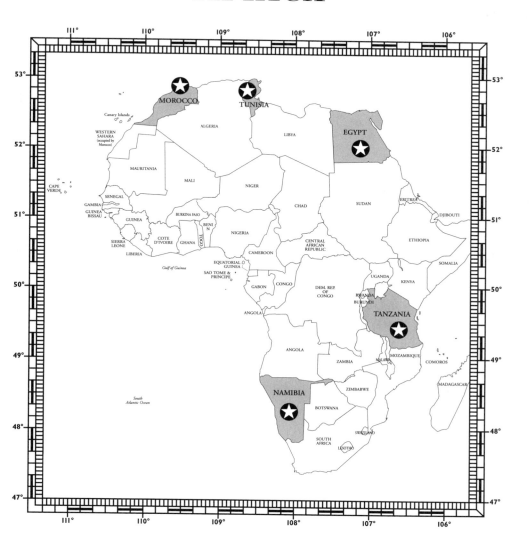

Alison and Will Nichols ride into the Sahara Desert from Zagora, Morocco.

CHAPTER 11

MOROCCO: ON THE ROAD THROUGH MOROCCO, FAMILY STYLE

FAMILY TRAVEL TO MOROCCO

"Don't worry, madame," whispered the turbaned man next to me, "that snake around your daughter's neck is not poisonous."

It couldn't have been more than 30 seconds since I had taken my eyes off my 12-year-old in Marrakech's throwback medieval square, Djemaa el-Fna. Yet in that time, a snake charmer had succeeded in wrapping the creature around my startled child, who now stood stone-still as the slithering serpent slowly wound its way up around her neck.

"Get that thing off her. Now," I ordered. As the snake's owner complied, my daughter shot me one of those if-looks-could-kill glances. (To Alison, being almost strangled by a snake was preferable to being embarrassed by her mother.) So on this, our first day in Morocco, the stage was set for Alison and her 9-year-old brother, Will. Surprise, intrigue and unrivaled family adventures would continue to mark our 12 days in this exotic North African country.

Friends had warned my husband, Bill, and me about our summer travel plans to Morocco, particularly since we really had no plans other than knowing we would rent a car in Marrakech and, *sans* guide, drive south through the High Atlas Mountains, ending up in the Sahara.

"Your kids will fry in the desert" . . . "You're bound to get lost on your own" . . . "The roads are treacherous" . . . were all phrases that fell on our unconcerned ears. Okay, I'll admit it. We did get lost a few times. But Morocco's well-developed system of roads was perfectly navigable. And neither Alison nor Will suffered heatstroke. While Morocco had the faraway allure of other countries already stamped in their passports—Thailand, Tanzania and Ecuador—it also offered a level of safety that allayed our parental concerns.

Morocco, slightly larger than California, is a North African country that lies within an arm's reach of Spain, across the Strait of Gibraltar. It is blessed with long coastlines bordering the Atlantic on the west and the Mediterranean on the north. The Atlas Mountains rim its eastern border, while the Sahara Desert lies south. Geographically shielded from the rest of Africa, Morocco's culture is an amalgam derived from numerous invaders and mixed with its indigenous people, the Berbers. Flavoring this rich cultural soup are remnants of French and Spanish colonization.

With a major economic stake in tourism, Morocco is a politically stable and socially liberal Moslem country and a staunch American ally. In fact, King Mohammed VI was one of the first to offer support in rallying the Arab world to fight terrorism after September 11th. It seems this pro-west posture may have played a role in the May 2003 terrorist bombings in Casablanca. The U.S. State Department nevertheless lists Morocco as a safe destination; religious extremism (with the notable exception above) is kept in check and violent crime and personally owned weapons of any kind are rare.

As for health issues, Morocco gained points when I told the kids that this country requires no immunizations—"Yes!" said Alison (although bottled water is recommended, and malaria pills may be prescribed for coastal areas).

Best of all, as we discovered, seeing the less traveled parts of the country at our own leisure was an experience not to be missed.

We began our adventure in Marrakech, a city of 600,000 that resonates with rich Moroccan traditions and is laced with European flair.

Since we knew our trip to the south would be extremely economical by U.S. standards, we decided to splurge our first two nights at the five-star Hotel La Mamounia, where two double rooms cost a total of $500.

One of the world's most legendary hotels, Mamounia earns its elite reputation. Our adjoining rooms featured expansive balconies looking out over 20 acres of lush gardens. And the kids immediately staked out their claim to a palm-island oasis in the middle of the hotel's gigantic swimming pool. (If they noticed the topless French ladies sunning poolside, they didn't show it.)

To lure the kids out of Mamounia to see the sites of Marrakech, we promised caleches, or horse-drawn carriages. For a hard-bargained price of 40 dirham (about $4), they clip-clopped from the hotel to the heart of Marrakech's main square—the Djemaa el-Fna—where we stepped right into medieval Morocco. With its jostling throngs of people, seductive scents of food and the ceaseless din of horn-honking, instrument-playing, and human bantering, Djemaa el-Fna awakens the senses.

Although it was quite intimidating to our kids (and their parents) at first, we soon began adapting to the square's bizarre rhythm. Musicians, magicians, acrobats, folk healers, fire eaters, storytellers, contortionists, snake charmers, monkey trainers, tooth extractors, henna artists, beggars and, of course, those who merely observe this amazing scene are among the crowd that converges here as the sun sets each evening. It's then that dozens of small mobile eateries are set up on the periphery, serving everything from traditional Moroccan lamb stew to couscous and pastries to steamed lamb heads replete with their most coveted delicacy, the eyeballs.

It was this latter food item that convinced us we would eat in a bona fide restaurant, Dar Marjana, about five minutes from the square. There, an elderly, bent-over man in a *djellaba*, or long robe, greeted us with a lantern in hand and led us down a dark, narrow alleyway opening onto a beautiful courtyard ringed by knee-high tables. We sat on a low bench surrounded by dozens of satin pillows, and were served a sumptuous meal of 11 hors d'oeuvres, couscous with grilled vegetables, fowl wrapped in a crepe and tagine (lamb stew)—all topped off with a huge brittle crepe dessert drenched with honey. The kids, after timidly testing each dish, imbibed in the full pleasures of this meal. We passed up the evening's traditional dancing entertainment and led our weary, overstuffed young travel mates out of the restaurant just as they began to melt into the comfort of the pillows.

Our second day in Marrakech, we hired an official guide for $20 in the hotel lobby. This was a necessity for our day's activity—visiting the souk, the ancient labyrinth of shops that teems with people, bicycles, and donkeys.

Bargaining in the souk is not only customary, it is expected. From a $1,000 silk rug to a $2 bracelet, every item demands intense negotiation. "Start at one-fourth the asking price and bargain patiently, aggressively and with humor," a guidebook advised. The kids immediately took to this game, learning to walk out of the shop if, after several rounds of haggling, no agreement on price was reached. Inevitably the shopkeeper, an expert at the retail ballet, called after them in a contrived, defeated tone, "OK, OK, what's your final price?"

Our third day, we left the splendid Mamounia and headed off in our rented Volvo to "Le Grand Sud," the southern region of Morocco, choosing the well-traveled Tizi n'Tichka, a winding but well-maintained two-lane route popular with tourists. We would climb 7,000 feet before dropping down into the oasis of Ouarzazate, about 120 miles (or four hours) from Marrakech.

Along the way, each switchback afforded a view more spectacular than the last. Mountain landscapes—from verdant green to stark lunar—and small mud villages built into the hillsides presented photo ops too precious to pass up. Only one other sight equaled this startling High Atlas panorama: the Berbers. As we drove through small villages, *djellaba*-clad men rested and chatted in the shade of mud buildings, or sat around tiny cafe tables drinking tea. The women, with their distinctive facial tattoos and garishly colored shawls and clothing, herded goats, carried massive bundles of straw on their backs, tended children, or drew water from wells.

At noon, we arrived at Ouarzazate, a lush oasis on the Draa River. As the center of Morocco's growing film-location industry, the city boasts of being the backdrop for scenes from *Lawrence of Arabia, Jesus of Nazareth, The Man Who Would Be King,* and numerous others. We stayed the night at the Berber Palace, one of several modern hotels in this rapidly developing town. Set amid well-maintained gardens and reasonably priced at $75 for a double room, the hotel offered a good restaurant with meals from the menu or buffet, and pizza selections wildly popular with Will and Alison.

On day four, we set out for Zagora, a town of 15,000 and gateway to the Sahara. Motoring on an unpronounceable road, the Tizi n'Tinififft, we snaked through spectacular mountain scenery before dropping down into the Draa Valley. Here many oasis dwellers live in *ksour,* fortified adobe-type villages built generations ago and occupied by multiple families.

Zagora, though unimpressive, is a good base from which to arrange a trip into the Sahara. We stayed at the Kasbah Asmaa, where the garishly decorated double rooms cost about $30 a night. A new hotel built around an inner courtyard, Asmaa also offers nomad wannabes two authentic Berber tents available for camping out on the hotel grounds. We passed on this, but did arrange with the hotel's front desk for a next-day camel trek and overnight in the Sahara. It would cost about $300 for the four of us, including camels, trek guide, the tent, dinner and breakfast, as well as the host, cook, and musicians, six or seven people in all.

The next day our guide, Naji, waited for us in the parking lot with our transport: four massive single-humped camels with saddles of thick, rolled-up woolen blankets from which protruded metal handlebars.

"Climb on," Naji glibly instructed, motioning to the four sitting dromedaries, their legs neatly folded beneath their hulking bodies. He neglected to warn us to hold on for dear life, though, while the camels reared up first on their long hind legs, keeping the front ones folded—a motion that sent us into a head-forward position almost parallel with the ground. Then straightening out their front legs, the animals jolted us back to vertical.

"Do you suppose the hotel has any bike helmets?" I asked Naji once I realized we were now five feet off the ground. The kids rolled their eyes as I started my usual lecture to the kids about head injuries. But Naji either didn't understand my request or chose to ignore it. As we bumped through the edge of Zagora, children chased after us and men drove stubborn mules overburdened with supplies along the narrow, dusty road. Low, flat houses of mud, many surrounded by thick adobe walls, disappeared as we entered the rocky, hilly countryside with its herds of grazing camels.

Three hours of riding across the rock-strewn desert put us at our evening's accommodation: a low-slung Berber tent made of goat hair. Our camp crew—a cook, an assistant and three musicians—welcomed us and then motioned to the kids to pat the camels. Dinner of couscous and tagine did not excite us, but the three musicians did with their offering of traditional songs played on tambourines, stringed instruments, and ceramic darbukas (cylindrical, goatskin-covered drums). We thanked them by singing a Nichols' rendition of "I've Been Working on the Railroad." Before turning in, we took a short hike but didn't stray far; the noiseless night was inky black, and aside from the occasional faint sounds of camels belching, there were no markers to lead us back to our camp.

In the morning, we awoke in time to watch the red sun edge its way over the endless sand dunes, where the only other signs of life were the tracks of scarab beetles.

Our next destination was the town of Erfoud, another four hours away. Although the drive was uneventful, our stay in Erfoud and the cozy Hotel Tazimi was not. This family-owned hotel is built around a center courtyard. The rooms, each with thick adobe walls, feature tasteful furnishings. The staff was gracious and friendly; the charming restaurant served excellent Moroccan, international, and French cuisine.

The first night at Tazimi we were all awakened at midnight by the haunting sound of women ululating. This wailing chant marked the beginning of a three-day wedding celebration for one of the owners. The next morning, the gracious groom invited us into his honeymoon suite to meet his wife, an exquisitely beautiful 17-year-old dressed in a white embroidered caftan. Her black hair was perfectly coifed, her heavy eye makeup meticulously applied, and her hands intricately decorated with rich, reddish-brown geometric designs.

In a country in which most marriages are arranged and result from social and economic contracts between families, men may legally take up to four wives. Our host, 32, was on his second. Had she remained single into her mid-20s his bride would have been referred to as a *meskin*—"poor thing."

The couple treated us to sweet cookies, dates, and nuts and invited us to the festivities that evening. We gladly accepted and hours later joined the celebration, where Alison and I sat segregated with the women in the parlor as they tended their babies, danced, and talked. They were dressed in elegant finery, and their hands bore intricate geometric designs similar to the young bride's. Bill and Will hung out in the courtyard with the men.

For our final day in Erfoud, we arranged for a guide to drive us at 4:00 A.M. to Erg Chebbi, Morocco's most massive dunes, about 40 miles south. Our intent was to scale these 10-story-high mountains of unforgiving, shifting sand in time to catch the sunrise. The kids and Bill tackled the dunes effortlessly. I watched as Alison and Will reverted to sandbox play, filling their shoes with sand, burying their legs, and creating sand angels. Making it almost to the top, my progress slowed and it seemed that for every few steps I took, I sunk back one. Suddenly a hand appeared and pulled me up the rest of the way. Thanks to the kindness of a young Berber man, I arrived at the peak of the dune in time to witness, with my family, the sun shedding its growing light on the Sahara for as far as the eye could see.

That afternoon back in Erfoud, our desert guide, Mohammed, invited us to his home, an old kasbah he shared with many other families. Once inside, he introduced us to Fatima—a henna artist with whom he had arranged a hand painting session for Alison and me. For the next two hours, we sat with Fatima while she meticulously drew elaborate geometric and floral designs on our hands and arms with a blunt-edged applicator, applying a mud-like concoction of powdered henna, sugar, and water. Mohammed's sisters and mother hurried in and out of the room serving us mint tea and small delicacies.

As we said goodbye to our host, his family—and soon to Morocco—Mohammed told us that the henna, which would remain on our hands for another few weeks, would bring us good fortune and beauty.

But indeed, we had already experienced that: The good fortune had come with traveling as a family in this gracious and intriguing part of the world. Long after the henna faded, the memories of family wanderings in Morocco would continue.

MOROCCO OVERVIEW

- Morocco: Approximately the size of California
- Population: 31 million
- Capital: Rabat (Population: 1.5 million)
- Ethnicity: 55% Arab, 44% Berber and 1% others
- Religious Affiliation: 98% Sunni Muslim, 1% Christian and 1% Jewish
- Language: Arabic (official), French: Language of business, government and diplomacy
- Currency: Moroccan Dirham.

PLANNING AND PREPARATION

Passports

A valid passport is necessary, however for Americans there are no visa requirements.

When to Go

Depends on where you go . . . areas on the coast have a pleasant climate year-round, while inland temperature is hotter and drier. From April to October average temperature is 86 degrees during the day and 59 degrees at night. The desert areas in the south are extremely hot and dry, while the nights can get cool. The mountainous regions are cool in summer, and from December to March, there is usually snow.

Health Issues

There are no health issues in Morocco, nor are any inoculations required. To make sure drinking water is safe, use bottled water. Use common sense and caution when purchasing food from street vendors.

Safety

Morocco has a level of safety that allays concerns. With a major economic stake in tourism, this politically stable and socially liberal Moslem country is a staunch American ally. In fact, King Mohammed VI was one of the first to offer support in rallying the Arab world to fight terrorism after September 11th. (See earlier comment about May 2003 terrorist bombings in Casablanca.) The U.S. State Department lists Morocco as a safe destination; religious extremism is kept in check and violent crime and personally owned weapons of any kind are rare.

What to Bring

Morocco is a Moslem country, hence clothing tends to be conservative, especially for women. Loose fitting dresses, skirts, and blouses are essential to bring. Also useful would be a light shawl as a cover up if you are wearing more revealing western clothes.

Hiring a Guide

On our second trip to Morocco, we hired a guide. We chose the destinations and Aziz, our knowledgeable guide, planned the timing and the events. The advantage was that we experienced places we never would have seen on our own, such as a visit to a Berber home, a nomad camp, and behind-the-scenes stops at shops in the souk, where employees took the kids and dressed them up in traditional Moroccan garb. Asiz, a former history teacher who was fluent in English, also shared stories with us on growing up in Morocco and provided an intriguing overview of the history of each site.

Questions to Ask a Guide

- What services do you provide?
- What is the daily cost? (The cost is usually negotiable. Be sure to give a tip.)
- Are you fluent in English?
- What activities can you arrange that are of interest to children of ages . . . ?
- What would a typical daily schedule look like?

Things to See and Do

Activities for Kids

- Children will view startling elements in Morocco. Have them observe and discuss architecture, mode of dress, markets, small shops in which the artisans are working, only men sitting in cafes, children working in the market and much more that will put a clear line between their way of life and a Moroccan's.
- As you walk through the market, stop to observe the craftsmen (there will be no women). Weavers, dyers, wood workers, shoe makers, and more ply their crafts.
- Have your kids draw their favorite market items, then ask your hotel concierge to label them in Arabic.

Camel Rides—A trip to Morocco is not complete without a camel trek. My family of four headed to Zagora: the gateway to the Sahara. We arranged our dromedary excursion through our Zagora hotel, the Kasbah Asmaa, then greeted our four humped traveling companions in the late afternoon. Then off we went for the bumpy and blissful ride through kasbahs and oases and eventually into the searing sands of the Sahara.

For $300, our price included our guide, a Berber tent, a cook, three musicians, and dinner and breakfast. After a three-hour ride, we arrived at our night's shelter: a low-slung tent made of woven camel hair rugs and set amidst undulating dunes.

In addition to arranging camel treks at Zagora hotels, tours can be booked online through The Best of Morocco, Ltd. (www.morocco-travel.com), a London based company that provides treks ranging from one to five nights.

Sleeping in a Desert Oasis—From Ouarzazate, families can journey in Land Rovers to an oasis set on the banks of the river Fint. Dining at small tables and stools placed on Berber rugs, parents and children are often entertained by men playing drums and stringed instruments as well as women in colorful, flowing costumes who hold hands, perform a tribal dance, and sing and ululate. Often, the male performers grab the men and the females the women to join them in a dance. Don't expect to dance with your mate though, as the two sexes deliberately do not mix. As a thank you for the entertainment, families can sing a joint popular American song to the performers, then bed down on the sand for a star-viewing extravaganza.

Stay at a Riad—At day's end Morocco embraces families by providing luxury and serenity in *riads*, traditional courtyard mansions refined to the highest architectural and decorative quality as lavish hotels, and which give a glimpse into this country's customs and artwork.

An example of two divine riads are *Riad Maison Bleue* in Fez, and *Riad Kaiss* in Marrakech. *Riad Maison Bleue* was built in 1900, by Sidi Mohamed Ben Arbi Aloui, an eminent citizen of Fez. The property remains in the possession of the family. Many of the furnishings of *Riad Maison Bleue* belonged to French General Lyautee, who ruled Morocco at the beginning of the 20th century, when France occupied the country. When the General moved back to France, he left the furnishing to his servants, who auctioned them off to the highest bidder—the Alouis. Room amenities included cable TV and air conditioning, while *riad* facilities offered a *hammam* steam bath, an exquisite library, swimming pool, and two terraces. *Riad Maison Bleue* is situated five minutes from Fez's medina or old walled city.

Riad Kaiss in Marrakech is located on the edge of medina. Built in 1860, this mansion was originally owned by the Ben Hivoun family whose father was a *wali*, or governor of Marrakech. It was purchased in 1998 by French architect and Asian hotel designer Christian Ferre who spent three years refurbishing it to a luxurious accommodation. This opulent, eight room *riad* houses traditional Moroccan furnishings and fabrics, a startling collection of modern art and traditional crafts.

Get a Henna Tattoo—Have your kids—or you—dreamed of getting a tattoo but were turned off by the life-long permanence? Now you dreams will come true in Morocco! Henna tattoos grace your skin for only a week to ten days . . . then *poof!* they fade away. Henna is made from a paste of dried leaves, then mixed with lemon juice, sugar, and hot water so it can suck up easily in a syringe whose tip has been cut off. Getting a henna tattoo is a safe technique that requires no skin piercing. Most henna artists carry pictures of previous artwork, so choose the best!

Marrakech—Marrakech, a city founded in 1062 AD, was once the capital of an empire that stretched from Toledo, Spain to Senegal. Today, this city of 1.5 million, holds an immediate and enduring allure for visitors with its endless activity, palpitating aura, and embracing culture. Shopping in Marrakech's souk is a must. In this winding labyrinth of shops each item claims its own section—food, carpets, jewelry, clothing, leather products, woodwork, and lanterns. Merchants try to lure shoppers in by saying, "Come into my shop. There are many bargains here."

In addition to the souk, visit the Jardin Majorelle Gardens which were created by Frenchman Jacque Majorelle who acquired the land in 1924 and landscaped it with vegetation from five continents. In

1947 this artist and architect opened his gardens to the public. Set amid the plants are fountains and vases painted in a brilliant hue called "Majorelle blue." When Majorelle died, the gardens were taken over by Yves Saint Laurent, whose house backs up on the gardens.

Fez—The historic city of Fez is a metropolis that resonates with Moroccan traditions and is revered as the intellectual and cultural heart of the country. Founded in the ninth century, this city of 600,000 is a gem of Spanish-Arab civilization. Don't miss the medina, or old walled city named as a World Heritage Site by UNESCO. The medina is a winding labyrinth of houses, workshops and booths, which jolts the senses with its hypnotizing sounds, sensual fragrances and brilliant colors. An endless swirl of activity captivates visitors . . . throngs of shoppers intermingle with the merchants of the small shops, while 30,000 craftsmen—including weavers, potters, wood crafters, shoe makers, tile artists, cloth workers, and leather workers—make traditional crafts. Be sure to visit the tanner's market. Here, over a hundred stone vats combine mordants—a chemical that combines with dye—with natural pigments to create color. Holding a sprig of mint under your noses to mask the odors, families can view workers in the vats dying the animal skins and the finished products drying on nearby roofs.

Hotels in Marrakech

La Mamounia—Cost: Double rooms $200–$500 and up. This is one of Marrakech's—and arguably Africa's—finest hotels. Classic North African architectural style with beautiful gardens in back. Swimming pool with palm tree island. Also has a squash court. Winston Churchill slept here. Bab el-Jedid, Marrakech; www.mamounia.com. Tel: (800) 223-6800 or (212) 4 448-981. Fax: (212) 4 444-044. Email: management@mamounia.com.

Hotels in Ouarzazate

Le Berbere Palace—Rates: Double room $100 and up. Located a short drive from Ouarzazate's major sites. Very high quality services.

Large swimming pool. Quartier Mansour Eddahbi. Tel: (212) 4 883-077. Fax: (212) 4 883-071.

Hotels in Erfoud

Kasbah Tizimi Hotel—Rates: Double $50–$100. Located on the edge of Erfoud with mostly desert on the south side. Built around a central courtyard with a refreshing swimming pool in the center. Route de Jorf. Tel: (212) 5 576-179, (212) 5 577-375.

Riads

Riad Kaiss—Rates: $140–$162. $216 for suite. Double occupancy, breakfast included. Located on a small alleyway, just five minutes by foot from Marrakech's central souk. This delightful riad has a small rooftop swimming pool. 65 Derb jdid, Marrakech, Morocco. Website: www.riadkaiss.com. Contact: Tel/Fax: (212) 4 444-0141. Email: riad@riadkaiss.com.

Riad Maison Bleue—Rates: $260.00 Double occupancy, breakfast included. Just minutes by foot from Fez's medina, in a converted mansion built around a courtyard with small swimming pool. Rooftop breakfast terrace. 33 Derb El Mitter, Fez, Morocco. www.maisonbleue.com. Tel: (212) 55 741-873. Fax (212) 55 740-686. Email: resa@maisonbleue.com.

Restaurants in Marrakech

Dar Essalam—170 Riad Zitoune El Kadim. Tel: (212) 44 44 35 20. Set in a superbly preserved 17th century palace in the heart of the medina. Moroccan menu includes pigeon and chicken *pastilla* (flaky pastry crust). Alfred Hitchcock and Sean Connery have dined here.

Safran et Canelle—40 Avenue Hassan II. Tel: (212) 44 43 59 69. Serves Moroccan specialties in an opulently decorated dining room. Located outside the old city walls in the new town.

Restaurants in Fez

Dar Saada—21 Souk el Attarin. Tel: (212) 5 63 73 70. In this 16th century palace with high ceilings and ornate woodwork, one can sample a range of traditional Moroccan dishes.

RESOURCES

Official Website

www.tourism-in-morocco.com

Other websites to book riads:
Riad2000.com—www.riad2000.com
Marrakech Holiday—www.marrakech-holiday.com

Books for Adults

Lonely Planet Morocco by Matt Fletcher
Knopf Guide Morocco

Books for Children

The Storytellers by Ted Lewin
Ali, Child of the Desert by Jonathan London

Videos and DVDs

Road to Morocco with Bing Crosby and Bob Hope
Globe Trekker: Morocco
Morocco: A Bridge Across Time

Audio CD

The Music of Morocco: In the Rif Berber Tradition by Nour Eddine
Songs and Dances from Morocco by Chalf Hassan

Will and Alison Nichols scan the horizon in the Serengeti.

CHAPTER 12

TANZANIA: SAFARI, WILDLIFE, AND CULTURE

FAMILY TRAVEL TO TANZANIA

I loathe camping . . . setting up tents, hiking to the bathroom, sleeping in bags on the ground. But everything I hate about camping, my two kids love. So when our travel agent suggested we camp on safari in Tanzania, my children were smitten with the idea. "It'll be an adventure," they crooned. "Come on, Mom, we just have to do it."

We don't have to do it, I thought, but I knew I was outnumbered. And if you can't beat 'em. . . .

The east African country of Tanzania, lying within an arm's reach of the Equator, is a kaleidoscopic paradise of savanna grasslands, shimmering lakes, and tropical forests. This East African gem devotes 25% of its land to conservation and is home to the most prolific wildlife on the planet. Additionally, the country's stability and economic growth make it an ideal family tourist destination.

We signed on with a local outfitter specializing in family safaris. Linked with three other families whom we had never met, we became part of a group of 14: seven children ages five to 15 and seven baby boomers. For 12 days, our group would share three safari vehicles, three drivers, one guide, as well as meals, binoculars, film, books, games, songs, stories, chocolate, toothpaste, and other necessities jammed into our safari bags.

We arrived at Kilimanjaro Airport in the shadow of Africa's tallest mountain—Mount Kilimanjaro. Once on the tarmac, my son Will got down on his knees and kissed the ground. "I've always wanted to come to Africa," he said, "and now I'm here!" Our guides greeted us, then drove our jet-lagged group to the city of Arusha, Tanzania's gateway to its northern safari circuit.

Our itinerary would take us to three of the country's most striking and animal-rich game parks: Tarangire National Park, Serengeti National Park, and Ngorongoro Conservation Area. Although some of our accommodations were in game lodges, it was the camping that appealed to the kids and put us in the heartbeat of Africa.

Tarangire National Park lies only 70 miles south, but a four-hour drive from Arusha. The park is a dry-season retreat for herds of plains-grazing animals that drink from the snaking Tarangire River, which cuts a swath through the length of this park. The Tarangire Safari Lodge, our permanent tented camp for the next two days, lines a high, sharp bluff overlooking the expansive, dry savanna below. My family was assigned two tents, and our kids immediately claimed theirs by throwing themselves onto the beds as a fleeting vision of flimsy camp cots collapsing under their weight flashed before me. But the sturdy wooden beds easily bore up. Night tables, sisal floor covering, a solar heated shower, and, thankfully, a flush toilet completed the tent's interior.

Outside, a veranda offered unobstructed and dazzling views of the savanna with giant baobab and feathery acacia trees dotting the landscape. But the true visual prize was the profuse wildlife that meandered below us: Gazelles, giraffes, elephants, zebras, and wildebeest wandered the plain. "We don't even need to drive around to see the animals," Will mused. "We can just watch them from our tents." Indeed, his theory proved correct as we pulled out the binoculars and viewed the rich life that lay before us.

But before too long, our rumbling stomachs led us from our verandas and into the lodge's spacious and airy dining room, where a delectable buffet of barbecued beef, vegetable curry, fresh fruit, salads, rice, and warm breads lined the room's long tables . . . a scrumptious feast that appealed to the kids. Hot cobbler, sweet cakes, and robust Tanzanian coffee were topped off by an unexpected treat that was to become a staple of our after-dinner fare: engaging safari tales, culled from 20 years of guiding, by our guide, Willie Hombo. These enchanting, informative stories of the wildlife and the local people were richly woven with glimpses into Hombo's own life growing up in Tanzania. As the adults lingered over their last cups of coffee and savored Hombo's words, the children, armed with flashlights, ran off to a nearby tent to spin a few yarns of their own by the dim light of kerosene lamps.

As we adults made our way back to our tents, the first unmistakable sounds of the African night broke the silence. In the distance we heard faint lion roars and hyena howling intermingled with the joyful giggles of our children.

The 6:30 A.M. wakeup call came all too early—especially for the teens. But Hombo's words from the night before resonated: "If you want to see lion, we leave by 7:30." Punctuality paid off; within a half hour—success! Three female lions and their cubs, partially hidden by the tall dry grass, sat feasting on a freshly killed wildebeest 20 feet from our vehicles. Undisturbed by our presence, the females tore at the flesh with their blood-smeared snouts and paws, their cubs almost disappearing into the carcass as they gorged. Around the kill, hyenas paced in the tall grass while vultures circled above, dutifully waiting their turn in this dining hierarchy. Hombo's keen awareness of the wildlife forever astonished us. "He must have binoculars in his eyes," one of the children marveled. Indeed, the day's yield included a lone leopard lazing in a sausage tree; a lion, belly to the ground, stalking two gazelles; and, atop a waist-high, chimney-shaped termite mound, a dozen pygmy mongooses no bigger than chipmunks. As we stopped to observe, the kids climbed up to the roofs of the vehicles and spotted the biggest find of the day: 15 elephants lumbering within an arm's reach of our vehicles.

After another day of spectacular game viewing in Tarangire, we were off to the Serengeti, a vast savanna habitat equal in size to Connecticut and host to an estimated three million animals, most of whom migrate in a seasonal event unrivaled in nature. Although our August visit missed the migration, the animals in this wildlife metropolis were not to disappoint us.

Midway through our six-hour drive over dusty, deeply pitted roads, we were blessed by what most perceive as an annoyance: a flat tire. As we climbed out to inspect, two teenage girls emerged from the rocky plain, barefoot and swathed in bright red cloth. As they came closer, we recognized them as Maasai, the most visible of Tanzania's 120 tribes. Elaborately beaded earrings dangled to their shoulders. Their earlobes were elongated through years of inserting progressively bigger wooden plugs into the pierced hole. More earrings were festooned from pencil-sized holes on the top of their ears. Coiled gold bracelets snaked up their thin arms and legs. And on their cheeks, for added beauty, were etched circular scars.

The girls motioned to our cameras, then posed. Not missing a beat, our group's intrepid photographer—the five-year-old—pulled out her Polaroid, snapped, and handed the pictures to the girls, who viewed in enraptured silence the magical unfolding of their own images. Then the girls once again pointed to our cameras and pulled our children over to stand with them. This time we adults snapped away at this priceless photo op.

Tire fixed, the journey continued. Almost instantly, the endless, golden dryness of the savanna turned a fertile green as we entered the Great Rift Valley. This dramatic fracture in the earth's crust results from 20 million years of tectonic movement and cuts a jagged scar thorough Tanzania as it squeezes and molds the land to form lakes, valleys, craters, and highlands.

Punctuating this varied countryside were lush fields of coffee, bananas, and beans surrounding small houses, many made of mud bricks. Outside our vehicle's windows, an eclectic array of people lined the narrow road—women balancing huge bundles on their heads, Maasai children herding errant goats, and Tanzanian boys riding Ben Hur-style atop wooden carts pulled by oxen. A roadside crafts booth with a zebra-skin-painted facade caught our eye.

Here, Alison honed her negotiating skills as she bargained over a Maasai necklace. "That's only $80," the clerk said as he noticed her admiring it.

"But I only have five," she said in earnest as she pulled the bill out of her pocket, anticipating immediate rebuke.

"Okay, it's yours," he quickly replied. Stunned, she accepted. This first, lucky deal bolstered her negotiating confidence so much that she attempted to dominate all future family transactions.

After a night's respite at yet another tented lodge above the flamingo-rimmed Lake Manyara, we arrived in Serengeti's Seronera Valley. Our camp was ready, having been set up the night before by a crew of six who had passed us in a cloud of dust during the flat tire episode. Nestled between two rocky outcroppings were 14 walk-in tents. The assemblage included seven boxy green tents for sleeping, a long narrow rectangular one for dining, and, set behind, six small blue tents resembling beach cabanas and used for showering and toilets. This time the youngsters did not claim their own tent and, thankfully, did not throw themselves onto their collapsible beds. "Now this is real camping," said Will.

The meals, prepared over open fire by our crew, were simple yet hearty and tasty. Meat and vegetarian entrees, vegetable curries, exotic fruits, rices or pastas, and occasional deserts graced our long, family-style dining table. The crew's daily ice run to the nearest lodge kept the stored food fresh.

Safaris, for all their joys, have one major drawback: lack of exercise. Land Rover lethargy, my husband called it. No jogging, no walking, no evening stroll—what's an active body to do? Spud, of course. Spud is a ball and tag game initiated by the children; it required throwing and catching, interspersed with short spurts of running. Dubbed "Serengeti Spud," by the kids, this was the major source of body movement for youngsters, adults, and even the crew. During the first day's game, we noticed that we humans were not alone in the camp. Perched on the surrounding rocks were 12 baboons, with a persistently intense interest in this frenzied human game. Their two-day spud fixation was interrupted only by occasional migrations of several baboons from one rock outcropping to another—to get a better view—or so we all thought.

These animals were not the only visitors to the camp. Hombo had warned us that although the proximity to the animals was one of the joys of camping, it could also be one of the hazards. "Don't be surprised if you hear rustling outside your tent," he warned. "Civets, hyenas, and other guests occasionally wander in. And lions have been known to visit. So zip up your tents." We immediately complied. And before long the sounds of the night creatures permeated the silence. Distant lion roars intermingled with haunting hyena howls brought a profound and immediate intimacy with the animals.

Two days of game drives in the Serengeti brought new and spectacular finds, including the *kopjes*—ancient granite formations left behind as the surrounding soil eroded and weathered. These jumbled boulder outcroppings dot the dry flatness of the Serengeti and provide shelter and protection to many animals. It was on the *kopjes* that we saw our first cheetah, a pride of eight lions, and small creatures called rock hyrax. "What is a rock hyrax?" Will asked Hombo as he photographed this rabbit-like creature.

"They are the closest living relation to the elephant."

This startling fact sent the kids scrambling for the nature guides to learn more about this odd animal.

Serengeti wildlife has taken an erratic course in the last 30 years. The wildebeest, or gnu, population has increased from a quarter million to over four times that; lions and cheetahs have doubled in number to approximately 3,000 and 1,000 respectively. But other animal populations in this area have not been so lucky. Wild dogs have been nearly eliminated by distemper, and black rhinos have been poached to near extinction.

Our final stop on the safari circuit was the Ngorongoro Conservation Area, a matchless marvel that contains volcanoes, mountains, rivers, forest, plains, and shifting sand dunes. One feature of this dramatic area is Olduvai Gorge, the renowned archeological site. Often called the "cradle of mankind," Olduvai is where anthropologist Mary Leakey discovered the skull of Australopithecus-Zinjanthropus Boisei, or "The Nutcracker Man." Just shy of two million years old, the skull was but one of Leakey's famous finds. The Olduvai park ranger allowed the children to dig for fossils in the gorge, with the understanding that any finds would be returned to the site's small museum on the way out. So within feet of the plaque marking Leakey's discovery, Alison and Will dug furiously and emerged with pockets of rocklike objects they relinquished to the park ranger. "You're holding a two-million-year-old lion's tooth," he told my young archeologist, Will. "You have a prehistoric tool made out of quartz," he told Alison as he collected all the fossils from our awestruck children who had—at least momentarily—held a bit of prehistory in their little hands.

Our final campsite in the Ngorongoro Conservation Area, again set up by the crew, was poised on the 7,600-foot-high rim of the Ngorongoro Crater. The near 40-degree night temperature was reason enough for the crew to break out a camping commodity never before seen by the children—hot water bottles for warming beds and bodies. "Please mom," Alison and Will begged after the first night with this rarity, "can we get one when we get home?" If only all requests could be so simple.

The early morning game drive, snaking down the crater's escarpment and onto its floor, put us in the sunken cone of the Ngorongoro Volcano, the world's largest intact caldera. Sometimes called "paradise on earth," and the "eighth wonder of the world," the crater is home to over 30,000 large mammals, and because of its size—only 10 miles in diameter—the wildlife feels dense and close, like a virtual Noah's Ark. Dotting the vista near and far were thousands of animals—zebra, wildebeest, cape buffalo, gazelle, eland, and hartebeest—grazing, roaming, and frolicking.

The vehicles frequently inched through, parting these masses of animals. As we stopped to watch a herd of zebras envelop and pass our vans, we spied across the plain something that parted the herds even more efficiently—the hyena. More than 400 of these ruthless, spotted predators live on the crater's floor, and the grazing wildlife takes them very seriously.

The crater itself is a microcosm of African wildlife. Open plains, grasslands, rolling hills, marshes, swamps, soda lakes, streams, and forest support a vast and varied array of animals and plant life. The find of the day was seeing three of the crater's 20 rhinos in one grouping! As we watched in silence, the male rhino marked his territory with a urine spray of firehose force. Two days of game drives convinced the kids that the Ngorongoro Crater earned yet another label: "The Garden of Eden."

Our last night in Africa went all too quickly, as the entire trip had. We had intimately experienced—in tents—the enchanting and mysterious bush of Tanzania, savoring the closeness of the animals and feeling a part of our surroundings. We had gotten to know the gracious Tanzanians who ate with us, told us stories . . . and even joined us in Serengeti Spud. And we had had a family travel adventure unrivaled by any other.

We drove back to Kilimanjaro Airport in satisfied silence—the kind you have when you've just experienced something magical and indescribable. "Can we come back someday, Mom?" Alison asked.

"We'll try," I said. "And when we do, we'll camp."

TANZANIA OVERVIEW

- Tanzania: The size of New Mexico and Texas combined
- Population: 36 million
- Capital: Dar es Salaam (Population: 2 million)
- Ethnicity: 99% Native African (represents 120 tribes), 1% European, Asian and Arab
- Religious Affiliation: 45% Christian, 45% Muslim and 10% indigenous beliefs
- Official Language: Swahili
- Language of Commerce: English (widely spoken)
- Currency: Tanzanian Shilling

PLANNING AND PREPARATION

Passports

A passport and visa are required for travel to Tanzania.

When to Go

Since Tanzania lies close to the equator, seasonal temperature variations are minimal. Wet and dry seasons have a much greater influence on when visitors choose to come to Tanzania. During the two dry seasons (July–October and December–March) animal viewing is at its best, because animals tend to congregate more densely near water holes. If possible, time your trip to observe the great annual herd migrations at the beginning each of these dry seasons.

Health Issues

The Centers for Disease Control and Prevention's Website provides up-to-the-minute information about health issues, as well as required and recommended vaccinations and medications for all foreign countries. Tanzania requires visitors to present an international certificate confirming they've been vaccinated against yellow fever. Kenya suggests vaccinations for yellow fever and cholera. When visiting all African countries, it's advisable to get hepatitis and typhus shots. Visitors should also consider taking antimalaria medication. Personal first aid kits should include insect repellent with DEET, an antihistamine for insect bites, and Imodium. For up-to-date information, call the Center for Disease Control in Atlanta at 800-237-3270 or visit their website (www.cdc.gov/travel).

Safety

Tanzania has a well developed tourist infrastructure that allows for generally safe travel in the country. However, the area near Tanzania's borders with Rwanda and Burundi has been the site of minor military clashes, and refugee flows across the borders into Tanzania continue. There have been a number of incidents of criminal and violent activity in the region. Travelers to this area should exercise caution. On August 7, 1998, terrorists bombed the U.S. Embassy in Dar es Salaam. The United States has had excellent cooperation with Tanzanian police and security forces since the bombing.

What to Bring

On safari, extremely casual, comfortable clothes are the norm. There is virtually no reason (nor opportunity) to dress up. At higher elevations, early mornings can be cool, so bring a light jacket. Of course bring photographic equipment, extra batteries, plenty of film, and binoculars.

Why go on Safari?

Safari means voyage in Swahili. And what a voyage it is——especially for families. The spirit of exploring a distinctly different country, observing animals, intermingling with diverse cultures and connecting with extraordinary nature makes safaris the perfect parent-kid adventure.

My family chose the country of Tanzania as our safari destination and headed off to this east African gem when Alison was 11 and Will was eight. We booked a tour with three other families, and immediately all the kids became friends: dining together, telling ghost stories at night, and even bumping along in their own Land Rover—with the parents trailing behind. Every aspect was an adventure to this enthusiastic group of young people. They delighted in camping out in the game reserves, observing at close range the plethora of animals, and socializing with other children as we visited local schools. They dug for fossils at the Oldavai Gorge, visited a Maasai village and shopped in outdoor markets.

Our safari was a voyage that will never be forgotten. My advice to other families? Gather your sense of adventure, your cameras and your kids, and prepare for an experience of a lifetime.

Safari Locations

Safaris occur in two regions of Africa: Southern Africa in the countries of South Africa, Botswana, Zimbabwe and Namibia, and East Africa in the countries of Tanzania and Kenya. Most safari operators recommend at least a week on safari, so families can have the opportunity to visit several game parks. Check with your tour operator to determine the best safari season in each of these countries.

We chose Tanzania, as it is one of Africa's most politically stable countries, free of political upheaval and tribal conflict. Tanzania boasts 120 different ethnic groups; more than any other African nation. And 25% of Tanzania's land is declared as National Parks or game reserves. This allotment is only surpassed by Costa Rica with 27%.

Safari Guides

A guide's knowledge of the terrain and animals is a key component for getting the most out of a safari. Top-notch safari companies hire guides who have training in environmental issues, natural history, and wildlife. The most amazing thing a guide does is spot an animal from afar when clients have not a clue that an animal is within miles. Our intrepid and knowledgeable guide, besides being a walking encyclopedia of wildlife behavior, entertained and educated us each night after dinner with stories of specific animals, insight about the local culture, and memories of his experiences growing up in Tanzania.

Accommodations

Accommodations on safaris include three types of tents as well as game lodges. The first type of tent is called a *walk-in tent*. It has twin beds, linens and a night table with a lamp . . . and since it's walk-in, you won't bump your head on the ceiling! The second style of tent is termed an *adventure tent* which safari members set up on their own. Both of these options have portable toilet and showering facilities shared by all. The third category of tents is called a *permanent tented camp* with canvas walls secured on a foundation. This accommodation is replete with private bathroom and shower. The last accommodation is a game lodge, often offering luxurious decor, ample bathrooms and a high level of services. Some lodges are constructed of natural material that blends with the surroundings and others are built on stilts or in treetops.

Food

Most safaris include three meals a day—after all, where would you find a restaurant in the middle of the Serengeti? Lodges and permanent tented camps tend to offer buffet style meals served in the restaurant, while walk-in and adventure tents provide meals prepared at the camping site by a cooking staff. No need to worry about freshness. Cooks make a daily run to purchase ingredients and prepare delicious meals served family style in a large dining tent.

Safari Vehicles

Safari vehicles are heavy and sturdy, four wheel drive Land Rovers or vans. Pot holes in dirt roads and traveling across land with no roads makes for a very bumpy ride. Many vehicles have large roof hatches that allow participants to stand up while in the vehicle and observe and/or photograph the animals. Be sure that the van is large enough to accommodate a window seat for each person.

Questions to ask Safari Companies

- How many families will be on the tour?
- Will each participant have a window seat in the vehicle?
- How many bags is each person allowed to bring?
- Is there special clothing or supplies that are recommended?
- What is the daily schedule?
- What is included in the cost?
- Is there contact with local people, such as school visits and stops at local villages?
- What are the range of accommodations? (Tents, game lodges etc.)
- What are the toilet and shower arrangements for the tents?
- What are the arrangements for meals and how do cooks respond to special diet requirements such as vegetarian needs?

Safari Companies

The following companies arrange family safaris to Tanzania (prices may vary seasonally).

- **Thomson Safaris**, based in Cambridge, Massachusetts, has specialized in Tanzanian safaris for 20 years. Scheduled and customized family safaris for 13 days: around $5,500 for adults and $4,500 for children 11 and under. Includes all meals, accommodations, land arrangements, and airfare from Boston or New York. Contact www.thomsonsafaris.com or call 800-235-0289.

- **Abercrombie and Kent**, based in Oak Brook, Illinois, offers a family safari to Tanzania. This 13-day episode starts at $4,425 for adults, $3,495 for children under 18, $2,750 for children under 12 (price varies according to season). Includes meals, accommodations, and land arrangements, but does not include airfare. Abercrombie offers a host of kid-perfect activities, including a visit with an elephant researcher, learning bush skills, and creating masks and beadwork. Contact www.aandktours.com or call 800-323-7308.

• **Maxim Tours, Uncommon Safaris**, based in Morristown, New Jersey, offers two family safaris to Tanzania. Their 12-day family adventure safari starts at $3,500 for adults and $3,100 for children, excluding airfare. Their "Classic Tanzania" safari is 11 days, starts at $3,900 per person, excluding airfare. Prices, which vary according to season, include all meals, accommodations and land arrangements. Contact www.uncommonsafaris.com or call 800-655-0222.

THINGS TO SEE AND DO
Activities for Kids
• Visit a Maasai school. If you plan to do this, pack a couple of children's books or some school supplies and let your kids give them to the teachers.
• Visit a Maasai village.
• Encourage your children to keep a journal of their safari. If they are inclined to, they could also have their parents write about their favorite safari day.
• Ask your children to draw and write about their favorite animal. They could also interview your guide for more information.

Go to Zanzibar—Zanzibar is an archipelago made up of Zanzibar and Pemba Islands, and several islets. Located in the Indian Ocean, it is 25 miles from the Tanzanian coast. Zanzibar Island is 60 miles long and 20 miles wide, and touts gorgeous sandy beaches with encircling coral reefs, and historic Stone Town—the only functioning ancient town in East Africa. Families can fly or go by boat to this island, and will delight in visiting spice plantations where cloves, nutmeg, cinnamon, and many other spices are grown. Zanzibar has some of the best diving in the world, and the coral reef structures ensure that the marine life is abundant. There are several dive centers on the island which handle all levels of divers, from beginner to expert.

Hike Mt. Kilimanjaro—Mt. Kilimanjaro is the highest walkable mountain in the world. There is no special equipment needed for the walk—except a good pair of hiking boots—because the routes allow a slow gradual hike. Once reaching the top, families can take in a view of East Africa. There are several routes families can choose from which vary in steepness and popularity. The Marangu, or "Coca-Cola" Route, is the easiest and the most frequented trail on Kilimanjaro. The Machame, or "Whiskey" Route is more physically demanding. All the routes grant spectacular views as you hike through a range of habitats—including low montane forest, cloud and rain forests, the alpine desert, and dazzling glacier walls. There are many tour companies which provide hikes.

Boat or Snorkel on Lake Tanganyika—Lake Tanganyika, also known as the Fossil Water Lake, sidles up on the west side of Tanzania. This lake fills a deep, 4,700 foot crevice formed by the Great Rift Valley. Lake Tanganyika is the second deepest lake in the world, and the majority of its water is thought to be 20 million years old. The lake's isolation makes it a unique eco-system which boasts 350 species of sea life. Amazing scenery and crystal-clear waters augment the beauty of this lake. Kigoma, a major town on the shores of Lake Tanganyika, offers a range of accommodations. Six miles south of Kigoma is the historic town of Ujiji, which also has accommodations.

Shop Indigenous Markets—Many villages and towns have colorful markets that offer a range of desirable objects to families including hand-crafted wood items and such Maasai artwork as beadwork, jewelry, and spears.

Visit a Maasai Village—If your tour guide has not planned a visit to a Maasai village, be sure to arrange one. These tall, proud people live in self-built homes constructed from cow dung and mud plastered over bent wood wands and twigs. We were invited into the house, then entertained on the grounds with singing, dancing, and a jumping contest among the males of the tribe.

RESOURCES

Official Websites
The United Republic of Tanzania—www.tanzania.go.tz
Tanzania Tourist Board—www.tanzania-web.com

Books for Adults
The Safari Companion: A Guide to Watching African Mammals by Richard Estes
Say It in Swahili by Sharifa Zawawi
On the Edge of the Great Rift: Three Novels of Africa by Paul Theroux
The World of a Maasai Warrior: An Autobiography by Ole Saitoti
Guide to Zanzibar by David Else

Books for Children
The Serengeti Migration: Animals on the Move by Linda Linblad
Tales from the African Plains by Anne Gatti
How It Was With Dooms: A True Story from Africa by Xan Hopcraft
The Maasai of East Africa by Jamie Hetfield

Videos and DVDs
Out of Africa
I Dream of Africa
Africa, The Serengeti
Gorillas in the Mist
Snows of Kilimanjaro

The Mitchell family stealthily approaches seals on the Skeleton Coast.

CHAPTER 13

NAMIBIA: SKELETONS ON THE COAST

BY CINDY MCDONELL MITCHELL

FAMILY TRAVEL TO NAMIBIA

If you want to really bond with your teenager, then take him or her to the Skeleton Coast in Namibia. There will be few outside influences to disrupt your bonding—no T.V., phones, electricity, running water, roads, nor in some parts, people. It will just be you, your family, and a pilot guide. This is the perfect place to spend some truly meaningful quality time, while having the adventure of a lifetime!

Namibia, a former German colony, is on the southwestern coast of Africa between South Africa and Angola. A sparsely populated and mostly desolate country, Namibia has some of the weirdest landscapes on the face of the earth. It also has exotic wildlife that has adapted to this bizarre landscape. Nature had a heyday when it created this land. It is a place of extremes, having the tallest dunes in the world as well as some of the reddest I have ever seen. It has longitudinal dunes, ripple dunes, roaring dunes, and saltpans. There are extinct volcanoes; pink, green and purple rocks; and more strange sights than one can imagine: lizards hopping on opposing front and rear legs to avoid standing for too long on hot desert sand, desert elephants playfully sliding down sand dunes on their rumps. . . .

Our introduction to Namibia came when my husband, 14-year-old son, and I flew into the capital, Windhoek. What a surprise! We found a small German city plopped down in the middle of a desert. Mercedes whipped down well-maintained roads, past half-timbered German-style houses. Some street and business signs were in German, others in English, even a few in Afrikaans. (South Africa was the colonial power that moved in when the Germans relinquished control after World War I.) We spent a day and night at the Windhoek Country Club, a four star hotel with nice restaurants, a water park, and a lively casino. But Windhoek was not our destination; the countryside was. So once acclimated after our 20-hour transit from Chicago, we set out to explore the country.

Given the lack of roads and substantial distances to cover, we chose to travel by air: we had booked a small charter plane with pilot guide. Early in the morning we drove to the airport to meet up with Helga, the only female pilot guide in all of Namibia, and got into our single engine plane. Little did we know the great and fantastic places this little plane would take us or how it could land on almost any flat surface: beaches, hard packed desert, dirt roads. . . .

Helga put our son to work immediately by having him check the oil. We were unaware that he would later learn to change tires, clean the windshield, turn the parked plane around to face into the wind, taxi, and ultimately, to take over as co-pilot to fly the plane!

We took off into a cloudless blue sky and aimed southwest toward Sossusvlei in Namib Naukluft Park. After landing, we got into a Land Rover and Helga drove us into the park where we climbed the highest dunes in the world. Rising nearly 1,000 feet, they are one of many kinds of strange and beautiful dunes scattered across this country. After a picnic lunch, we took off again, flying low along the coast of Conception Bay. We landed again to once more hike up some dunes, but these were bright red. Wonderful little green beetles and hot-footed lizards scurried across the red sand. The entire scene was contrasted by the bright blue sky.

Again, we took off in our plane, flying low over the wreck of the *Edward Bohlen*, a large rusted ship which capsized on the shore over 30 years ago. Just offshore, a red tide wove its way in and out of the breaking waves, adding to the effect. Nearby, thousands of pink flamingoes fed in a shallow pool. A short time later, flying low over Cape Cross, a breeding reserve for thousands of Cape fur seals, we buzzed a huge colony of seals, then flew over the Ugab Formations, a nearly lifeless moonscape of black ridges contrasting with the white desert floor.

By the end of the day, we had fallen in love with our small plane and the great opportunity it gave us to fly low over inaccessible landscapes, unlike anything we imagined on earth. And Helga was a gem! Her knowledge and love of both the landscape and the strange animals was obvious, and her piloting skills were as good as they come. She would set us down on most any flat surface and she would expertly dodge the occasional thunder cloud. That night we landed on a small dirt strip where a Land Rover was waiting for us. With Helga at the wheel, we drove to the Huab Valley to spend the night at Camp Kuidas. Little wooden huts and a small dinner tent made up the entire camp. Helga had brought our own perishable supplies, and the camp caretakers—members of a local tribe—turned those supplies into a surprisingly great dinner. That night we sat under a beautiful starlit sky where we were tutored on the constellations of the southern hemisphere.

The next morning brought a Land Rover drive further into the Huab River area. We learned about the *Welwitschia Mirabilis*, a 1,000-year-old dwarf tree which was probably the ugliest little mess ever to be called a tree. This evergreen lays low along the ground and derives its moisture from sea fog dew. The oldest specimens may even approach 2,000 years in age. Hundreds of tiny red beetles lived within the tree. A necessary resident for its survival, they offer their pollination services. The diversity and strangeness of all the flora and fauna was extraordinary.

That afternoon, our son got his first lesson in turning the parked plane into the wind. For someone not old enough to drive a car, this was just his first step in learning to "co-pilot." Later, flying along

Terrace Bay, we landed to inspect the beached shipwrecks of the *Montrose* and *Henrietta*. Scattered around these wrecks were thousands of bones of seals and whales. No wonder they call this the Skeleton Coast! We also observed partially eaten seal carcasses, evidence that even lions and hyenas inhabit this strange desert environment.

We then headed off for a beach hike. It was cold and windy—rather normal for this desert at this time of the year. The beach was covered by small pebbles that were bright green, purple, yellow, red, and orange. Our son collected a multi-colored selection of these round rocks as a souvenir.

While flying to our next camp we swept low to observe a herd of small desert elephants making their way across the sand. Helga pointed out slide marks down the side of a dune where they had been playfully sliding. Later we would spot ostriches and a few solitary impala . . . there were no great herds since the very sparse vegetation could not support them.

Our next camp was in the Hoarusib Valley. Members of the Herero tribe run this little camp. Each woman was bedecked in a full-length, brightly colored hoop dress. Puffy sleeves, and a large matching hat completed the outfit. It was surreal to see. Why would women dress like this in the middle of this remote desert? In the late 19th century, Victorian-era missionaries came to Namibia and introduced this attire to bring "modesty" to the mostly nude tribe. The missionaries are long gone, but the dress has become tradition. The Herero at our camp spoke little English, but somehow we managed to communicate.

The next morning, we set out to visit a nomadic tribe, the Himba. Their homes are small, round, mud and wattle huts. The women stay in camp while the men herd goats and cattle. Clad only in a leather skirt, each woman wears a white conch shell between her breasts. They cover their (mostly) exposed skin and hair with a red dirt, rancid butter fat, and aromatic resin mixture. By rubbing this concoction on themselves, they are protected from the sun and from insect pests while looking most fashionable within their culture. They weave straw baskets in natural tan and black colors and also carve human faces and nature scenes into the surface of indigenous nuts. We bought a few of each. The men wear little more than a leather loin covering. Sadly the 6,000 member Himba tribe is dwindling in number due to a very high AIDS incidence.

Back in our plane, we flew along the coast, landing again on the beach. Here Helga instructed us in the fine art of getting into the middle of a huge seal colony. The trick was to drop down on our knees and crawl the 50 or so yards into the middle of the very loud and smelly colony. This became a problem when we realized that we were being tracked by a jackal. Not much larger than a Cocker Spaniel, it posed absolutely no threat to us. However, the comic scene caused fits of laughter which disturbed the seals who waddled into the sea just as we reached them. Oh well, maybe next time!

After our seal encounter we drove towards the Angola border to our final camp. Called Otza, it is perched on a cliff overlooking the Kunene River which separates Namibia from Angola. In the late afternoon we spied a troop of baboons across the water. After a great night's sleep we woke to a beautiful day with the promise of illegal activity! We boarded a little yellow raft and rowed 100 yards across the river to Angola. After beaching our craft, my son, Helga and I went hiking in the hills of Angola, a country which requires a visa to enter. Few tourists feel compelled to visit this sometimes war torn nation, so this made it all the more exciting. Realistically, we were hundreds of miles form any danger of combat; we merely wanted to be able to say that we visited Angola. I suppose we risked encountering a rare border guard who would throw us in jail for all eternity. However, our visit was calm and the land there was uninhabited. The only sound we heard was the chirping of birds.

The time had come to drive back to our little plane and fly to Windhoek for our homeward-bound connections. As we returned to the aircraft, Helga asked our son if he wanted to learn how to fly! After take-off, Helga instructed our son in the fine art of flying. With white knuckles, he took over the controls. For over four hours, he flew the plane through huge thunderclouds, around rough weather systems, and all along the coast. The small aircraft bumped up and down, tossed by wind and air. I wondered if I had lost my mind!

Thankfully, we arrived home safe and sound. Would we do it again? You bet! And did our son decide to become a pilot? No way!

NAMIBIA OVERVIEW

- Namibia: Larger than Texas
- Population: 2.4 million
- Capital: Windhoek (Population 126,000)
- Ethnicity: 50% Ovambo, 44% other tribes, 6% White
- Religious Affiliation: 90% Christian (mostly Lutheran), 10% other
- Language: English (official), Ovambo
- Currency: Namibian dollar

PLANNING AND PREPARATION

Passports

Americans are required to have a valid passport to enter Namibia. A visa is not required for U.S. passport holders.

When to Go

Namibia can be visited most any time of year. It has a sunny and dry climate with an average of 300 sunny days a year, hot in the interior and cooler at the coast. Winter days are mild to warm, so you should bring light summer clothes. Nights can be quite chilly—even in summer at the coast.

Health Issues

The Centers for Disease Control and Prevention's Website provides up-to-the-minute information about health issues, as well as required and recommended vaccinations and medications for all foreign countries. When visiting all Sub-Saharan countries, it's advisable to get hepatitis and typhus shots. Visitors should also consider taking anti-malaria medication, especially if visiting the northern part of Namibia. Personal first aid kits should include insect repellent with DEET, an antihistamine for insect bites, and Imodium. AIDS is widespread in the countries of southern Africa. For up-to-date information, call the Center for Disease Control in Atlanta at 800-237-3270 or visit their website (www.cdc.gov/travel).

All water from taps is purified. Medical facilities are relatively modern, especially in the city of Windhoek, however they are mostly non-existent in the countryside where visitors typically go on safari.

Safety

Namibia is a safe country with a low crime rate. It has a politically stable environment. As in most countries, some petty crime occurs, so one must be observant in tourist centers and in Windhoek. The U.S. State Department reports some incidents of banditry along the northern border with Angola.

What to Bring

On safari, extremely casual, comfortable clothes are the norm. There is virtually no reason (nor opportunity) to dress up. In the southern winter and along the coast—even in the summer—the temperature can be cool. Warm clothes are thus a necessity. A good pair of sunglasses, sunscreen, and a sun hat are also useful. Of course, bring photographic equipment, extra batteries, plenty of film, and binoculars.

Tour and Safari Operators

While it is possible to conduct a self-drive vacation in Namibia, traveling with a tour company will allow the traveler to see much more, learn much more—and if air travel is included—cover much more of this large country. Tour and safari options include self-drive routes, pre-packaged (fixed itinerary) programs, and customized itinerary trips. One must chose a tour with the type of accommodation that appeals to his/her family: camping, permanent tented camps, or lodges. Many tours include a mix of accommodation types.

Also, your mode of transportation will define the type of tour you take. If you and your family can stomach small single engine planes, then you will see a much broader array of terrain, people, and animals.

An excellent website that offers links to many of the tour and safari operators active in Namibia is The Online Guide to Namibia, www.namibweb.com/. Additionally, you may ask you travel agent to recommend a tour program or local operator that your agent is familiar with.

Tour Guides

A guide's knowledge of the local tribes, terrain, and animals is a key component for getting the most out of a tour or safari. Top-notch safari companies hire guides who have training in environmental issues, natural history, and wildlife.

Accommodations

Accommodations in the countryside range from rough campsites to permanent tented camps to quite comfortable, but rustic, lodges. The cost of lodging rises as one moves from rough campsite to tented camp to lodge.

Food

Most tours and safaris include three meals a day—after all, there are not a lot of restaurants on the dunes of the Skeleton Coast! Lodges often offer buffet-style meals served in their restaurant, while camping adventures provide meals prepared at the camping site by a cooking staff.

Vehicles

Safari vehicles are heavy and sturdy, four-wheel-drive Land Rovers or similar. Pot holes in dirt roads and traveling across land with no roads makes for a very bumpy ride. Be sure that the vehicle is large enough to accommodate a window seat for each person.

Questions to Ask Tour and Safari Companies

- What modes of transportation will be used? (Small plane, Land Rover, etc.)
- How many families will be on the tour?
- Will each participant have a window seat in the vehicle?
- How many bags is each person allowed to bring?
- Is there special clothing or supplies that are recommended?
- What is the daily schedule?
- What is included in the cost?
- Is there contact with local people, such as school visits and stops at local villages?
- What are the range of accommodations? (Tents, lodges etc.)
- What are the toilet and shower arrangements for the tents?
- What are the arrangements for meals and how do cooks respond to special diet requirements such as vegetarian needs?

THINGS TO SEE AND DO

Activities for Kids

- Let your kids collect a selection of brightly colored pebbles. Have your guide explain the source of the many colors.
- With you children, inspect seal bones on the Skeleton Coast. Look for signs of lion or hyena having eaten the seals (e.g. gnaw marks on the bones, partially eaten carcasses).
- Have your kids draw pictures of the different types of clothing worn by the tribes they visited (e.g. Himba women covered with red dirt and butter fat, Herero women dressed in Victorian era hoop dresses).

Fly to the Skeleton Coast—This 30-mile-wide strip of land stretches some 400 miles from the central coast, north to the Angolan border. Dense coastal fog and cold ocean currents attract fish, which in turn attract seals and whales whose bones are scattered up and down the coast, along with the "bones" of several beached shipwrecks. The terrain is a fascinating mix of windswept dunes, rugged canyon walls, volcanic rock, mountain ranges, and even small colorful pebbles. The northern section has been designated a wilderness area where tourists can enter only via exclusive fly-in safaris. Ask if your tour operator includes this destination in his itinerary.

Climb the sand dunes at Sossusvlei—These dunes in the Namibian desert are nearly 1,000 feet high, among the highest in the world. Nearby are several otherworldly features: red dunes, camel thorn trees, and deep narrow canyons. The desert here receives meaningful rainfall infrequently, at which time clear blue pools—"vlei" is the local term—form in the hollows between dunes. Visitors may fly in on charter planes or travel by road from Windhoek. Those seeking to spend the night can stay at the beautiful Sossusvlei Lodge or the popular Sossusvlei Mountain Lodge.

Camp in Etosha National Park—Etosha is 320 miles north of Windhoek. Several lodges offer accommodations as well as campsites; included are Namutoni, Halali, and Okaukuejo. The park is home to over 340 bird, 110 reptile, and 100 mammal species, including elephant, black rhino, wildebeest, zebra, and several antelope species. Lion, cheetah, and leopard can also be seen, as can huge flocks of flamingoes. The rainy season, between December and April, offers the greatest congregations of animals. An excellent network of roads within the national park makes travel quite manageable.

RESOURCES

Official Website
www.republicofnamibia.com

Useful tourism website: The Online Guide to Namibia www.namibweb.com/

Books for Adults

Sands of Silence: On Safari in Namibia by Peter Hathaway Capstick
Lonely Planet Namibia by Deanna Swaney

Books for Kids

Have Yourself a Thornberry Little Christmas by Barry Goldberg
Misoso: Once Upon a Time Tales from Africa by Verna Aardema

Videos and DVDs

National Geographic's Survivors of the Skeleton Coast

Graham and Cindy Mitchell share a camel while Steve gets his own at Pyramids of Giza.

CHAPTER 14

EGYPT: CRUISING THE NILE

BY CINDY MCDONELL MITCHELL

FAMILY TRAVEL TO EGYPT

Egypt, the land of mystery. The land of the legendary King of Gold, Tutankhamen. Nevertheless, what am I doing here? I hate temples and tombs. Our teenage son is going to be bored to death. He has no interest in hieroglyphs and ancient reliefs. And the airline has lost my luggage. I think I want to go home.

We have just landed in Cairo. It is one o'clock in the morning and we are driving through the darkened streets of the city to our hotel for four hours of sleep before we catch an early morning flight to Aswan, where we will board our boat for a six day cruise on the Nile. I have no clothes. This is not a good start.

Before dawn, we head back to the airport where I expect to board a small shuttle plane, but instead we are herded onto a 747 with hundreds of other weary tourists. We land at Abu Simbel and are transported to our boat; and then things immediately begin to look a little better. It is a small boat with just a handful of cabins and a great crew. Maybe this won't be so bad after all. The boat has comfortable cabins, a well appointed dining room, and a welcoming deck for just relaxing and watching the world of the Nile pass by.

We began our exploration of the antiquities at Abu Simbel, a great example of old and new. These rock-hewn temples of Ramses II and the beautiful Queen Nefertari had been carved in a sandstone cliff. When the Aswan Dam was built in the 1960s, Egypt appealed to the world community through UNESCO to help move these monuments from their ancient site which was to be submerged under the soon-to-be created Lake Nasser. Over 30 nations assisted in this endeavor. The end result, to quote our teenage son, was "awesome." The two temples were dismantled and raised over 180 feet up the sandstone cliff where they had been built more than 3,000 years before. Here they were reassembled, in the exact same relationship to each other and the sun, and set in a cliff in an artificial mountain. This new mountain was built over an 80-foot high dome. The interior of the new dome is as amazing as the ancient towering figures. Both celebrate the great minds and creativity of man and they exist in perfect harmony.

As we began to make our way down the river, we were entranced. It was not all about tombs and temples, but about the everyday life along this eternal river, one of the cradles of civilization and one which has changed very little over the centuries. The pace was slow and the sights were enthralling. Perched on deck, binoculars in hand, we watched the daily life of people whose existence depend on this river. People were bathing, washing breakfast dishes, drawing water from their wells, and fishing from small sailboats. Life was going on unchanged. We took hundreds of photos over the days as we attempted to capture this ever-changing, but constant scene.

At day's end, we anchored and wandered into a small town. Could I possibly find something to replace my dirty, "jet-lagged" clothes? We walked down the dark, tiny main street and I wondered if I would have to wear these same dirty clothes for two more weeks. Then, what should appear, but a Benetton's. And it was still open. I bought a brown skirt and white top. I had clothes now. And, I would soon learn that I cannot only survive with just two sets of clothes (laundered daily by our crew), but realize this is a great way to travel. No luggage, no hassle.

On the southern reaches of Lake Nasser we stopped at the Granite Quarry where most of the stone used in Egypt's ancient monuments was sourced. It is a strange place, frozen in the past, as if the workers simply laid down their tools one day and walked away. An unfinished obelisk lay on its side. It was huge, weighing over 1,100 tons and 126 feet in length. Did they just abandon it? How were they going to transport it? How would they raise it up at its final spot?

As we moved down the river, we began to really enjoy our boat and fellow passengers. The food was great and, over dinner, we discovered that one of the passengers was a real "English Lady" of the royal sort. This was topped only by a man who joined us later in the trip. He was a high profile accused murderer who was found innocent in a well-publicized trial. Things just kept getting more interesting.

Next on the temple route was the Greco-Roman temple of Kom Omba. Beautifully sited along the river, the ruins of this lovely building stand in solitude. Very rarely in Egypt does one see any of the historic sites not surrounded by 20th-century buildings and towns. This was a pleasant exception. Built to honor two gods, Haroeris (the sun god), and Sobek (the crocodile god), the temple included a hidden corridor which led to a trap door for a priest to enter below ground level. It is believed that crocodiles used to be kept in the temple. Hundreds of mummified ones were found there during excavations in the 1960s.

In the town of Edfu we stopped at the Temple of Korus, the hawk god. Erected by the Greeks from 237 BC to 57 BC, it is covered with beautiful reliefs, although many have been defaced by later Christians who lived in the temple.

Just when we would feel that we had seen too many hieroglyphs, we would get back on our boat and drift down the Nile. Our son loved these times, especially watching the *felucca*, the flat-bottomed sailing boats still used on the Nile.

The Nile was also our son's first introduction to in-your-face, and often crushing, poverty. He was deeply affected by the many small children dressed in rags whom we saw daily as they scavenged through garbage or begged for coins when we docked. This put a face on the facts he studied in school about living standards around the world and how they differ from ours back in the U.S.

Next up was the Temple of Khnum, an unusual place which basically has a modern town built on top of it. Dozens of houses had been erected upon the temple after centuries of sand had covered it. Now the temple is exposed, but surrounded by the cliffs of the foundation of the town.

Towards the end of our Nile journey, we reached the famed site of ancient Thebes. Modern Luxor is now what surrounds the home of the greatest remnants of Egypt's heritage. Our small boat docked in the river, but not on the banks of the Nile. Rather, we were the fifth boat docked out from the banks, and to get to shore we walked through the main cabins of four huge boats.

Thebes, for over 400 years from 1567–1085 BC, was the center of the ancient world. Left behind as proof of its greatness are the Colossi of Memnon and the Temple of Hatshepsut, Egypt's only female pharaoh. Also at Thebes is the Valley of the Kings, with 64 tombs discovered to date, including King Tut's tomb. The greatest rulers of Egypt each left his mark. Scores of tombs, eerie and fascinating, are hidden away in the dry desert landscape. But after viewing too many hieroglyphs, columns, and statues, everything began to all look alike. So we were ready to move on, to get back to the modern and hectic. On to Cairo.

Describing Cairo is difficult. It is huge. The traffic defies comprehension. But even being stuck in traffic can be a wonder. One afternoon, we were stopped by a herd of camels, hundreds in number, being led through the center of town. This was taken in stride by car and horse-cart drivers alike. There was no honking or angry fists.

Enjoying our elegant hotel after days on a small boat, we settled in for some deserved relaxation, until our son came down with a virulent stomach bug and fever. We called for the hotel doctor, but with some trepidation. Would he speak English, would he know what to do, would he have modern medicines? All our fears evaporated when he came to our room. A graduate of Harvard Medical School, he diagnosed the problem in no time and administered a "miracle" shot which eliminated all of the symptoms in about one hour. Whatever this shot was, I wish it were available back home!

Perhaps everyone has at some time dreamed of seeing the Great Pyramid and Sphinx of Giza. As we approached them, they shimmered in the distance. So close to the city of Cairo, it is hard to believe they are real. When we neared, camel drivers offered us (for a steep fee) the chance to approach by camel. As we negotiated, our son realized we were only talking about hiring two camels and there were three of us. Something was wrong with this picture and the fault was mine. I was unwilling to let my 13-year-old son—even though he was bigger and stronger that I—ride alone on his own camel. No way would I give in. Humiliation and mortification set in as our son climbed on and shared my camel. Never will I live this down and never will I take down the photo on our kitchen wall memorializing the moment.

And so we plodded through the sand to Giza. There was the famed Sphinx, but something had happened between imagination and reality. The Sphinx shrank! Although over 240 feet long and 66 feet high, it was nowhere near the giant figure I had envisioned. Over 4,500 years old and carved of a single block of limestone, it is thought to be a portrait of Chephren, a king from the Fourth Dynasty. Next on the agenda was the museum housing the funerary boat of Cheops. This is the oldest intact boat in the world. It is in almost perfect condition, even though it is older than 4,500 years. (We would later walk back to visit this fascinating museum.)

And finally, the pyramids. Nothing prepares one for the great bulk of these monuments. The Pyramid of the Great Cheops is made up of over 16 million tons of stone. It stands 482 feet high. There is a shaft penetrating into this pyramid, a narrow, poorly lit space where adventurous tourists can go. Did I even consider it? No way. However, our son was first in line to descend with the other brave souls into this bit of hell. He loved it and he loved teasing me about my fears and phobias. He described the musty smells, the single light bulbs hanging from a wire, and the bats (which he actually didn't see, but added for the effect).

We explored hectic, mesmerizing Cairo for yet another day: modern and ancient, markets and street scenes. However, the memories seared deepest in our minds were from our week-long float down the Nile. Ancient history lesson and modern social observation made a perfect pair of themes for our family trip. And, of course, our son has vowed never to share a camel with his mother again.

EGYPT OVERVIEW

- Egypt: 50% larger than Texas
- Population: 64.2 million
- Capital: Cairo (Population 9.9 million)
- Ethnicity: 99% Egyptian, 1% other
- Religious Affiliation: 94% Sunni Muslim, 6% Coptic Christian
- Languages: Arabic (official), French, English
- Currency: Pound

PLANNING AND PREPARATION

Passports

Americans must have a valid passport and a visa to enter Egypt. A renewable 30-day tourist visa can be obtained at any port of entry, except Taba and Rafah, for a fee of U.S. $15.

When to Go

Egypt is one of the warmest and sunniest countries in the world. Although the areas along the Mediterranean coast experience a few showers here or there, most of the nation sees little rainfall. High temperatures are the norm, but Cairo and the northern half of Egypt's Red Sea coast can be cool in January and February.

Health Issues

Traveler's diarrhea, caused by bacteria or viruses contaminating food and water, is the most common complaint of travelers to North Africa. Lower your risk by only drinking bottled, boiled, or carbonated drinks, and frequently washing your hands with soap and water. If possible, avoid tap water, fountain drinks, and ice cubes. A limited risk of malaria exists in parts of Egypt, but it is not necessary to take an antimalarial drug as the risk for travelers is considered low. However, it is important to use insect repellent to prevent mosquito bites which cause malaria. Modern pharmacies and medical facilities are accessible throughout most of the country. Check with the Center for Disease Control for the recommended inoculations for travelers to Egypt (North Africa) www.cdc.gov/travel/nafrica.htm.

Safety

Crime in Egypt is comparable to Western countries. In fact, many would argue that walking the streets of Egypt is actually safer than in some Western countries. In the past few years, thefts from hotel rooms, including in-room safes, seem to be on the rise. It is best to keep your money and valuables on you at all times. In the Middle East and North Africa terrorism is always a possibility. At this time, Americans are cautioned to be on heightened alert for terrorist attacks.

What to Bring

Egypt is a Moslem country, hence clothing tends to be conservative, especially for women. Loose-fitting dresses, skirts, and blouses are essential to bring. Also useful would be a light shawl as a cover-up if you are wearing more revealing Western clothes. And it would be wise to bring along a wide-brimmed hat and a high SPF sunscreen whenever you go. Pack a lightweight jacket or windbreaker if you plan to visit the northern half of Egypt's Red Sea Coast.

THINGS TO SEE AND DO

Activities for Kids

- While on the boat, have your kids observe a scene on the shore using binoculars, then write a story about what they see.

182 of 360 EXOTIC TRAVEL DESTINATIONS FOR FAMILIES

- Before renting a camel, let your children watch other customers negotiating a price, then let them bargain with the camel drivers. (In the worst case it will only cost you a few bucks of overpricing.)
- Ask your kids to design their own pyramid—including figuring out what materials to use, how these will be transported, etc. Encourage them to draw a plan.

Choosing a cruise

Perhaps the best way to experience ancient and modern Egypt is by taking a boat cruise on the Nile. After all, the Nile defines Egypt. Length of cruise, sites visited, type of vessel, and price are the key elements that influence a traveler's selection of a cruise. Prices generally range from $200 to $300 per person per day. However fares as low as $50 and as high as $500 are also available. Here is a sampling of cruise options:

Movenpick: The Radamis—Movenpick Cruiser docks either in Luxor (Mövenpick Resort) or in Aswan, depending on the three-, four-, or seven-day cruise schedule. It cruises the Nile between these two cities. The boat offers 70 individually air conditioned deluxe cabins, eight of which are connected in pairs to form four suites with balconies. The deluxe cabins all have private bathrooms and come with minibars. The Radamis has a sundeck, swimming pool, fitness area, gift shop, and beauty salon, as well as a bar, restaurant, lounge, and disco. Tel: (20) 10-107-7438. Email: Info@EgyptReservation.com.

Sonesta Nile Cruises—The Sonesta Nile Goddess is one of three ships operated by Sonesta on the Nile between Aswan and Luxor on four- and six-night itineraries. The Nile Goddess features 63 standard cabins and two presidential suites with private lounges. All cabins have broad panoramic windows, private direct-dial phones, three channel music systems, television, and video remote control. Bathrooms are equipped with full-size bathtubs. On board are restaurants, bars, a disco, and an outdoor swimming pool with bar. Tel: (20) 2-262-8111. Email: reservations@sonestacruises.com.

Felucca Sailing on the Nile—The Royal Cleopatra is a traditional wind-driven sailing craft that cruises the Nile on five-, seven-, or fourteen-day soft-adventure tours. The 14 day itinerary includes an overnight train journey on the Nile Express. Facilities include a spacious lounge with breakfast area and a small library. An Egyptologist is onboard to answer any questions the travelers may have. Tel: (888) 466-8242.

Abercrombie and Kent—At about $500 per person per day, this is the high end of Nile cruising. The 11- and 12-day itineraries begin and end in Cairo and include a cruise between Luxor and Aswan onboard the Sun Boat IV. Also included is a flight to Abu Simbel for sightseeing. The ship has 36 superior double rooms, two Presidential suits and two Royal suites. All cabins face outside with two picture windows and have full bathrooms with shower and hairdryer. Each cabin comes with individually controlled air conditioning, color television, international telephone access, individual CD player, and minibar. A resident fleet physician is on call 24 hours a day. Cooking lessons are offered whenever a group of children is on board. www.abercrombiekent.com/programs/activities/cruising/images/sunboat4_deck_big.gif. Mobile phone use is banned aboard the ship. Tel: (800) 323-7308.

Hotels in Cairo

Mena House Oberoi—Cost: Double room $150–$250. One of the most elegant and historic hotels in the country, the Mena was once the royal lodge of Khedive Ismail, the ruler of Egypt from 1863–1869. It is ideally situated at the foot of the Pyramids. www.oberoihotels.com/oberoi/Egypt/Mena/index.htm. Tel: (800) 562-3764.

Nile Hilton—Cost: Double room $65–$165. Popular hotel for families. Located on the banks of the Nile River, adjacent to the Egyptian Museum and within walking distance to the major shopping and business districts of Cairo. Tahrir Square, Cairo. www.hilton.com/en/hi/hotels/index.jhtml?ctyhocn=CAIHITW. Tel: (800) 445-8667.

Windsor Hotel—Cost: Double room $39–$60. This delightful hotel, oozing with character, has been featured in Hollywood movies and was once a colonial British officers' club. An eclectic mix of furnishings and fixtures from antique bathtubs to the lavish lift in the lobby make it a fun, although somewhat faded, place to stay. Close to shopping and all the city's major attractions. 19 Alfi Bei Street, Cairo. www.windsorcairo.com/mainpage.htm. Tel: (20) 2-5915810. Fax: (20) 2-5921621.

Hotels in Aswan

Sofitel Old Cataract Hotel—Cost: Double room U.S. $175–$300. The grande dame of Aswan, this historic and luxurious hotel is surrounded by breathtaking gardens and boasts spectacular views of the Nile. It's located within walking distance of the city center. Abtal El Tahrir Street, Aswan. www.sofitel.com/sofitel/fichehotel/gb/sof/1666/fiche_hotel.shtml. Tel: (20) 97-316-000. Fax:(20) 97-316-011.

Restaurants in Cairo

Cafe Riche—17 Talaat Harb. Traditional Egyptian food including a delicious chicken fatta: juicy slices of chicken over rice, baked together and served with garlic bread.

Khan El Khalili—5 El Badistan Lane, Khan el Khalili Bazaar. Located in the heart of Cairo's colorful bazaar, the restaurant serves a traditional Middle Eastern menu. Open daily 12:00 noon to midnight.

RESOURCES

Official Website
www.touregypt.net/

Books for Adults
Lonely Planet Egypt by Humphries Andrew
The Geology of Egypt: A Traveller's Guide by Bonnie M. Sampsell

Secrets of the Great Pyramid by Peter Tompkins
In an Antique Land by Amitav Ghosh

Books for Children
Adventures in Ancient Egypt (The Good Times Travel Agency) by Linda Bailey
Welcome to Egypt (Welcome to My Country) by Nicole Frank, Leslie Jermyn, Leslie L. Wilson
Escape from Egypt: A Novel by Sonia Levitin

Videos and DVDs
The Prince of Egypt
National Geographic's the Mysteries of Egypt
Napoleon's Obsession: Quest for Egypt

Lisa and Jeff Sachs between a rock and a hard place in Carthage, Tunisia.

CHAPTER 15

TUNISIA: MODERN AND ANCIENT CIVILIZATIONS

BY MARY NICHOLS SANDOVAL

FAMILY TRAVEL TO TUNISIA

We were driving along the coastal highway between Tunis and Carthage in our rental car with our two young children. The Mediterranean was a deep blue to our right and to our left, the green rolling hills stretched as far as one could see. We had arrived in Tunisia the night before and were on our way to visit the famous Phoenician ruins at Carthage. Up ahead we could see a man at the side of the road, waving his arms frantically. His car was parked on the shoulder with a very flat tire. I was driving at the time and I slowed down to see if we could help him.

"What are you doing?" shouted my husband, "Can't you see that no one else is stopping? No one from his own country, no Arabic speakers are stopping. Doesn't that seem strange to you?"

"But Dad, if *we* had a flat tire . . ." began our son.

"You've always told us we should help people," added our daughter.

"Don't stop!" said my husband, in his firmest voice, so I didn't.

When we were past the man with the flat tire, he continued, "Someone from the office told me about this trick. You pull over and he asks for a ride to the nearest town, which just happens to be where he lives. He's so grateful that he invites you to his home to meet the entire family, including the aged Bedouin grandmother, and you drink mint tea and eat Tunisian almond pastries. After you tell the family about your plans to visit Tunisia and where you'll be staying next, it turns out that the grateful man has a cousin/uncle/brother/brother-in-law who just happens to live very close to your hotel and who will be your devoted guide for as many days as you like. The next day when your devoted guide shows up at your hotel, he just happens to have a cousin/uncle/brother/brother-in-law himself, who is the best rug merchant in all of Tunisia. After you've purchased many more rugs than you'll ever need, it turns out that the rug merchant also has a cousin/uncle/brother/brother-in-law who has the finest collection of silver Bedouin jewelry in all of Tunisia. . . ."

"O.K., O.K." we all say. "We get the point."

We saw many flat tires on our week-long drive through Tunisia and we also saw many tourists pulling over, but no Tunisians. Even if one happens to fall for the scam, there is usually no danger involved. It's all a part of Tunisian marketing.

The stop at Carthage was well worth the trip, once we managed to get past the vendors who were digging "Pre-Roman" treasures of bronze out of the ground, right before our very eyes, cleaning them off with delicate brushes and whispering furtively, "Don't let the authorities see you buying this. These are more than 2,000 years old." The most beautiful sensation one feels in Carthage is being able to wander among the fallen marble columns as the tall cypress trees sway in the breeze with the deep blue Mediterranean stretching off into the distance. Even the children were in awe of the grandeur of it all, and were full of questions about the Carthaginians, the Punic Wars, the Greeks and the Romans, and we were glad to have taken along a guide book with a brief history to consult. We sometimes find that hired guides may not have information that is interesting to young children, and so we prefer to do a bit of research and explain certain things ourselves.

Sidi Bou Said, a short drive north of the capital city, is a whitewashed village on a hillside overlooking the sea. It is famous for the varied designs of its green-, turquoise-, and ochre-colored doors, and we spent the entire morning walking the narrow winding streets, looking for eye-popping doorways around each corner. The children photographed the doors they liked best and we also bought a poster of "The Doors of Sidi Bou Said." The children especially enjoyed a visit to a typical Tunisian cafe where one sits on elevated carpeted platforms, sips mint tea, and watches others smoke the hubbly bubbly pipes. As a non-smoker, I was never tempted to try and, at any rate, women don't usually smoke these pipes in public. My husband sat with a group of Tunisians and said the pipe had the taste of apple peels. We had read that these water pipes can be filled with many types of dried fruits. My husband wasn't squeamish about putting something in his mouth that had been passed around a circle of strangers, so I vowed not to give it a second thought. . . .

We stayed at the Sheraton in Hammamet. It was exactly what you see in the travel brochures—a kidney shaped pool shaded by date palms with a floating bar in the middle and a barman with white jacket and black bow tie. We saw something one doesn't usually see in the brochures, though. A very blond Nordic female tourist, wearing just the barest expression of a mono-kini, was happily sipping an elaborate drink as she stood waist deep in the pool, chatting animatedly with a Saudi female tourist who was also standing waist deep in the kidney shaped pool, sipping a cup of tea, clad from head to foot in her black robes, head scarf, and face veil. Our children were fascinated. They were, of course, more concerned about the "lady with all of her clothes on" in the water than by the "lady with all her clothes off," as my daughter put it. That one image of ancient and modern, Eastern and Western, will always be a part of my memory of Tunisia.

Hammamet is perhaps one of the more touristy Tunisian towns with modern resort-style hotels and long, sandy beaches. A beach is a beach, and for our children, they had plenty of fun in the sand and water, while I would have wished for something a bit more exotic. While my husband and kids were playing in the waves, I did see an old Bedouin gentleman, white bearded and turbaned, leading his camel along the sand. That could have been my "exotic" image of Hammamet, were it not for the tourist riding atop the camel. She was wearing only the bottom part of her suit and her ample breasts bounced up and down to the loping gait of the camel. I had, and still have, mixed feelings about that image.

From Hammamet we continued down the coast to the city of Sousse. The "medina," or old center of the city is well preserved and filled with little shops featuring Tunisian crafts. Tunisia is known for its blue and white pottery and we bought some in Sousse, but the children were fascinated by two things in particular: delicate bird cages, painted white with blue doors, which came in all sizes, ranging from very tiny to more than three feet high; and handmade Tunisian dolls, with carved wooden heads and clothes made out of scraps of cloth, wielding dangerous-looking daggers. Very near to the city of Sousse is Port Al Kantaoui, where the wealthy berth their yachts. The white and blue village, with thousands of masts and sails in the foreground, is a beautiful sight. As night fell, the aroma of jasmine blossoms filled the air. We all bought necklaces of these blossoms from the street vendors to wear around our necks. I am always pleased when my children are happy with some small token.

From Sousse we drove inland towards the holy city of Kairouan, said to be the fourth holiest city in the Islamic world (after Mecca, Medina, and Jerusalem). The countryside was much as it had been along the coast—green rolling hills and white villages—until we got closer to Kairouan, where we saw ochre plains and the city shimmering a bit like a mirage in the distance.

The great mosque of Kairouan is reputed to have the oldest standing minaret in the world, dating from the 8th century. From the large esplanade in front of the mosque one can observe the graceful columns with ornately carved capitals, but this wasn't of much interest to the children. What they did enjoy was the visit to the "Bi'r Barouta," an ancient well in the center of the city where a blind camel walks in circles all day, pulling the waterwheel which brings the water up from the well. A legend says that Uqba bin Nafi Al Fihri, a Muslim conqueror of the 8th century, had lost a golden cup in a sacred well in Mecca and when he and his troops arrived months later in Kairouan and went to the local well to drink, he found his cup floating in the water. This miracle was thought by some to mean that there was an underground river flowing directly from Mecca to Kairouan. The children found the well, the legend, and especially the blind camel to be extremely interesting.

We returned to the capital city, Tunis, for the last days of our stay. Some of the tourists we spoke to along the way had been quite frightened in the main souk in Tunis, and said we should never venture in "there" with our children. In the souk, there is a feeling of very narrow streets, a crush of people, vendors calling to you in six languages from every stall, a mingling of unusual sounds and smells, and a slight strangeness that can be overwhelming. Many Tunisians in the souk reached to stroke the heads of our light-haired children. We are an adventurous family, though, and we walked through every corner, especially off-the-beaten path away from the main tourist stalls.

We did experience one minor incident when a young man tried to grab my camera. He did not get it, nevertheless the Tunisians nearby shouted at the man and several chased him down a narrow street. One man hit the would-be thief with a broom. The children were duly impressed by this scene and a bit frightened as well. We always do our best not to alarm the children and to leave them with a positive impression of every place we visit. I had to explain to the children that there are poor people in almost all countries who don't have as many things as we do. There was, of course, that inevitable question, "Why didn't you just give your camera to the man if he was so poor?" We explained that most Tunisians want foreigners to have a good experience and they have no patience with people who try to take things from tourists. Needless to say, the camera incident was talked about for days afterwards.

The visit to the truly local part of the souk was fascinating. Women bargained for vegetables and fruits, vendors unfurled bolt after bolt of glittering cloth, and men crouched on the elevated platforms of the cafes, smoking the hubbly bubblies. The aromas of the spice market evoked scenes of camel caravans and endless dunes. We bought unusual things: comic books in Arabic, because the children wanted to see how one reads from right to left; a "miswak," a stick which people chew on as a way to brush their teeth; spices like cinnamon bark, cloves, coriander, and cumin; fancy hair bobbles with sequins and lace; kohl for painting the eyes; and frankincense in amber-colored chunks.

Outside of the "tourist" streets, which are fascinating and colorful in their own way, the souk is divided into sectors by the trades practiced there. We watched gold and silversmiths at work, cabinet makers and carpenters, weavers, potters, tanners, coopers, shoemakers . . . I can't think of any modern western city where one can still see artisans practicing age old trades. There is a medieval flavor in the souk and we had the feeling that we could find anything in the world we needed, if we only knew in which narrow lane to look.

Our visit to Tunisia was just "exotic" enough to keep me interested, problem free for traveling with young children, and we balanced our beach and pool time with cultural visits, so that the whole family enjoyed the trip.

TUNISIA OVERVIEW

- Tunisia: About the size of Wisconsin
- Population: 10 million
- Capital: Tunis (Population 1.8 million)
- Ethnicity: 98% Arab, 1% Berber, 1% French
- Religious Affiliation: 99% Muslim
- Languages: Arabic (official), French
- Currency: Dinar

PLANNING AND PREPARATION

Passports

Americans are required to have a valid passport to enter Tunisia.

When to Go

In the summer months, hot weather brings sun-seeking northern Europeans to Tunisia by the planeloads. The spring and fall bring somewhat milder, although still warm, temperatures and fewer crowds. The winter can be wet. Pack an umbrella and rain gear if you plan to visit during this time of year.

Health Issues

A yellow fever vaccination certificate is required from travelers over 1 year of age coming from infected areas. The tap water is safe to drink in Tunisia, however travelers are often put off by the strong chlorinated flavor. Bottled water is available almost everywhere. For a list of recommended immunizations when traveling to Tunisia (North Africa) consult the Center for Disease Control. www.cdc.gov/travel/nafrica.htm.

Safety

Tunisia has a relatively low rate of street crime and prides itself on being a safe destination for families. Exercise caution in larger cities, like Tunis, where pickpockets and petty thieves tend to congregate.

What to Bring

Like most Moslem countries, clothing tends to be conservative, especially for women. Loose-fitting dresses, skirts, and blouses are essential to bring. Also useful would be a light shawl as a cover up if you are wearing more revealing western clothes.

THINGS TO SEE AND DO

Activities for Kids

- Have your kids either draw pictures or take photographs of the doorways in Sidi Bou Said, and make an album to share with friends at home.
- In the souk, ask your kids to find five products that cannot be found at home and have them find information about each.
- Have your kids write a short story about a day in the life of an ancient Carthage citizen.

Tunis' ancient medina and souk—As you enter the narrow streets you will feel as if you have stepped back centuries in time. Small shops offer their treasures of brass, olive wood, leather, and carpets. Brightly colored garments spill out into the street. Souvenirs, antiques, Berber jewelry, and pottery vie for your attention. Make your way to the heart of the medina, the Mosque of the Olive Tree, or Ez Zitouna. Rebuilt in the 9th century, the Ez Zitouna was the focal point of life in the city. Custom decreed the location the different trades were placed around the mosque. Booksellers, perfumeries, dried fruit sellers, and cloth merchants held the privilege of proximity. Today, one can still see traces of this tradition: the Souk of the perfumes, traditional clothing shops, and almond and spice sellers are still located alongside the mosque walls. The medina is a wealth of ancient palaces, mosques, and centers of trade and learning; for your family it is a living museum.

Kairouan—Roughly 100 miles south of Tunis and one hour inland from the coast lies one of Islam's holiest cities. Sometimes called "the city of 50 mosques," Kairouan is the spiritual home of Tunisians. The city of ocher and beige buildings represents 13 centuries of Islamic culture. Especially interesting is the old city or "medina," with its imposing walls and monumental gates. Within the walls are lovely mosques and hundreds of shops where carpets of pure wool are woven and sold and where the visitor can admire handicrafts of copper and leather. The Artisanat Center provides an excellent exhibit on carpets and carpet weaving. Be sure to see the "Bi'r Barouta," an ancient well in the center of the city, where a blind camel walks in circles all day, pulling the waterwheel which brings the water up from the well.

Carthage—Carthage has been around since the 9th century BC when the Phoenicians called it "Kart Hadasht" (the new town). These famous ruins lie on the Mediterranean, nine miles north of Tunis via an excellent paved road. Wander the extensive site to view vestiges of the Punic and Roman empires, baths, dwellings, temples, shrines, and the fabulous naval port of the Carthaginians. Be sure to visit the Antoinine Thermal baths, one of the largest built under the Roman empire, and featuring the "cool room" an amazing 47-meters long and 15-meters high. The Roman theater is still used today for the summer festival of Carthage.

Sidi Bou Said—This lovely blue and white village is perched on cliffs overlooking the Bay of Tunis a short distance from Carthage. Cobblestone streets wind up the hillside past shops offering carpets, pottery, bird cages, and perfumes. During the warm summer evenings concerts of traditional Tunisian music—"malouf"—attract visitors and Tunisians alike. At the foot of the cliffs lies the Port of Sidi Bou Said, a modern marina with restaurants and hotels. If you come in July you will be able to view the Kharja, a religious festival in honor of Sidi Bou Said, the city's namesake saint.

Hotels in Tunis

Abou Nawas Tunis—Cost: Double room $185. This five-star hotel is located in the city center, close to the business and shopping districts, and to the Palais des Congres. B.P. 355-Place des Droits de l'homme Av. Mohamed V-1080, Tunis. www.abounawas.com/en/tunis.htm. Tel: (216) 1 350 355. Fax: (216) 1 352 882.

Le Palace Tunis—Cost: Double room $156–$274. A bit further out from the city, but close to the beach, this hotel offers clean, comfortable rooms and amenities such as numerous restaurants, a large swimming pool, and a modern fitness center. 2078 La Marsa des Cotes de Carthage, Tunisia. www.lepalace.com.tn/htmla/homepganglais.htm. Tel: (216) 1 91 2000. Fax: (216) 1 91 1442.

Hotels near Carthage/ Sidi Bou Said

The Golden Tulip Carthage Tunis—Cost: Double room $156–$180. A sprawling five-star hotel, with architecture inspired by ancient Greece, located in the hills of Gammarth about three miles from Carthage and Sidi Bou Said. Avenue De La Promenade BP 606, 2078 La Marsa. www.goldentulip.com/site/PropertySearch.asp. Tel: (216) 71 913000.

Hotels in Hammamet

Sheraton Hammamet Resort—Cost: Double room $103– $200. A luxurious seaside resort that features large rooms, with domed-brick ceilings, decorated in the Tunisian style using local designs and fabrics. Avenue Moncef Bay, Hammamet. www.starwood. com/sheraton. Tel: 888-625-5144.

Restaurants in Tunis

Restaurant La Victoire—1 Ave Franklin Roosevelt, Tunis. A popular eatery that serves traditional Tunisian fare. Try the couscous with veal, lamb, or fish.

Restaurants in Sidi Bou Said

Restaurant Le Pirate—Rue Hedi Zarrouk. Located by the marina, it's a great spot for seafood.

RESOURCES

Official Website

www.tourismtunisia.com/

Books for Adults

The Rough Guide Tunisia by Peter Morris
Footprint Tunisia Handbook by Justin McGuinness
Tunisia: The Story of a Country That Works by Georgie Anne Geyer

Books for Children

Tunisia (Enchantment of the World) by Mary Virginia Fox

Videos and DVDs

Dizzy Gillespie: A Night in Tunisia
Travel the World by Train: Africa—Morocco, Tunisia, Egypt, Kenya, Uganda, South Africa

Islands

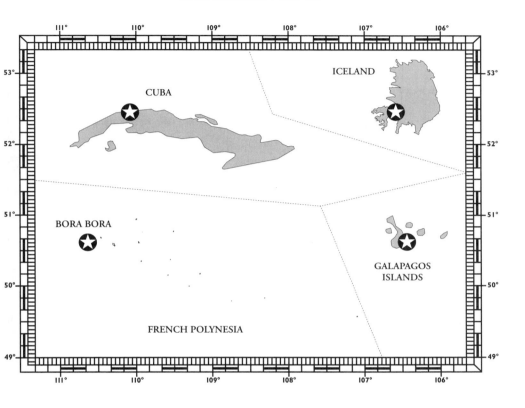

Bill, Will, and Alison Nichols head out to sea in Bora Bora.

CHAPTER 16

Bora Bora: Tropical Paradise for Active Families

Family Travel to Bora Bora

Among the most treasured experiences in Bora Bora were the late afternoon shore walks with my daughter, Alison. "I wish we could stay here all summer," she sighed as we stood stone still in the crystal clear water with thousands of tiny fish tickling our ankles. "I love everything about this place."

"I know you do," I said, holding her hand and wading deeper into this wondrous sea world. Bora Bora had captivated us both—and for a change, our opinions about the family vacation were in sync. Well . . . almost. Alison dreamed of staying on this alluring island gem till summer's end. But my fantasy? To stay forever. Who wouldn't in paradise?

Bora Bora. It's everything to everyone. Often called the "pearl of the Pacific," this island belongs to the Society archipelago of which Tahiti is the recognizable anchor. Novelist James Michener praised Bora Bora as the most beautiful island in the world; an accolade endorsed by others who added tributes on paper and canvas—Paul Gaugin, Robert Louis Stevenson, and Herman Melville. With towering volcanic peaks, lush palms, emerald green hills and pristinely white beaches, all encircled by a translucent turquoise lagoon . . . Bora Bora mesmerizes.

After an eight hour flight from Los Angeles, my husband, Bill, thirteen year-old Alison and ten year-old Will, arrived in Papeete, Tahiti; the region's major airport and jumping off point for touring the other islands in French Polynesia. The usual torture of waiting in a customs line was made palatable by a group of local musicians who serenaded us, while traditionally dressed women draped us with a fragrant welcoming lei of frangipani. "Are you married?" one gorgeous woman asked Bill as I eyed her suspiciously. As he shook his head obediently up and down, she placed a flower behind his left ear to show that he was taken.

We quickly headed to Air Tahiti for a 45-minute flight to Bora Bora. Circling low over this island, we spied towering volcanic peaks, topped by sheer black rock and crowned by billowy clouds. Midway down, the volcanic rock became carpeted by lush palms, before finally spilling into pristinely white beaches. Encircling this scene was a translucent lagoon painted with brilliant hues of blues and turquoises. This waterworld was enclosed by small *motus*, or islands, on one side, and a coral reef on the other.

Landing on a tiny island connected to Bora Bora, we boarded a boat for a half hour ride to Vaitape, the main village of Bora Bora, then hopped on "Le Truck," an open, flat roofed bus, that took us to our destination: Club Med.

We've never been big fans of the Club, so when our seasoned travel agent proposed, "Try the Club Med on Bora Bora," my husband shrieked, "What? Is she crazy?"

But once digesting the costs of the other hotels in Bora Bora—the ones with the glass bottomed coffee tables which provided a look into the sea—it was clear: Paradise had a price tag. Club Med would not break the bank. Using this lagoon-situated hotel as a base, families can bask in the unrivaled beauty and culture of the island, while engaging in activities that tantalize all ages. For the active, there's snorkeling, scuba diving, windsurfing, kayaking, and water skiing. For the adventurous, there's biking, climbing a volcano, and treating local sharks to a mid-morning snack. And for the laid back, there's swinging in a hammock strung between two coconut trees' . . . an opportunity to bask in dreamland.

Billed as a Club Med village for everyone, it graciously welcomes children. However, your kids are not whisked away for circus training, arts and crafts lessons, or the pool for a 12-hour adventure *sans* parents. There are no kids' clubs at the Bora Bora Club Med. Although much of the instruction of various activities is child-oriented, parents are solely responsible for their offspring. The club provides kid-sized windsurf boards and patient instructors in sports such windsurfing, scuba and kayaking.

One advantage of this club is that most activities can be booked instantly. My son, Will, was constantly on the move. His days were occupied with snorkeling, windsurfing, archery, and, before dinner, games of soccer and basketball with young men from all over the world. "Those guys are really good," he marveled one evening after playing with young men from France, Spain, Italy, and Australia.

The Club Med village skirts a lagoon with bungalows lining the edge. We had two adjacent bungalows, each spacious and furnished tastefully with king-sized beds, a desk, and offering a large dressing room and bathroom. Our ample decks extended over the lagoon and offered dazzling views of the endless turquoise water world before us, with its distinctive palm-covered islets called *motus*, each ringed with white sand. I luxuriated during my down time each day in a lounge chair overlooking the water—reading, writing, and dreaming of ways to stay forever.

This was the first family vacation where we had no trouble rousing the kids from bed. They were up and dressed by 7:30, at breakfast by 8:30, and ready to start the day's activities by 9:00.

We were in culinary heaven! The main area contains two large dining areas, each with massive thatched roofs, a bar, and theater for the evening entertainment. One night we participated in an authentic sandpit barbecue and traditional dances performed by local villagers.

Each lavishly displayed meal included a wide variety of fish that was grilled, baked, fried, and kebabed. Evening fare featured a theme, such as Italian or Mexican night. We even had a dessert night with rich chocolate tortes, and chocolate-dipped strawberries. Bread night featured breads of all sorts and shapes, including those shaped like books, snakes, flowers, and even a giant alligator.

Luckily, this Club Med did not assign seating, a custom of many other clubs. The dining room featured long tables for socializing, but also tables for two and four. One evening we were feeling particularly social, so we sat with the staff member whose job was Hygiene Director. "That sounds like a job you'd be good at, Mom," Will said after hearing the string of responsibilities this guy had, which included checking the coconut trees for signs of nuts on the verge of falling.

"You'd be surprised at how many people are seriously injured from falling coconuts in Polynesia," this young Frenchman said. Hmmm. That's *one* danger of exotic foreign travel that had never crossed my mind . . . but I did catch myself looking upwards more often than usual.

The distance around Bora Bora is only 18 miles; manageable for a three hour bike ride with the kids. Leaving the hotel on rented bikes, we headed to Vaitape, Bora Bora's largest—and only—town. On the way, we passed the ultra deluxe Hotel Bora Bora, while next to it stood a small thatched roof hut with stray dogs wandering, and clothes drying on a line. We stopped at the famous Bloody Mary Restaurant where the names of celebrities are carved on a sign, including Diana Ross, John Denver, and Prince Ranier.

While in Viatepe, I wanted to secretly slip into a tattoo studio as I planned to write about the exquisite works of inky black art displayed on the human canvas of the Polynesian body. Chests bore intricate seared necklaces; hips and shoulders were emblazoned with bold designs; and encircling arms, legs, and thighs were startling geometric shapes, some intertwined with images of indigenous animals.

I hit pay dirt: I entered Bernard's Tatau Studio, owned by the island's self-appointed tattoo expert, Bernard. The skin and ink business was thriving. A dozen Polynesian and French customers clustered around a table, poring over Bernard's portfolios of tattoos. Some were clearly there to gawk; giggling nervously as they pointed to parts of their bodies, speculating where a particular skin design might find a home. But most were serious consumers, thoughtfully marking portfolio pages that featured their dream designs—the ones Bernard would soon sear onto their skins for life.

Staring through the window was my family, so what could I do but invite them in? And what an education they got. A curtain separated Bernard's workroom from his customers. Bernard's small, muscular body—itself a portfolio of tattoo designs—was bent over the back of a young woman stretched out on a cot. In two hours, she would emerge from under a piercing, high-speed tattoo instrument with a long, gracefully winding strand of delicate flowers etched onto her lower back. As Bernard paused to dab droplets of blood from his flesh canvas, his client eyed the progress in a nearby mirror. "*C'est magnifique,*" she said.

"*Je sais,* I know." Definitely not a modest man, Bernard explained that he had started out as a painter of murals in France. "But when I came to Tahiti and Bora Bora, there were no walls," he said, "so I started tattooing." Bernard claimed that his designs and ability made him the most popular tattoo artist on the island.

But skill accounts for only part of Bernard's success . . . the rest is attributed to location. In few places throughout history has the art of tattooing been so integral to the social, sexual, and religious mores of a people as here on the islands of French Polynesia. Today, the Polynesian tattoo is not only a mark of personal identity, but also a renewal of cultural pride and tradition—and perhaps for some bearers, a challenge to colonial powers. Bernard contributes to the art with his re-creation of traditional designs, and his tattooing of many Polynesians.

But there are other purveyors. Hidden from island visitors are the fluent speakers of this skin language: the indigenous Polynesian tattoo artists. "There's one for every ten households here," Bernard claimed. They are the repositories of the traditional designs, many which still carry their original names—*matahoata, pepehipu, paka-nui*—words as obscure to the outsider as this ancient language of the skin itself. As I gazed out the door, past the village of Viatape and into the lush island hills, I imagined these itinerant artists canvassing this paradise.

As we observed and listened to Bernard's stories of this ancient art form, we were struck by his information and now have tattoos permanently seared . . . at least in memory.

The next day, we tried the pinnacle of all water activities—scuba diving. The manager of the program agreed to take Will and Alison, providing that both had their own instructor. "But you have to hold on to the instructor the entire dive," he said. So off we went accompanied by three diving instructors. We headed between two lush motus, in the shadow of the island's volcanic peak. The kids, dressed in wet suits, were exhilarated by this adventure. The dive master provided careful instruction on the equipment, stopping to question them or asking them to repeat important information to be sure they understood. He also showed them hand signals to use while in the water. Then, with their teachers in hand, the kids and Bill went overboard while I photographed. "You should have gone, Mom," they said breathlessly after they ascended. I know. Next time. "We saw a manna ray as long as my room!" Will screamed.

The following morning, we hopped on a boat with other guests and headed off for a wild adventure: feeding sharks. Once reaching our destination we climbed out of the boat into waist-high water. Carefully keeping our extremities behind a rope-boundary marker, we watched underwater as our guide dropped chum (chopped fish) in the water. The sharks lightly grabbed it. Luckily no one was missing a hand as they got back on the boat. That afternoon, to calm us, we went to a pareo tying session. Pareos are traditional garb worn in French Polynesia. Brightly painted, they are generally two yards long by one yard wide and often have fringe on the edge. There are many ways to tie pareos—each offering a totally different style. They can even be tied as shorts for men. After viewing all the possibilities, we rushed to the store and bought our own pareos, then went back to our rooms for a personal fashion show.

As we huddled around the dinner table on our final night, Bill and the kids made a matrix of all the activities we had done . . . tennis, archery, horseback riding, wind surfing, snorkeling, scuba diving, water skiing, biking, jogging, kayaking, catamaran sailing, shark feeding, basketball, soccer, volleyball, and pareo tying.

It had indeed been a busy time in paradise.

BORA BORA OVERVIEW

- Location: Midway between Los Angeles and Sydney, Australia
- One of the Society Islands, French Polynesia
- Capital of French Polynesia: Papette, Tahiti
- Population of Bora Bora: Approximately 5,400
- Ethnicity of French Polynesia: 78% Polynesian, 12% Chinese, 10% French
- Religious Affiliation of French Polynesia: 54% Protestant, 30% Roman Catholic, 16% other
- French Polynesia has been an overseas territory of France since 1946.
- Official Languages: French and Tahitian. English is spoken at major hotels and restaurants.
- Currency: Pacific French Franc
- Circumnavigating Bora Bora: 18 miles

PLANNING AND PREPARATION

Passports

A valid passport and a return airline ticket are required of U.S. citizens.

When to Go

Anytime! French Polynesia offers warm, tropical weather 12 months a year. The climate of these islands is sunny and pleasant, because the area is cooled by the gentle breezes of the Pacific. There are two seasons, however. From November through May the climate is more humid, with temperatures around 85 degrees. There is occasional rain during this season. From June through October the climate is drier with daily temperatures of about 82 degrees. Temperatures seldom get below 70 degrees. Ocean temperature is in the low 80s.

Health Issues

Most of French Polynesia has a high level of health facilities, including medical care, pharmacies, and private clinics. There is a large government hospital in Tahiti. Necessary medications should be brought from your home, as pharmacies are not always close to hotels. Water is generally safe to drink, but to avoid taking chances, drink bottled water.

Safety

Bora Bora and the other islands are very safe. Violent crime is a rare. Theft can happen, but is rare, and families should take sensible precautions taken on any trip.

What to Bring

Casual, informal clothing is standard in French Polynesia. Women can dress in shorts, slacks, or sundresses. One typical, attractive item to wear are pareos, a wrap-around cloth garment which can be tied in many different ways. Men customarily wear shorts, although take along a couple pairs of slacks for dinner. Children should take casual clothing as well. Families should take comfortable footwear, sun hats, and bathing suits. If scuba diving, families should take rubber-soled shoes for walking on rocky areas underwater.

THINGS TO SEE AND DO

Activities for Kids

- Dressing in Pareos—Pareos are brightly painted material two yards long by one yard wide. Many stores have smaller ones for children. Polynesian women wear them as dresses and skirts and sometimes men wear them tied at the waist. There are many ways to drape pareos, and children will enjoy learning the traditional ways to tie them. Hotels often offer lessons on pareo-tying. There are also brochures that teach this art.
- Point out the differences of jobs on Bora Bora balanced against those at home, and encourage children to compare and contrast the differences. They will observe people fishing and working in the fields. And they will see many people working in the tourism industry.

Bora Bora

Sunset Dinner Cruise—Seafood and entertainment are the offerings for this cruise that lasts 3 1/2 hours on a double-decker outrigger. The cruise takes you around Bora Bora. Cost: $85 per person. Tel: 689-69-40-00.

Travel to Other Islands

Flying Air Tahiti—Air Tahiti is the domestic carrier of French Tahiti. It provides flights to over 35 islands. Tel: 800-781-9356. Website: www.airtahiti.com.

Tahiti—Tahiti is the most recognizable and largest of French Polynesia's 115 islands and atolls. Encompassing this island, which is called "the island of love," are translucent waters, coral reefs, and black sand beaches. This magnificent island is landscaped with volcanic peaks surrounded by thick rainforests. Tahiti is made up of two islands: Tahiti-Nui (big Tahiti) and Tahiti-Iti (little Tahiti) which are joined by an isthmus called Plateau of Taravao. The capital of Tahiti and French Polynesia is Papeete, a city of 70,000 that bustles with activity all day long and into the night. Families can keep very busy in this spectacular city by shopping, imbibing in local cuisine and walking along the bustling shore where hundreds of eye-popping yachts are docked. Families will also enjoy the indoor market, which offers an array of traditional crafts and traditional food items. The market is open daily, except Sunday, from 5:00 A.M. to 6:00 P.M. Be sure to drive into the suburbs to view the many styles of homes.

Children will enjoy the Museum Of Tahiti And Her Islands, located at Pointe des Pecheurs, Punaauia and open daily, except Monday, 9:00 A.M. to 5:00 P.M. This museum displays a variety of objects from Polynesian history and culture. After visiting this museum, we went behind the building to watch hoards of surfers ride the gigantic waves. Families will also be interested in the Paul Gauguin Museum, located at PK 51,200 Papeari. Open daily, 9:00 A.M. to 5:00 P.M. This startling museum features original works and reproductions from this famous French artist.

Huahine—Called the garden island, Huahine is a small, beautiful place for families who want to relax. We flew to Huahine to "chill," as the kids said, from all of our activities on Bora Bora. We took long walks on the pristinely white beaches, arose early to watch the fishermen sell their catch, and biked around the island. We also visited Huahine Local Motion Farm located at Vaiorea Bay. Open daily, except Sunday, from 9:00 A.M. to 4:00 P.M., this farm is filled with fruit trees and stunning flowers. Here families can taste unique cuisine and refreshments.

Hotels on Bora Bora

Club Med Bora Bora—Weekly prices start at $1,400 per person, double occupancy; air fare not included. Price includes three meals a day, most activities, and evening entertainment. There are no children's clubs at this club. Contact information: Website: www.clubmed.com.

Le Meridien Bora Bora—Cost: Double room $575–$623. Lower price for beachfront bungalow, higher price for over the water bungalow with glass-bottom floor. Located on the tip of a Polynesian islet. Resort offers many activities, including serenades by local musicians, fish watching, star-gazing, snorkeling. Motu Tape, Bora Bora, BP 190, French Polynesia. www.lemeridien.com/french_polynesia/bora_bora/information_pf1657.shtml. Tel: 800 543 4300.

Restaurants

Bloody Mary's (Bay de Pofai)—This is Bora Bora's most exotic restaurant for local fish dishes. It is also a hot spot for famous people, as evidenced by the large sign in front that features their names. Diners can choose from many dishes, including steak, chicken, or vegetarian meals. Prices range from $20–$50. Reservations are necessary. Closed Sundays. Tel: (689) 67-72-86.

RESOURCES

Official Websites

www.boraboraisland.com
www.gotahiti.com

Books for Adults

Insight Compact Guide: Tahiti and French Polynesia by Francis Dorai
Open Road Tahiti and French Polynesia Guide by Jan Prince
Tahiti Tattoos by Gian Paolo Barbieri
Pauk Gaugin: Images from the South Seas by Eckhard Hollmann

Videos and DVDs

Mutiny on the Bounty
Globe Trekker: Tahiti, French Polynesia and Samoa
Laura McKenzie's Travel Tips: Tahiti and French Polynesia

Will, Bill, and Alison Nichols on the rocks in Stykkisholmur, Iceland.

CHAPTER 17

ICELAND:
IT'S SO COOL, IT'S HOT

FAMILY TRAVEL TO ICELAND

"You're going to love this country," a native Icelander enthused to my family. "And once you come here, you've been bitten—you will come back." After spending five days in Iceland, this man's predictions became apparent. This North Atlantic island-nation had captivated, entertained, and educated us. When we reluctantly departed, we longed for more. Iceland had indeed bitten us . . . hard.

My husband, two teens and I headed off to Iceland at the end of May, a perfect time of year when the temperature hovers in the low 50s and the sun hangs around for about 20 hours a day—allowing ample time to soak up the unrivaled beauty, dramatic landscape, and captivating activities that this country offers both adults and children.

Iceland, with a population of 270,000, is suspended in the North Atlantic and within an arm's reach of the Arctic Circle. Touring Iceland doesn't require a complex traveling strategy. Hotels and services are easy to book, there are no traffic jams, no crowds, and in this efficiently run country, everything seems to work.

Add to these benefits Iceland's unspoiled, dazzling landscape that is unrivaled anyplace else in the world. With 200 volcanoes, 10,000 waterfalls, imposing glaciers, craggy lava fields, steamy geysers, innumerable geothermal pools, and bubbling mud pots, the terrain constantly awes the visitor who never knows what will pop up—literally—around the next bend.

This island-nation is an enticing enigma for the kids. Boasting one of the highest standards of living in the world, there is no poverty . . . yet there is no blatant wealth, either. The country also has the highest literacy rate in the world, and the greatest number of books published per capita . . . yet over 50% of this educated population believes in elves. And Iceland claims the highest per capita Internet connection in the world . . . yet in this technologically savvy European country, computer is *ios tolva* or translated into English: number soothsayer.

We landed at Iceland's Keflavik International Airport, hopped into a rented car, and began our five-day adventure by heading to the western peninsula of Snaefellsnes. This wind-swept, 40-mile-long finger of land is so unearthly, that Jules Verne chose a volcano under a glacier here to serve as the entrance to the planet's core in his classic adventure, *Journey to the Center of the Earth.*

Our destination was Grundarfjordur, a charming fishing village of 1,000 resting alongside the fjord by the same name. We based ourselves at Hotel Framnes, one of three accommodations in the village. Built on the site of an old fishing hut and surrounded by fish factories—*sans* a telltale fishy scent—Hotel Framnes has a full-service restaurant serving homemade breads and an array of delectable fish dishes made from the fresh catch from a nearby bay. The hotel offers comfortable rooms and weekend Icelandic singing performances in the bar.

After lunching in the hotel dining room, the kids wanted to absorb the local culture by touring the fish factory across the street. Fishing, which accounts for 75% of Iceland's exports, employs 12% of the Icelandic population.

A robust, curly haired fisherman named Gisli Olafsson owns the small, family-run factory specializing in salt cod. Gisli's relatives, decked out in brightly colored rain slickers, salted and packed the cod in crates, while Gisli proudly demonstrated his craft. Slapping a two-foot-long cod on a table, he deftly slit it open, removed the innards, and then provided the kids with a true hands-on experience . . . presenting the creature's bone-like tongue and brain, which they carefully wrapped in Kleenex and politely pocketed. After observing all the stages of fish processing, our tour concluded with sampling dried cod strips, touted by Gisli as the fuel responsible for the Viking's successful explorations. "Without this dried cod," claimed Gisli, "the Vikings never would have made it."

Fortified with Viking stamina, we left Gisli and set off on our own explorations. Heading west from Grundarfjordur, and circling the edge of the peninsula, we arrived at Arnarstapi. This fishing village is the head-quarters for snowmobile tours and hikes to the Snaefellsjokull glacier, the lure of author Jules Verne. Die-hard skiers can ski on this glacier through June. Due to fog and mist, however, we passed on the glacier offerings and instead opted to hike a nearby bluff where thousands of cliff birds nested. A total of over 300 different species of birds have been observed in Iceland. Thankfully we had packed a pair of binoculars and an ornithology guide. Otherwise, we might have missed identifying Iceland's winged wonders, including the most common Icelandic bird, the photogenic puffin, with a population of over eight million.

The second day on Snaefellsnes, we headed off to the northern-most jutting of the peninsula, and the town of Stykkisholmur with a population of 1,200. Here, we experienced the unexpected and the mystical. The unexpected occurred when my husband and I walked right into a building we just knew was a museum. Alison and Will refused to come in. "Are you sure that's a museum?" Alison asked.

"Of course it is," I said. We entered and gazed at intriguing photo-graphs, paintings, and furniture, but found no place to pay and no brochures. What kind of museum was this, anyway? Suddenly, we heard quick footsteps on the stairs. A woman appeared with a confused, somewhat annoyed look. "May I help you?"

"Is this a museum?" we asked.

"No," she said curtly. "It's a private home."

Apologizing profusely, we made a bolt for the door. In our 30 years of travels, this was a first—and a blunder that Alison and Will have yet to let us live down. But it *really* looked like a museum....

The mystical experience? We drove 15 minutes to Helgafell, or Holy Mountain, which figures prominently in Icelandic history and literature. Ascending this 240-foot hill, with its rocky, winding path, grants the climber three benevolent wishes, but only if certain conditions are met: do not look back; do not utter a word; and once reaching the stone ruins of a chapel at the summit, cast your eyes eastward. The kids followed these rules religiously... but I broke the rules by trying to pry their wishes from them. They remained tight-lipped. Time will tell if our wishes come true.

Driving 10 miles from Helgafell, and skirting the coast, we arrived at Bjarnarhoefn farm, owned by an elderly Icelandic man who harvests and prepares shark meat and other sea products including seal and sea birds. As we walked around the farm observing an array of shark bones and fishing supplies, the owner appeared. He motioned us to come to a large table on which lay a massive shark. Demonstrating his craft, he sliced the huge milk-colored creature into sections, then directed us to two sheds where slabs of shark meat hung by hooks to dry. After the shark is cut up, the pieces are buried in sand for several months, then hung to dry to let the powerful flavors develop. This process produces an Icelandic delicacy known as *hakark*—or putrefied shark meat. Fortunately, the kids did not want to taste this specialty... nor did we.

The third day, we left Grundarfjordur early and drove an hour south to Snorrastadir farm, the starting point for a two mile hike to a massive volcanic crater. As we exited the car, our guide appeared—a black and white dog that led the way up the narrow trail snaking through a lava field. After an hour, we scrambled up the steep volcanic slope—behind our guide dog—and viewed the crater. Wide as a football field and 150 feet deep, it was full of black lava and blanketed with thin, green grass. When our canine guide pushed his head into Will's behind, we assumed it was time to descend. We never discovered where this dog came from, but the kids tipped him with a big pat on the head.

Although this crater had seen its day millions of years ago, there are still 25 active volcanoes in Iceland. On average, the country experiences an eruption every five years, many occurring deep beneath the glacier Vatnajokull, the largest icecap in Europe.

At midday, we arrived in Reykjavik, Europe's northernmost capital and home to over half the country's population. Reykjavik differs substantially from most other European capitals. Driving into the city, we saw no mansions, no blatant wealth, no slums, no poverty, no skyscrapers, and few monuments. "Look at all those boxy, colored houses," Alison said as we gazed out over the gently rolling landscape. "I've never seen anything like that!" She was right. A vast assortment of square buildings, painted in bright primary colors, were shielded in corrugated metal siding— a protection against the North Atlantic winters. One additional difference from many world capitals is a total lack of pollution. Iceland harnesses its natural resources: over 85% of Reykjavik's homes and buildings are heated geothermally, thus removing the need for fossil fuels.

We stayed at the Hotel Borg, in the center of Old Town. Several notables had preceded us, including Charles Lindbergh, Clark Gable, and Marlene Dietrich. Our luxurious suite, recently renovated in retro 1930's style, had all the amenities and pleasures one would expect in a luxury hotel. There was one exception, however. An invasive egg smell permeated the bathroom each time the hot water was turned on. The geothermally heated water carries the minerals and aroma of its underground source.

We dined at Einar Ben Restaurant, one of the city's 200 restaurants. With an extensive native menu—including grilled lobster, whale steak, wild bird, and monkfish—Einar Ben more than satisfied.

Our fourth Icelandic day was devoted entirely to exploring Reykjavik. The first activity the kids requested was shopping, and we willingly complied. Hotel Borg lies in the center of a choice shopping area, featuring a prime selection of Icelandic items ranging from gorgeous wool sweaters to sheepskin gloves, hats, shawls, and blankets.

One item that lured the kids were tiny replicas of trolls and related books about these odd creatures. According to surveys, over half the Icelandic population believes in supernatural beings, which include trolls, elves, dwarfs, light-fairies, and "hidden folk"—human-like creatures that live in rocks. Each of these critters has a distinct appearance, special characteristics, and habitats. And they command respect. Highway crews frequently build roads around certain boulders said to be inhabited by these creatures. Occasionally, construction stops completely until these tenants can find new accommodations. The Reykjavik Tourist Office offers elf tours Monday through Friday at 3:00 P.M. Additionally, the Icelandic Elf School in Reykjavik offers a three hour session granting participants an elf degree upon completion of the course.

Reykjavik's main shopping area, Laugavegur Street, touts a collection of chic shops and restaurants. And if you're searching for a panoply of items, the Kolaportid Flea Market is the place to go on Fridays and the weekends. Under one roof, vendors sell everything from clothing to artwork, as well as food items including traditional dried fish, cured shark, and, when in season, rams' testicles. We passed on this latter item.

In addition to shopping, our day in the capital also included a visit to The Culture House to observe a Viking exhibit; a climb to the pinnacle of Reykjavik's landmark church, Hallgrimskirkja; a bus ride from one end of the city to the other; and a walk along the nature path on the western edge of the city. We also viewed the Volcano Show, a film shot by two volcano enthusiasts, who, over the last 50 years, have rushed to the site of every Icelandic volcanic eruption, including the eruption of the island of Surtsey out of the sea in 1963. After all that fire, the kids needed to cool down, so we took them for afternoon drinks at the Paris Café, then in the evening, dined at an Italian restaurant—one of many ethnic offerings in the city. Twenty hours of daylight suited us just fine.

Arriving back at Hotel Borg, my daughter Alison dashed to the lobby's phone booth. "I just read that the phone book is listed by first name, and I had to see it," she said. As we peered over her shoulder, she was right. Hans Gunnarsson was followed by Hans Kristjánsson . . . and so on. The "son" on the end of both last names results from Iceland's patronymic system for naming; a process that tracks heritage by recognizing who was the father. Males' last names combine their father's first name with "son" while females combine it with "dottir." Thus, Hans, son of Gunnar, is Hans Gunnarsson, while his sister is Sophia Gunnarsdottir.

Our fifth and final day in Iceland, we left Hotel Borg promptly at 9:00 A.M. so we could squeeze in three essentials—steam vents, bubbling mud pots, and the Blue Lagoon.

Driving southwest of Reykjavik, we headed for the Reykjanes Peninsula, a small promontory on which the international airport is located. Driving through a lunar-like, treeless landscape, we spied wisps of steam emerged from the edge of Lake Kelfa. "Yech! This smells like rotten eggs!" Will yelled as he got out of the car and inhaled the overpowering odor of the sulfur laden steam. The unearthly experience of playing with the steam delighted the kids as they walked into it, almost disappearing, then emerged once again, fully intact. And, we had hit pay dirt, as surrounding the steam vents were bubbling mud pots—dancing globs of mud resembling black pearl necklaces that jumped up to six inches from the ground.

We continued to the Blue Lagoon, one of Iceland's most celebrated attractions. This silky-like, luxurious pool of natural, mineral-rich geothermal seawater, is carved out of a volcanic slag. Created by the runoff from the nearby Svartsengi Geothermal plant, the lagoon is a healthy mix of blue-green algae and white silica mud. This combination forms soothing, oozy, mud-like sediment on the bottom and gives the water its milky aquamarine color. I saw only the bobbing heads of my kids as they submerged their bodies in 104 degree water. The Blue Lagoon is an immensely calming experience and also good for one's health. Icelanders enjoy one of the highest life expectancies in the world. One possible factor is the perpetual supply of geothermal water that controls symptoms of arthritis, asthma, skin problems, and alleviates stress.

Healthier and happier, we reluctantly left the Blue Lagoon and made our way to the airport. Recalling the last five days in this alluring and intriguing country, we harkened back to the Icelandic man's prediction. We would return to Iceland . . . it *had* bitten us hard.

ICELAND OVERVIEW

- Iceland: Size of Kentucky
- Population: 280,000

- Capital: Reykjavik (Population: 175,000)
- Ethnicity: Homogeneous mixture of descendants of Norse and Celts
- Religious Affiliation: 93% Lutheran, 7% Protestant and Roman Catholic
- Official language: Icelandic, however most Icelanders speak fluent English
- Currency: Icelandic Krona
- Literacy rate: 99.9%, highest in the world

Planning and Preparation

Passports

Americans are required to have a valid passport to enter Iceland.

When to Go

Despite Iceland's frozen-laden name, this country is warmer than New York in the winter. Despite this, many tourist sites close by the end of September, except the tourist industry in Reykjavik.

Health Issues

There are no health risks in Iceland and no immunizations required. Families are not at risk for eating any food, in markets, on the streets, or in restaurants. Medical care in this country is equal to that of America.

Safety

One of the safest countries in the world, period.

What to Bring

Dress for the climate. Even in summer months, be sure to bring a lightweight jacket. One essential item to pack: a bathing suit. Even in the dead of winter, families will want to swim in a geothermal pool. Also take a sturdy pair of shoes for walking.

Getting There

Icelandair flies from Baltimore/Washington, Boston, New York, Minneapolis/St. Paul and Orlando. Check Icelandair (www.Iceland air.com) for details.

Getting Around

The four-wheel-drive vehicle is the preferred car in Iceland. The majority of Icelandic roads are two lanes, with many consisting of hard-packed, well-maintained gravel. The Ministry of Tourism publishes an updated map of roads that is available in tourist information centers. Car rental is expensive, and should be arranged before arriving in Iceland.

THINGS TO SEE AND DO

Activities for Kids

- Have your kids look inside a phone book to view the listing of names. Ask what the difference is between the U.S. phone book and the Icelandic phone book. (The Icelandic phone book is listed by the first name.) Ask what the two endings are on most of the names ("son" and "dottir"). Explain that the "son" and "dottir" on the end of last names results from Iceland's patronymic system for naming; a process that tracks heritage by recognizing who was the father. Have your children put their names in the patronymic system.
- After viewing the wide range of trolls available in many stores, encourage your children to create and draw a troll, and give it a distinct personality.
- Tour a fish factory.
- Hop on a public bus and ride it to the end of the line, then back again to get a sweeping view of Reykjavik.

Reykjavik

Álfaskólinn or The Icelandic Elf School—Go to Elf School and you will get the inside scoop on elves, hidden people, trolls, dwarfs, gnomes, light-fairies, mountain spirits and other invisible beings that inhabit Iceland, numbering between 7,000 to 20,000 residents. With a set curriculum, the Elf School grants diplomas to those completing the three-hour course. Location: Sidumuli 31, 108 Reykjavik, Iceland. Tel: +011-354-894-4014. Fax: +011-354-588-6055. Email: mhs@vortex.is.

Árbæjarsafn Open-Air Museum—Open June through August, this museum offers a collection of old houses from Iceland's past, including turf-roofed and corrugated iron buildings. Resting on the site of an ancient farm from the 1400s, this museum gives glimpse into the lifestyle, arts, and skills of the Icelandic people from ages past.

Hallgrímskirkja—This imposing church was designed to look like a mountain of lava. Hallgrímskirkja, named after Iceland's premier poet, Hallgrímur Pétursson, was begun in the late 1940s took over 25 years to complete. Families can climb or take an elevator to the pinnacle—a 246 foot high tower which affords magnificent views of Reykjavik.

Volcano Show—The Volcano Show, located in a refurbished building in the backyard of a house, features films shot by two volcano enthusiasts who, over the last 50 years, have darted to every Icelandic volcanic eruption, including the eruption of the island of Surtsey out of the sea in 1963. Shown every day at 3:00 P.M. and 8:00 P.M. in English. Tickets can be purchased at The Tourist Information Center in Reykjavik.

Near Reykjavik

The Blue Lagoon—The Blue Lagoon is not to be missed. With its silky-like, mineral rich geothermal seawater, the pool is carved out of a volcanic slag, and can accommodate 700 people. There are changing and showering facilities as well as lockers for personal items. The complex also includes a restaurant, a health product store and a health clinic. Cost: $11.00/adults. Children under 12 free when accompanied by adult. $6.00/12–15 years. Times: September 1–May 14: 10:00 A.M.–7:30 P.M. May 15–August 31: 9:00 A.M.–9:00 P.M. Website: www.bluelagoon.is.

The Western Peninsula of Snaefellsnes

Helgafell Holy Mountain—Hekgafell holds a significant place in the history and literature of Iceland. Follow the three rules and you may see your wishes come true. This 240-foot hill is located three miles south of the town of Stykkishólmur.

Snaefellsjokull Glacier—Snaefellsjokull Glacier is one the most massive and startling glaciers in the world. The glacier is purported to be a major global energy center. Writer Jules Verne selected it as his entrance into the earth in his novel *Journey to the Center of the Earth*. There are multiple ways to view the glacier. A ski lift carries visitors to the top, but only on weekends in winter. If your family loves to hike, then a four-hour trek to the top is possible.

Hotels in Reykjavik

Hotel Borg—Cost: Double rooms $160–$220, breakfast, taxes and service included. Children under 12 sharing room with parents free of charge. Beautiful classic hotel in the center of town. Pósthússtræti 11, 121 Reykjavik, Iceland. www.hotelborg.is. Tel: (354) 551-1440. Fax: (354) 551-1420. Email: hotelborg@hotelborg.is.

Hotels in Grundarfjordur

Hotel Framnes—Cost: Double rooms, $100 with breakfast. Studio apartments, sleeping 2–5 people begin at $150. Located on the wharf, near a fish factory... but this is really a quite intriguing location. Nesvegi 6-8, 350 Grundarfjordur, Iceland. www.simnet.is/framnes. Tel: (354) 438-6893. Fax: (354) 438-6930. Email: framnes@simnet.is.

Restaurants in Reykjavik

Einar Ben—Restaurant & Bar, Veltusund 1. Expensive. Traditional Icelandic food including fish, seabirds, wild game and lamb.

Carpe Diem Restaurant—Raudararstigur 18, International Cuisine. Special lunch-time salad bar buffet and soup, as well as home-made bread and a choice of fish and meat dishes.

Naust Restaurant—Vesturgata 6-8. Modern European Cuisine accompanied by an Icelandic Saga evening with Icelandic folk songs.

Resources

Official Websites
www.goiceland.org
www.icetourist.is

The Icelandic Tourist Board can be reached in New York at 212-885-9786, or call the Icelandic Tourist Bureau at (212) 949-2333, fax: (212) 983-5260, and ask for "Iceland A to Z," a useful planning tool.

The North American website of The Icelandic Tourist Board is www.icelandtouristboard.com.

Additional information: For a daily update of events and weather in Iceland, log on to Iceland's Daily English Newspaper: www.malog menning.mm.is/icenewsis/.

Books for Adults
Insight Guide Iceland by Jane Simmonds
Iceland by Jim Krusoe
Iceland: Land of the Sagas by David Roberts
Landmark Visitors Guide Iceland by Cathy Harlow
The Anthropology of Iceland by E. Paul Durrenberger

Books for Children
Surtsey: The Newest Place on Earth by Kathryn Lasky
Nights of the Pufflings by Bruce McMillan
Iceland: Enchantment of the World by Barbara A. Somervill

Videos and DVDs

The Turtle Expedition Explores Iceland: Land of Fire and Ice
Globe Trekker: Iceland

Patrick Sandoval posing with a banner featuring
Cuban revolutionaries in Caya Coco.

CHAPTER 18

CUBA:
REVOLUTION AND RESORTS

BY MARY NICHOLS SANDOVAL

FAMILY TRAVEL TO CUBA

During our children's teenage years, we usually found it difficult to agree on a family holiday destination. There were worries that the place might be "boring" or "isolated" or "just for older people" or "packed with little kids." I was amazed when I suggested Cuba and everyone agreed immediately.

I had wanted to visit Cuba since I was 10 years old. Maybe it was because it was a "prohibited" island, or maybe it was because I was learning Spanish, or maybe it was because of the Cuban refugee children who had come to live in our neighborhood until their families could leave Cuba. I loved practicing my basic Spanish with them and hearing about the beaches and the mango groves they talked about.

Years went by, though, and Cuba was off limits to most U.S. travelers, so I never could fulfill my dream. It wasn't until decades later, when I had a Spanish husband and teenage children, that I finally visited my "mango grove" island. My husband, like many Spaniards, had historical and even family ties to Cuba, because of 500 years of shared history. My son, who is studying Political Science in college, wanted to see the results of a people's revolution first-hand, and my daughter, who was about to graduate from high school, was doing an honors course in photography and couldn't think of a better place to spend a holiday and work on her final project.

My only words of caution about traveling to Cuba with a family are: Know what to expect before you go, expect a few *problemitas* (tiny, little problems), and take everything in stride. If you are looking for a tropical paradise with luxury hotels where solicitous waiters bring you drinks in coconut shells, you had best choose another destination.

Cuba is not a poor country. In fact, it has a much higher level of basic coverage in medical care, literacy, and social security for all its population than most other Central American countries. The "wealth" is uniformly spread throughout the population and there is little left over to create extra luxury for the tourists. Your hotel room may look very nice, but you might not have hot water, or any water at all, some of the time. In fact, your hotel might not even turn out to be the one you had booked through your travel agent! Once in Cuba, all travel arrangements are taken over by the Cuban National Travel Agency and changes in lodging and itinerary can be made without consulting the interested party. Transportation to and from the airport may take a bit longer than expected—you might sit on the bus to your hotel waiting for the next three international flights to arrive so the bus can be filled before it leaves for the hotel. This is due to gasoline shortages, but no one tells you that.

Knowing what to expect before you go means knowing what to take with you. Take plenty of medications, including simple things like aspirin. Take medicines that you might hypothetically need like antacid tablets or diarrhea tablets. You can leave them behind for people you meet if you haven't used them. Shelves in Cuban pharmacies are noticeably bare. Take tampons and sanitary pads. Neither are readily available.

Expect a healthy but basic diet—salad, grilled chicken or pork and fruit. Don't be fooled by an extensive menu in a tourist restaurant, because, after graciously taking your order, the waiter will return to your table a short time later to tell you there is a *problemita*. The items you ordered were served at a wedding banquet just before you arrived, but of course you can still order salad and chicken or pork and fruit.

Plan to walk a lot or pay for tourist taxis with U.S. dollars. The taxis are not expensive by U.S. standards and public transportation is almost non-existent in Cuba. Gasoline shortages are part of the reason, but some Cubans told us that the government didn't provide adequate bus transportation between provinces in order to limit the people's mobility. As a tourist, however, you can rent a car and drive freely around the country. You will see Cubans standing along the roadsides, holding up bills in their hands and hoping to hitch a ride. Though we did not rent a car, many of our friends had done so and said that driving across country and picking up passengers was a perfect way to meet people, who often invited them into their homes.

We began our journey in Havana, where we spent our first four days. The city is safe, crowded with people almost around the clock, and Old Havana is absolutely beautiful by night. Our hotel, La Florida, was right in the heart of the old city. It is a recently restored 18th century mansion. There were several *problemitas* associated with this otherwise lovely hotel. For example, our street was too narrow for the airport bus and we had to walk for five blocks from a wider street, carrying our luggage to the hotel.

Our children found plenty to do in Havana just wandering the streets, talking to people, and taking photographs. La Habana Vieja (Old Havana) is one of the most beautiful cities we have ever seen. A government agency, the "Office of the Historian," is responsible for studying historic documents and architectural drawings, and restoring Old Havana to its former splendor. Simply walking in the old city at night, by the light of the gas lamps, with Latin jazz drifting out of the music bars on every corner, is worth the visit to Cuba.

After four days, we flew to Cayo Coco, a beautiful resort on the northern or Atlantic coast, about an hour's flight east from Havana. The plane was a Russian propeller model from the '60s, and our luggage, and everyone else's, traveled in the passenger cabin with us, on empty seats, along the central aisle and piled to the roof of the cabin at the front of the aircraft. When we arrived at Cayo Coco and disembarked into a tiny thatched hut, we were immediately attacked by swarms of mosquitoes, but were rescued by swarms of Cuban soldiers who, with no previous warning, sprayed us from head to foot with something I suspect was pure DDT. We were later told that there is a *problemita* with dengue fever and the government takes extra care in tourist areas to keep the mosquitoes under control.

Our hotel complex was beautiful, spread over many acres along the beach with pools and gardens and numerous restaurants and, of course, bars where mixed drinks with rum were served at all hours. The basic fare was chicken and salad, though there was more variety than in the restaurants in Havana. There was, as to be expected, a *problemita*. There was no hot water while we were there. If the staff had simply said, "We're sorry, but we have a problem in a water main and we have no spare parts to repair it," we would have accepted our fate and taken the cold showers somewhat more cheerfully. As it was, the employees, from the chambermaid to the hotel manager, pretended that the *problemita* had *just* occurred (even after we had been there for five days) and that it would be fixed in the immediate future.

In addition to beautiful beaches and swimming pools, our resort offered bicycle rentals, tennis courts, exercise classes, and nightly entertainment for the whole family. The hotel also provided excursions to nearby points of interest. My husband and children signed up for a trip in a four wheel drive vehicle to visit the beach where Earnest Hemmingway had been inspired to write *The Old Man and the Sea*. When the three of them arrived at the main lobby to get into the jeeps, there was a *problemita*. None of the vehicles had drivers. The drivers were to be chosen from among the tourists who had signed up for the excursion. Since many of those who had signed up were families with young children, there weren't enough drivers to go around.

My teenage son, who didn't yet have his driver's license, was one of those asked to drive. My husband put his foot down, of course, and said that his son would have to be a passenger. After more than an hour of arrangements, Cuban drivers were finally brought in. There is obviously a different sense in Cuba of what we might consider insurance liability.

We spent New Year's Eve in Cayo Coco, rang in the New Year with a champagne fountain, danced in a discotheque, and flew the next day back to Havana.

When we boarded the plane the next morning, after another shower of DDT in the aerodrome, we were told that there was a *problemita*. There was not enough fuel for the flight back to Havana and we would have to make a stop enroute to get gas and then continue. We did indeed stop at another airport to refuel. In a bizarre twist, the other airport lay in the opposite direction from Havana. Presumably there are some government regulations that ration fuel to each province.

From Havana, we left on our mini-van tour. There were six passengers, our driver, and our guide. Driving in Cuba is a calm experience because there is so little traffic on the roads. My husband was interested in the economic aspects of life in Cuba since his company and other Spanish companies have built many large industrial projects there. My daughter and I asked about social and cultural affairs and my son couldn't get enough political information. Our driver and guide were a wealth of information and gladly answered all questions.

Our first stop was Santa Clara, 167 miles east of Havana. We visited a massive monument to Che Guévara and saw sites in the city where several important moments of the revolution had occurred after Fidel Castro had come down from the mountains with his guerilla fighters. Our daughter was interested in photographing typical street scenes rather than monuments, and though the guides never said that she shouldn't, we sensed they weren't entirely happy that she wandered away from "main attractions" to take pictures of the "less developed" aspects of Cuban street life. Our son made up for our daughter's indiscretions by asking politically correct questions about Che Guévara, the revolution, the U.S. embargo, the cutoff of Russian (Soviet) aid, etc.

From Santa Clara we continued south to Trinidad, over a breathtaking mountain pass shrouded in fog, and dotted with mango groves and typical mountain houses with thatched roofs. Trinidad is a Spanish-era colonial city of whitewashed buildings with pastel trim. It reminded us of a wedding cake. We stayed at a beach resort on the coast just outside the city. The complex had been built in the '60s to reward workers from the ex-Soviet republics who were given trips to Cuba for exceeding quotas. The bungalows reminded us of typical U.S. motels from the '50s, with no up-grades since, but we could easily imagine how someone from Kiev or Minsk would have been enthralled by such a spot on a tropical beach. There are no more Soviet workers, but Cuban workers today are also rewarded for exceeding production quotas with weekend stays at such resorts. In fact, that is the only time Cubans are allowed into such tourist complexes. Even if they have enough money to pay for their stay, Cubans may not enter tourist hotel areas, either in Havana or on the coasts.

One afternoon we returned from a long day of sightseeing in Trinidad and opened the doors to our bungalows. Our daughter gave a blood curdling scream and backed away from the door. We ran to her aid. There, in the shadows of her room, were two cadavers propped up on the beds. We were also taken aback, but, looking more closely, we saw that the chamber maids had stuffed the kids' pajamas with towels, scarecrow-style, and even rolled towels to make convincing heads! In our room there was a magnificent towel-constructed swan swimming on one bed and a big rabbit sitting on the other.

While my husband and son had done the dutiful round of colonial museums in Trinidad with our guides, my daughter and I had wandered the side streets, and saw little shops with shelves bare except for a lone bottle of shampoo or a single box of detergent. We spotted groups of uniformed school girls with the shortest skirts we'd ever seen anywhere and were told that the fabric to make school uniforms is rationed and the students get as many skirts as possible out of their cloth ration.

We watched while nearly 100 men and women pushed and shoved to get close to the door of a building. Over an hour later we passed by again to find the same crowd now dispersing from the doorway, a few of them gripping plastic bags. We learned that a shipment of fish had arrived and people were willing to wait more than an hour in hopes of getting some. It remained unclear exactly how many of the 100 people actually got the fish.

We were surprised by the number of men and women on the streets all day long and were told that they "were enjoying a few extra days of Christmas vacation" but more likely they were "enjoying" an extremely high rate of unemployment. We didn't see beggars as one sees in many large cities around the world, but we were occasionally approached by women asking us for U.S. dollars. The only men who approached us were offering cigars, which, surprisingly, are less expensive outside of Cuba.

From Trinidad we traveled along the southern coast to Cienfuegos, a large and not especially interesting city. Sociologically, though, everything we saw during our stay in Cuba was interesting, from the municipal market places where the stands boasted a lone bunch of carrots, a head of lettuce, several bananas and a plucked chicken; to the public schools, which were well equipped and filled with smiling, uniformed students; to the movie theaters, where the audience wandered in and out during the film, shouted catcalls to the bad guys and whistled at the attractive girls. We of course saw many U.S. cars from the '50s and '60s, waxed to perfection. There seemed to be a uniform level of lack of prosperity in Cuba, but no real poverty.

We were anxious to return to Havana, walk along the *malecón*, or waterfront, explore the charming corners of the old city, sit in an outdoor cafe and listen to Latin jazz bands. We saw the Havana that tourists see and we also saw working class neighborhoods with high rise apartment buildings, the university, sports facilities, the beautiful but rundown streets where the embassies are located, the famous Plaza de la Revolución with hundreds of school children practicing marching and singing patriotic songs, the tourist market, where you can buy junk with U.S. dollars, the renovated churches and monasteries from the Spanish colonial period, the Marina Hemmingway where the wealthy from around the Caribbean dock their yachts, and Chinatown, with market stalls offering more variety than elsewhere on the island.

My daughter and I took a ride in one of the "bicycle-taxis," something I really didn't want to do, since it seemed like a demeaning job for the man who had to pedal us. But he assured us that he was able to support his family because of his job and that he loved talking to the tourists.

When we returned to Havana from our road trip, there was as usual, a *problemita*. Our hotel was no longer the one we had booked and had stayed in when we began our Cuban travels. Though we arrived at midnight carrying our luggage five blocks from the wider street, we were told that arrangements had been made for us to stay elsewhere. No amount of protest was able to change anyone's mind, so we lifted our suitcases once again and walked to our new hotel, El Comendador, also a restored colonial building but not nearly as nice as La Florida. Friends who have traveled to Cuba on more expensive tours directly to beach resorts did not encounter the *problemitas* we did. One taking a family trip to Cuba might want to keep this in mind.

Nevertheless, we departed Cuba with wonderful memories. My daughter's photographs were highly acclaimed in the school art show, my son fulfilled his dream of visiting a country with an on-going revolution, my husband saw beautiful vestiges of his Spanish heritage, and I finally visited the "forbidden" island with the mango groves. Despite the *problemitas*, we would all go back again. In fact, my son already has!

CUBA OVERVIEW
  - Cuba: Slightly smaller than Alabama
  - Population: 11.5 million
  - Capital: Havana (Population: 2.2 million)
  - Ethnicity: 66% White, 22% Mulatto, 12% Black
  - Religious Affiliation: 40% Roman Catholic, 3% Protestant
  - Language: Spanish (official)
  - Currency: Cuban Peso (U.S. dollars widely accepted)

PLANNING AND PREPARATION

Passports

Americans are required to have a valid passport and visa to enter Cuba. While it is not illegal for U.S. citizens to travel to Cuba, U.S. Treasury regulations prohibit most Americans from spending any money in Cuba. This, in effect, is a "travel ban." The Treasury Department grants licenses for educational travel and certain humanitarian trips, particularly those organized by religious groups; however, sometimes these licenses are denied. Failure to comply with Department of Treasury regulations may result in civil penalties and criminal prosecution upon return to the United States. For more information, contact the Office of Foreign Assets Control, U.S. Department of the Treasury, 1500 Pennsylvania Ave. NW, Treasury Annex, Washington, DC 20220. Tel: (202) 622-2480; www.treas.gov/ofac.

When to Go

Cuba's climate is most agreeable during the dry season, November through April. Daytime highs range from 75 to 80 degrees. The resorts are heavily booked during the Christmas and Easter holidays. May through October is the rainy season and temperatures tend to be higher. The peak of hurricane season is September and October.

Health Issues

The Cuban Revolution gave the country a health care system that is the envy of much of the rest of Latin America. Most tropical diseases have been eliminated. Some, such as dengue fever exist but are uncommon. Foreign travelers who need medical care will be treated in international clinics or public hospitals and will be required to pay in dollars. Pharmacies tend to be poorly stocked so bring needed and potentially needed medications with you. No vaccinations are required for entry into the country from the U.S.

Safety

Cuba is a very safe travel destination. Naturally, tourists should practice common sense and be aware of pickpockets at major tourist sites and on public transportation.

What to Bring

A lot of $1 and $5 bills. Cubans love American currency and travelers can tip, pay for incidental items, or even use dollars as a way to get special treatment when the Cuban bureaucracy grinds to a halt.

Travel Service Providers

For most Americans who wish to travel to Cuba (legally), travel arrangements must be made by authorized Travel Service Providers. Four experienced TSPs are:

Cuba Cultural Travel—Tel: (949) 646-1229; www.cubacultural travel.com

Global Exchange—Tel: (415) 255-7296; www.globalexchange.org

Marazul Tours—Tel: (800) 223-5334; www.marazultours.com

Tico Travel—Tel: (954) 493-8426; www.destinationcuba.com

THINGS TO SEE AND DO

Activities for Kids

• Let your children select a Latin jazz session to attend by walking the streets of La Habana Vieja and picking the most promising corner music bar.

• Take the kids on a ride in a bicycle-taxi through downtown Havana.

• Familiarize your kids with the Cuban Revolution and discuss the benefits (e.g., improved universal medical care) and the detriments (e.g., lack of personal freedoms).

Havana

La Habana Vieja (Old Havana)—This is the old heart of the city. It was declared a UNESCO World Heritage Site in 1982. Since then the monuments and major buildings, as well as old shops and ordinary homes, have been beautifully restored. The area is far from a museum piece however. Hotels, restaurants, music bars, and shops make Old Havana a very active quarter day and night.

Miramar—Take a walk through Havana's most elegant neighborhood. Many of the mansions built here around the turn of the last century are now foreign embassies and government ministries. Several luxury hotels are also in this neighborhood.

Marina Hemingway—This Marina serves as a free port. Boats from Florida and the Caribbean are offered safe access, and no visas are required. Have your kids observe the many pricey yachts berthed here. Marina Hemingway is regularly organizing billfish and marlin fishing tournaments and regattas for nautical sports-loving people.

Trinidad

Like Havana, Trinidad (founded in 1514) was an important Spanish city in colonial Cuba. It was a slave trading and sugar producing center. And like Old Havana, Trinidad is a UNESCO World Heritage Site. The old buildings and cobblestone streets in the city lead the visitor to imagine that he has stepped back to the colonial era.

Hotels in Havana

NH Parque Central Hotel—Cost: Double room $100–$150. In Habana Vieja near the Capitol Building. A mix of Art Deco and modern architecture. Tel: (53) 786 066 27. Fax: (53) 786 066 30.

Hotel Florida—Cost: Double room $130–$180. Located in a colonial mansion dating from 1836 in Habana Vieja. Tel: (53) 762 4127. Fax: (53) 762 4117.

Hotel on Cayo Coco

Melia Cayo Coco—Cost: Double room (high season) $250. Large resort on a fine white sand beach. Just 1/2 mile from a coral reef. Numerous activities and excursions offered. Tel: 888-956-3542. www.meliacayococo.solmelia.com/.

Hotel in Trinidad

Hotel Ancón—Cost: Double room (high season) $105. Located on beautiful Ancón beach. Has a delightful garden with free form swimming pool. Tel: (53) 419 4011.

Restaurants in Havana

La Cocina de Liliam—Calle 48 No. 1311 entre 13 y 15. Playa. Tel: (53) 720 965 14. Popular restaurant with excellent traditional cooking.

El Patio—San Ignacio No. 54 esq. Empedrado, Plaza de la Catedral, Habana Vieja. Cuban and international cuisine in a former palace.

Restaurant in Trinidad

Restaurante El Jigue—Ruben M. Villena esquina P. Guinart. Tel: (53) 419 4033. Cuban and international cuisine in a well-preserved eighteenth century homestead with a stuccoed Moorish motif.

RESOURCES

Official Website

www.cubatravel.cu/

Books for Adults

Lonely Planet Cuba by David Stanley
Cuba Diaries: An American Housewife in Havana by Isadora Tattlin
Cuba on the Verge: An Island in Transition by Terry McCoy (Editor)

Books for Children

Under the Royal Palms: A Childhood in Cuba by Alma Ada

Videos and DVDs

Buena Vista Social Club
Before Night Falls
Cuba (documentary), directed by John Holod

Will and Alison Nichols are co-captains in the Galapagos Islands.

CHAPTER 19

Galapagos Islands, Ecuador: Evolution's Classroom

Family Travel to the Galapagos Islands

"Mom, look at me," my daughter called out as she lay stone still on a sandy shore. "A bird is walking over my arm—and it's not even afraid of me!"

This was not the first friendly acquaintance with animals that Alison and her brother Will experienced in the Galapagos Islands. Swimming with sea lions, gazing eye to eye with a giant tortoise, and gingerly stepping over lazing iguanas were the stuff of dreams. They also observed animal species found nowhere else on the planet, viewed finches that Charles Darwin researched for his theory of evolution, and saw the last of a remaining giant tortoise species in the world, Lonesome George.

Journeying with the kids to the Galapagos is an educational animal extravaganza, as gracing these enchanted islands are other distinguished residents, including the world's only species of marine reptile as well as the world's largest colony of red-footed boobies—not to mention 30% of the world's blue-footed boobies, flightless cormorants, penguins (on the equator, no less!), and dozens of species of reptiles, birds, and sea life.

Kids, animals, and the Galapagos are a perfect triumvirate.

The Galapagos are of volcanic origin. They are mere babies in geological age, ranging from 500,000 to 5 million years old. After first emerging above the ocean's surface, bacteria, fungi, and algae were the sole life of these islands. But through time—and by chance—plants and animals began to establish a foothold. Their modes of transportation were varied. Plant life either blew in with the wind, hitched a ride on the feathers of birds, or floated ashore in the endless rush of tides. Much of the animal life arrived by flying or by floating on vegetation rafts—large, tangled collections of plant and animal life. Some of the heartier species simply propelled their way across the expanse of rolling sea and arrived, where they slowly adapted to their new environment and began to propagate.

One such arrival was the *galapago* (Spanish for tortoise), and the namesake of the Galapagos Islands. These massive, hardy creatures—many weighing 300 to 600 pounds—possessed a strong resistance to the effects of the sun and the ability to go for long periods of time without food and water. These traits helped them survive not only the ravages of the sea but also the obstacles of their harsh new surroundings.

My husband, two children, and I spent five days aboard a 38-foot ketch, weaving our way to six islands in the Galapagos, each with diverse wildlife and vegetation. A crew of three accompanied us: a cook, the boat's captain, and a nature guide. Each morning, we would rise at 7:00 A.M. and have breakfast on the deck of the boat while our guide provided a description of the day's events, and the animals we were to see. Arriving at each island we would view a diversity of wildlife and vegetation, with each island distinctly different than its archipelago pals.

Among the most startling sights we viewed were the species that Charles Darwin researched on a journey to the Galapagos in 1835. Darwin found the islands sparsely settled with humans but teeming with wildlife, which provided a rich laboratory for him to examine animal adaptations and begin to form his theory of evolution. He found, for example, that each species of tortoise was different from the others, and that each species adapted to the type of vegetation unique to its island. Tortoises who had to raise their heads up to snatch a high branch developed long necks and a hood-like shell, or carapace, that allowed for this neck movement. Those that fed on low vegetation developed dome-shaped shells close to the neck. As children (and adults) observe these wonders, the complicated theory of evolution slowly sinks in. Darwin also found that the animals showed little, if any, fear of their intruders. In fact, writing in his journal, he reported of holding a dove in his hat while striding calmly beside one of the giant tortoises to measure its speed.

To this day, most animals in the Galapagos are fearless of their human intruders—even excited children. Respecting a reasonable distance, our children observed the beauty and behavior of the abundant wildlife. Iguanas, lizards, birds, sea lions and tortoises went about their lives unafraid of Alison and Will's extremely close inspection of their appearance, habits, and movements.

The most startling discovery for the kids was observing the finches that were instrumental in Darwin's shaping of his theory of evolution. Examining a chart of the 13 finches and then observing on the islands the distinctive anatomy of several finches, particularly beak size and shape, was a lifetime lesson. As Alison and Will observed the differences at close range, our guide instructed, "The bill adapts to the vegetation on different islands and is used to peck wood, crush seeds, and probe flowers for nectar."

Although much remains the same on the islands as when Darwin visited, some things have changed—unfortunately for the worse. Before the island came under the protection of the Galapagos National Park Service, humans and the species they introduced almost devastated the tortoise population. Between 100,000 to 200,000 of these gentle giants were slaughtered for their meat or oil. Pirates found the tortoises tasty fare. They kept the harmless animals tethered, sometimes stacked upside down aboard ship for up to a year without food or water, using them as a source of fresh meat. Even tortoises able to avoid the snare of their human predators weren't safe. Black rats, pigs, and dogs, all introduced by humans to the islands, ravaged the eggs and hatchlings. Goats, cattle, and burros competed with the tortoises for food. Now, fewer than 15,000 of these magnificent giants survive. Three of the original 14 species are extinct. And, of course, Lonesome George, the sole progenitor of his subspecies, hangs on patiently. He waits for a mate with which to begin the slow, deliberate repopulation of his almost lost species.

We wanted the kids to see George, so we sailed to the island of Santa Cruz, and the Charles Darwin Research Center. George shares the island with about 10,000 humans, the largest population in the archipelago. The Research Center, established in 1961, is managed by the Galapagos National Park Service. Its mission is to educate the public about conservation and environmental issues, as well as to control and eliminate the ravaging effects of introduced species on the islands' indigenous life. As we hiked the trail to the Center, the kids were able to view at close range a common animal that typically scurries away when humans are in the vicinity—the lizard.

The Research Center also breeds certain tortoise species that would otherwise have become extinct. One startling success story is the Hood Island subspecies, which had dwindled to just three males and 11 females. Through the efforts of the center, there are now more than 200 Hood Island tortoises surviving in their native habitats. The center also collects and incubates tortoise eggs from many islands in the archipelago. Hatchlings are nurtured until they are strong enough to withstand their predators, then repatriated to their original habitats.

The center also provides a safe haven for tortoises whose origin cannot be identified. Three pens house these unknowns, and they are the only animal life in the entire archipelago that visitors can touch. The children were ecstatic to finally pet an animal after days of longing to caress sea lions, pat lava lizards, and stroke the feathers of nesting boobies. But the wait was worth it. The tortoises remained calm and still as the children lovingly stroked their rough, elongated necks.

And what about Lonesome George? Although the idea of a $10,000 reward for finding him a mate lured the children and us to his spacious pen, we were unprepared for the powerful and significant message he provided. Here we were, looking at this magnificent and lone animal that was the last remaining one of his kind. "I'd even find him a mate for free," Alison whispered. We couldn't have agreed more. We gazed at and admired Lonesome George for a long time before we reluctantly moved on. But the message he provided, of the fragility of Galapagos life and the human responsibility for its preservation, has continued to resonate.

GALAPAGOS OVERVIEW

- The Galapagos Islands: Belong to Ecuador
- The Galapagos Archipelago: Consists of 61 islands and islets, with 13 main islands
- Location: 600 miles to the west of Ecuador's coast
- Formation of the Islands: Began five million years ago due to volcanic activity; the youngest islands are 500,000 years old.
- Official Language: Spanish
- Galapagos Currency: U. S. Dollar
- Arrival Fee: $100 per person upon arriving at the airport

PLANNING AND PREPARATION

Passports

Americans must have a valid passport, but visas are not required. Upon arriving in the Galapagos, visitors must pay $100 entry fee per person.

When to Go

Year round. Given the location of the Galapagos on the equator, temperatures are relatively constant through the year, with seasons influenced by the ocean current. You will never swelter or freeze on the Galapagos. Slightly warmer temperatures with the possibility of afternoon showers occur December to June with temperatures ranging between 72 and 90 degrees. Marginally cooler and drier weather typifies July to November with temperatures 65 to 75 degrees.

Health Issues

The Center for Disease Control (CDC) recommends yellow fever immunization if traveling to certain parts of Ecuador, particularly for those traveling to rural areas. There is a risk of malaria in areas with an altitude under 4,900 feet. There is no risk, however, in the cities of Guayaquil and Quito, the central highland tourist areas, and the Galápagos Islands.

Safety

The Galapagos are quite safe. There is little crime and there are no real population centers to generate crime in the first place.

What to Bring

Let your boat be your guide. You can wear just about anything on single family boats, however cruise ships are more formal and you should check with your tour operator regarding proper clothing. Be sure to bring a sweatshirt or light jacket for evenings. Cart along a good pair of hiking boots and snorkeling equipment.

On Board the Boat

Our family booked a trip of five days and five nights aboard a 38–foot ketch—a two-masted sailboat with an auxiliary engine. We ate, showered, and slept on the boat, which was managed by a crew of three; a cook, a guide and a captain. The kids' bedroom was in the bow of the boat, while ours was the main area. Because of the mild, predictable weather, we always dined on the deck of the ship, so we didn't miss a moment of scenery.

Boats for cruising the islands vary between our ketch, which catered to one family, to cruise ships that accommodate over 100. With most tour companies, the choice is yours. Once the vessels dock, passengers are ferried to the islands by small boats called *pangas*. Occasionally, you might have to wade through knee-deep water to make your way ashore.

Galapagos Naturalist Guides

At all times when touring the islands you must be accompanied by a trained, naturalist guide that is an employee of the Galapagos National Park Service. Before guides escort clients ashore, they provide detailed information on the flora and fauna of each island, and offer a wealth of wisdom once visitors step ashore. Boats are assigned particular islands at the discretion of the National Park Service, as too many people on an island disturb and disrupt the wildlife.

The Food

All meals are freshly prepared onboard the boat with no worry about contamination of food or water. Galleys are stocked with fresh produce, which is kept on ice. Our captain often caught fresh fish from the ocean, which the cook prepared. Meals were basic but delicious. On our last evening, we were surprised by a going-away cake that was decorated with all of our names.

A Typical Day

Tour boats in the Galapagos maximize time for visitors to explore by traveling longer distances between islands at night, when tourists are asleep. That leaves the daylight hours for two daily hikes, one at 7:00 A.M. (after breakfast) and another around 3:00 P.M. (after siesta). It also leaves time for an activity wildly popular with the kids: swimming with sea lions. Our watchful crew provided life preservers so the youngsters and their parents could float among these playful, friendly creatures. While we frolicked, the captain and guide kept a close watch for the bull sea lions, who could be trouble if encountered. When we were not swimming or hiking, daylight hours were spent on board the boat relaxing, reading, writing in our journals, playing cards, or just enjoying the scenery. Since the number of visitors on the islands is strictly controlled by the Galapagos National Park Service, we seldom crossed paths with other humans. Our two- to three-hour walks on the islands were private, leisurely, informative, and afforded plenty of time to observe, ask questions of our guide, and just sit and absorb the sights.

Questions to Ask Tour Operators
- What types of boats are available?

- If electing to go on a group tour, how many families are on board?
- What is included in the cost?
- Which islands are on the itinerary?
- What is the daily schedule?
- How many years of experience does the captain have sailing in this area?
- How many crew are on board?
- What clothing and water gear are recommended?

THINGS TO SEE AND DO

Activities for Kids

- Buy your children a journal with pages to write and draw. Prompt them to write their impressions of each day's events, interesting facts, and questions. What island did they visit? What animals did they observe?
- If your kids saw finches or tortoises, what were the physical differences from the ones they saw on other islands? Encourage them to draw the animals and ask the guide what vegetation they consumed and how this influenced their beak shapes or tortoise shells.
- Encourage them to draw their favorite animal from each day—parents should contribute to this artwork by also drawing their favorite creature.

The Islands

Santa Cruz Island—As the center of the islands' tourism industry, Santa Cruz has the largest town of the Galapagos—Puerto Ayora. This island also has a must see: the Charles Darwin Research Station, where the giant tortoise captive breeding program operates. Families can view, close-up, the pens to see these startling animals. The Station is also the home of Lonesome George—the only remaining member of the Pinta species of giant turtle. Trekking inland, families have the opportunity to view giant tortoises in the wild. Puerto Ayora is one of a handful of places where tourists can shop for souvenirs, postcards, and stamps.

North Seymour Island—This small island harbors a large colony of blue-footed boobies, frigate birds, and swallow-tailed gulls. Families can observe sea lions and marine iguana.

Bartolome Island—On this small island, families can climb a long wooden staircase for panoramic views of Pinnacle Rock and Santiago (James) Island, and examine various lava formations.

Santiago (James) Island—This island is a premier sight for viewing sea lions and marine iguanas, and there are a wide variety of sea birds that frequent the shores.

Genovesa (Tower) Island (Darwin Bay)—Hoards of animals frequent this island, including red-footed and masked boobies, gulls, frigate birds, finches, herons, and mockingbirds. Families can swim and snorkel from the beach.

Genovesa (Tower) Island (Prince Philip's Steps)—The island has large colonies of masked boobies, frigate birds, and storm petrels. Here, you can also observe the short-eared owl.

Isabela Island (Urbina Bay)—Land iguana and giant tortoises can be viewed on this island and families can swim and snorkel from the beach.

Isabela Island (Punta Moreno)—Hiking here requires families to walk over large beds of lava and in the shadows of impressive volcanoes. This walk requires a watchful eye as families have to make their way through sharp lava, which compromises balance. Keep an eye out for flamingos on the small lagoons.

Fernandina Island (Punta Espinoza)—This is the youngest island—formed by an active volcano in the area. Keep an eye out for Galapagos penguins.

Espanola (Hood) Island (Gardner Bay)—There are no marked trails on this island which contains a startling beach with white sand, and is frequented by mockingbirds and finches. Here, families can swim with sea lions. Large, red marine iguanas inhabit rocky outcrops while turtles frolic in the shallow waters.

Espanola (Hood) Island (Punta Suarez)—Families can view unusual bird colonies as they hike this lava terrain. Keep an eye out for the Galapagos waved albatrosses who has an awkward walk on land but once airborne, gracefully soars. Then spy seawater exploding from a famed blowhole nestled in the rocky cliffs.

Tour Companies

Among the companies offering family tours to the Galapagos are:
- Rascals in Paradise: Family Travel Specialists, One Daniel Burnham Court, Suite 105-C, San Francisco, CA 94109. Tel: (415) 775-0900. Website: www.rascalsinparadise.com.
- Galapagos Tours and Cruises, 1467 Industrial Ave., Escondido, CA 92029. Tel: (866) 672-4533. Website: www.galapagos-inc.com.
- Expedition Trips.com, 4509 Interlake Ave. N #179, Seattle WA 98103. Tel: (206) 547-0700. Website: www.expeditiontrips.com.

RESOURCES

Official Websites

Galapagos Chamber of Tourism:
www.galapagoschamberoftourism.org
Charles Darwin Foundation www.darwinfoundation.org

Books for Adults

Galapagos, A Natural History Guide by M.H. Jackson
Galapagos, Islands Born of Fire by Tui de Roy
The Voyage of the Beagle by Charles Darwin
Spectacular Galapagos: Exploring an Extraordinary World by Tui de Roy
Culture Shock! Ecuador by Crowder

Books for Children

Nilo and the Tortoise by Ted Lewin

Galapagos in 3-D by Marc Blum

Charles Darwin and the Evolution Revolution by Rebecca Stefoff

Videos and DVDs

Galapagos—Beyond Darwin

Galapagos—IMAX

ASIA

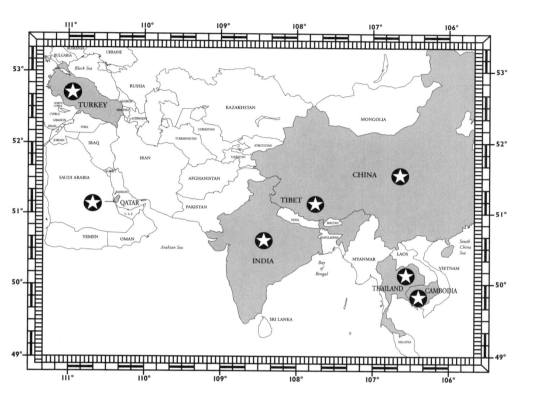

Alison, Jennifer, and Will Nichols take a break in Ayuthaya, Thailand.

CHAPTER 20

THAILAND: BEACHES, BUDDHISM, AND BARGAINS

FAMILY TRAVEL TO THAILAND

Our journey to Thailand began with two *bonks* on the head. After traveling more than 24 hours from Boston to Bangkok, we checked into our hotel, raced up to the room to change clothes, and then raced back down to hail a cab to take us to a snazzy restaurant. After all, why waste time resting in Bangkok when there's so much to see? On the way to the restaurant, Alison walked into a plate glass window, and after ordering, Will fell off his chair—both in a sleep-deprived stupor. All survived—the window included. Two bonks on the head. Two guilty parents. Lesson learned? Give into jet lag, even in one of the world's most captivating cities.

Once we caught up on our sleep, we set a fast pace to experience the intriguing offerings in this southeastern Asian country.

Thailand, once called the Kingdom of Siam, borders Cambodia, Laos, Malaysia, and Burma. Thais are 95% Buddhists, and this religion dominates cities and countrysides with elaborate temples and statues of Buddha. Most males become saffron-draped monks for a few days or years. This country is a lure to families with its gracious people, spectacular sights, and delectable food.

Bangkok, the nation's capital, has one hurdle: congested downtown traffic, which moves at a snail's pace. No problem! Water taxis, called longtails, can take you most anywhere. Our first day in

Bangkok, we hopped on the Chao Phraya River Express and got the lay of the river and saw many of Bangkok's most startling sites.

Temples, temples, and more temples are an encompassing attraction of Bangkok. We climbed to the top of some and examined the artwork, architecture, and sculptures of others. We started our temple tour at Wat Pho (also known as Wat Phra Jetupho), where we viewed the largest reclining Buddha in the country . . . or perhaps the world. This massive religious figure is 151 feet long! After walking around this mammoth gold statue, we headed to the Wat Pho School of Traditional Medicine and got in line for a massage. Will, who had gauze and tape stuck all over his legs, from an infected American poison ivy, drew suspicious stares from the masseurs. Not wanting to be thrown out for fear of some dreaded disease, I pointed to a leave in a bouquet, then to Will's leg. Obviously my sign language worked, as the masseurs clapped their hands then plied their craft: an eternally relaxing one-hour massage . . . all for $6 per person.

Our next stop was the Grand Palace, with its array of magnificent buildings. Initiated by King Rama I in 1782, he built the palace and a walled city. Other monarchs enlarged the compound. We walked around the complex gazing at the glorious structures, each in a different architectural style. These royal buildings are still used for regal ceremonies and government occasions, so tourists cannot enter. The king's official palace is the Chakri Maha Prasart, which occasionally welcomes visitors on special occasions.

On our way back to the hotel, we passed through a park. On a table were a dozen wooden birdcages with small birds inside and a sign that read, "Please set free these birds. You will be happy and prosperous." Alison and Will wanted to give all the birds their freedom, but we settled on two. After paying a dollar for each, they sat with the cages in their laps, studied the birds, opened the door and away they flew. The kids were indeed happy but time will tell if they become prosperous!

The next three days were filled with activities galore. The kids wanted to go to more temples. This was a request easy to fill. We shopped, enjoyed our hotel (Shangri La), went to Bangkok's Chinatown, and, of course, rode on the longtail boats.

Our last evening, we took a water taxi to a restaurant that offered traditional Thai entertainment, with instruments and dancing. As we sat on the floor imbibing in sumptuous Thai cuisine, two of the performers approached the table and asked if our kids could come up to the stage. Will declined, but Alison complied. They motioned for her to sit on the floor, then handed her a small drum and she became part of the entourage as she kept pace with the beat.

The next day we took a night train to Chiang Mai, the second largest city in Thailand. We checked into the Mae Sa Valley Resort, an accommodation surrounded by lush gardens. Each room at this resort is a traditional Thai hut made of bamboo with a thatched roof. As we checked into our hut, two Thai women pointed their cameras at us. We knew what this meant, so all four of us posed on the steps of our room and offered really huge smiles. But the women politely signaled for Bill and I to leave so they could only photograph our two blond kids. Our moment of fame lasted only a few seconds.

That evening, we went to the Night Bazaar, one of the lures of Chiang Mai. The area swarms with shops along the street and in buildings—selling paintings, antiques, lacquerware, clothing, wood-work, and traditional Thai items. Alison bought a traditional silk jacket and Will a small wooden chess set that folded up with the pieces inside. I purchased a jacket to match Alison's so we could be twins, and a jeweled antique neckpiece as well. Bill, being the practical guy that he is, purchased a silk tie with elephants on it.

Speaking of elephants, this animal is the pride of Thailand, and so we had to experience riding them. The next day, we headed off to The Center for Elephants at Work, a half hour drive from Chiang Mai. This Center is an elephant farm where families can view these mammoth beasts working and being bathed in a river. But the best part was riding them through a dense forest. We climbed up on a ramp that put us even with the saddles or *howdahs* that resembled a wooden couch with triangular legs. Each saddle accommodated two riders . . . and there was a third rider—a young Thai man who rode on the elephant's head. After an hour of bumpy riding we disembarked and the kids were presented with coconuts with a straw sticking out of the center . . . a perfect apparatus for slurping the juice.

That afternoon, we drove up a winding, pot-holed road to visit a hill tribe. These tribes are ethnic minorities living in mountainous regions. It is estimated that there are 20 hill tribes with a population over 500,000. Each tribe differs in its spiritual beliefs, language, customs and way of dress. Upon arriving, we were greeted by half a dozen children who accompanied us to their village of small huts. We were invited into a home, which was a single room for all the members of the family, then toured the grounds with the children trailing behind. For my kids, this was a valuable experience—seeing the way these children played, worked, and lived.

Chiang Mai was a non-stop offering of activities. The next day we visited an umbrella factory where dozens of artists painted gorgeous designs on paper umbrellas. These colorful, open, rain-catchers surrounded us as we brushed past them and viewed the artists hard at work. As the kids purchased their favorite umbrellas, the artists called them over and poised a brush above their jeans, implying that they wanted to paint their pants. They willingly complied and both left the factory with beautiful artwork seared into their jeans. The day was an artful one as we visited a lacquer factory and a silk studio.

We couldn't leave Chiang Mai without trying a real Thai delicacy: bugs. We hailed a cab and went across town to a restaurant that we heard served the little critters. The menu offered unusual entrees, including cobra and fried bamboo worms. We ordered both of these dishes. The bamboo worms came heaped high on an oval shaped plate. There must have been a thousand of these inch-long, skinny insects. Three of us munched down on a spoonful of worms, but my husband Bill devoured the remainder. No surprise . . . he's always been into natural foods!

Thailand Overview
- Thailand: Slightly more than twice the size of Wyoming
- Population: 62 million
- Capital: Bangkok (Population: 9.4 million)
- Ethnicity: 75% Thai, 14% Chinese, 11% other

- Religious Affiliation: 95% Buddhism, 4% Muslim, 1% other
- Languages: Thai, English (secondary language of the elite)
- Currency: Thai Baht

PLANNING AND PREPARATION

Passports

U.S. citizens are required to have a valid passport and a return ticket. Those staying longer than thirty days must have a visa. When departing the country through international airports, an exit fee of 500 bahts (approximately $11) must be paid.

When to Go

Bangkok's hottest month is April while the rainiest is October. The most popular months are December and August, while May, June, and September see the lowest number of tourists. The southern part of Thailand is the best, weather-wise, from March to May, while in the north the ideal time is from November to early December.

Health Issues

Do not drink tap water in Thailand. Drink only bottled water. Make sure your family only eats at restaurants which look busy and clean. There is a risk when eating in markets or on the street. Medical care in Thailand is good. There is excellent health care in Bangkok, where facilities exist for routine, long-term and emergency health care are present.

Immunizations are advised for hepatitis A, typhoid, and hepatitis B. Tetanus/diphtheria, polio and measles vaccinations should be current. Check with your travel clinic regarding anti-malarial medication. Also protect against mosquito bites as they can cause Dengue fever.

Safety

In recent years, street crime, such as pick-pocketing and purse-snatching, have risen in major cities in Thailand, but the incidents remain much lower than in American cities.

The Cambodian and Myanmar (Burma) borders have harbored land mines, bandits, smugglers, and rebels. Families journeying to these regions should contact the embassy to get news on latest security in these areas.

What to Bring

Thailand is hot year round, and often muggy. Consequently, bring cool, lightweight clothing. Fortunately Thailand is very casual, so informal clothing is quite acceptable. If you are planning a visit to Thailand's beaches and islands, you might consider bringing your own snorkel equipment.

THINGS TO SEE AND DO

Activities for Kids

- Ride an elephant. There are many elephant centers in Thailand, and most offer activities such as observing the animals at work and elephant shows.
- Visit an umbrella factory and ask if the artists will paint your children's jeans.
- Visit Buddhist temples and observe the architecture, artwork, and sculptures. Encourage your kids to sketch some of their favorite sculptures.

Bangkok

Chinatown—This bustling part of Bangkok is worth a family visit. When you gaze down the streets, you will see red lanterns and Chinese signs. Chinatown also offers an wide array of shops and many restaurants. The Thieves Market on Yaowarat Road is enjoyable to browse. Chinatown is located near the Hualamphong Railway Station and the Chao Phraya River.

Dusit Zoo—Here families can view a host of animals and kids can even ride elephants. Known also as Khao Din Wana, this zoo is located on Ratchawithi Rd., Bangkok. Tel: 02-281-002. Open daily from 8:30 A.M.–6:00 P.M.

Pasteur Institute—This snake farm, established by the Thai Red Cross, offers snake milking sessions Monday–Friday at 11:00 A.M. (The staff milks the snakes, not the visitors.) Families can also view slide shows and handlers working with deadly snakes. Located at 1871 Rama IV Rd., Bangkok. Tel: 02-252-0161. Monday–Friday 8:30 A.M.–4:30 P.M.

National Museum—This museum houses the world's premier collection of Southeast Asian art. Families can view Thailand's long history as evidenced by artwork, ceramic utensils, bronzeware, and many other artifacts. Tours in English are free and last for an hour and a half. They are offered Wednesday and Thursday at 9:30 A.M. and begin at the bookshop. Located on Na Phra That Rd., Bangkok. Tel: 02-224-1333. Times: 9:00 A.M.–4:00 P.M. Wednesday to Sunday.

Temples

Wat Pho—Golden, reclining Buddha—151 feet long. Also has a place where families can get a massage.

Wat Benjamabophit—Statues of Buddha line the courtyard. Popular with monks.

Wat Phra Keo—On the grounds of the Grand Palace. Extremely ornate temple with an emerald Buddha.

Wat Saket—Climb 318 steps for an amazing view of Bangkok.

Wat Traimitr—This temple contains the world's largest, solid-gold Buddha, weighing 5 ½ tons.

Hotels in Bangkok

Shangri La Hotel—Cost: Standard room $245–$265, Deluxe room $285–$330. Frequently rated as one the world's leading hotels, this deluxe-class hotel sits on the banks of the Chao Phraya. The property includes a spacious garden with lovely tropical vegetation. Equipped with numerous amenities including babysitting services, a fitness facility, outdoor pool, sauna, tennis courts, and whirlpool. 89 Soi Wat Suan Plu New Road. www.shangri-la.com/eng/hotel. Tel: (66) 2 236 7777. Fax: (66) 2 236 8579. Email: slbk@shangri-la.com.

Sheraton Grande Sukhumvit—Cost: Standard room $130–$185, Deluxe Room $150–$205. Located in the center of Bangkok, this hotel is set amidst shops, department stores, restaurants, pubs, and entertainment venues. Fitness facility with whirlpool and hot tub. 250 Sukhumvit Road, Bangkok. Email: grande.sukhumvit@luxurycollection. com. Tel: (66) 2 653 0333. Fax: (66) 2 653 0400.

Royal Orchid Sheraton Hotel and Towers—Cost: Standard room $100–$150. Deluxe Room $110–$155. River views from many of the rooms. Hotel has five restaurants and lounges, a tennis court, and swimming pool. Renovated during the summer of 2003. Siphya Road, 2 Captain Bush Lane, Bangkok. Tel: (66) 2 266 0123. Fax: (66) 2 236 8320.

Hotels in Chiang Mai
Mae Sa Valley Resort—Standard $30. Deluxe $43. Suite $60. www.chiangmaihoteltravel.com/mae_sa_valley.htm. Among the many activities offered are ceramic painting, silk work, biking and yoga.

The Westin Chiangmai—Cost: Standard room $60–$127. Deluxe room $93–$200. Hotel is located southeast of the city on the banks of the Ping River. Spacious guest rooms are furnished with fine teak and exotic carpets. 318/1 Chiang Mai-Lampoon Road, Chiang Mai. Tel: (66) 53 275 300. Fax: (66) 53 275 299.

Restaurants in Bangkok
Vientiane Kitchen—This restaurant is an excellent place to see a real piece of Bangkok. The food is mainly from the Isaan province and Laos. Ask for really spicy food if you like it. A live band plays traditional music, and the open air atmosphere makes for a special evening. Sukhumvit Soi 36.

Pierside Seafood Restaurant—Located adjacent to the Chao Praya River, in the River City Shopping Centre next to the Royal Orchid Hotel & Towers. Restaurant offers both indoor and outdoor dining. Tel: (66) 237 0077-8.

Restaurants in Chiangmai

The Khum Kaew Palace Khantoke—Features northern Thai cooking and performances of northern Thai dancing and singing. 252/19-23 Phra Poklao Road, Chiangmai 50200 Thailand. Tel: (66) 53 210663-4.

RESOURCES

Official Website

www.tourismthailand.org

Books for Adults

Travelers' Tales Thailand: True Stories by James O'Reilly
Real Thai: The Best of Thailand's Regional Cooking by Nancie McDermott
Frommer's Thailand by Jennifer Eveland

Books for Children

The Breath of the Dragon by Gail Giles
Thailand: Countries and Cultures by Tracey Boraas
Thailand: Cultures of the World by Jim Goodman
Hush! A Thai Lullaby by Minfong Ho
The Girl Who Wore Too Much: A Folktale from Thailand by Margaret Read MacDonald
The Man Who Caught Fish by Walter Lynn Krudop

Videos and DVDs

Exploring Thailand and Cambodia directed by Sheryl Brakey

Sonia and Hannah Sachs become objects of curiosity at Tonlee Sap, Cambodia.

CHAPTER 21

CAMBODIA: VISITING THE KHMER COURT

BY SONIA EHRLICH SACHS

FAMILY TRAVEL TO CAMBODIA

Hannah, almost seven, wanted to go to Disney World instead of Cambodia, which is where we were taking her and her 17-year-old brother. Her reluctance to let go of the Magic Kingdom was somewhat mitigated by my telling her that Cambodia has a king, a queen, princes, and princesses. In fact, we had read in the newspaper about one such princess and her involvement in environmental issues. My daughter became excited by this modern update of her fairy tale vision. However, I wondered if her excitement would be tempered if she found out that her Disney-type princess (a very young girl with long blond hair and a ball-gown) was actually a very accomplished, erudite, and charming French Jew, married to the half-brother of the current king. Nonetheless, Hannah gave up her Disney demand and willingly accompanied us on a fascinating trip to Cambodia.

Fortunately, our 17-year-old son, Adam, had outgrown his attachment to amusement parks, and now he was the one most anxious to get out and see as much as he could—including museums. We went to see the National Museum with our guide and received a tutorial on the history of the Khmer civilization. We were surprised to learn that the Khmer people blended some aspects of Hinduism with many aspects of Buddhism. There was a beautiful statue of Vishnu from the 6th century, with Indochinese facial features. Many Westerners would recognize Vishnu as the Hindu deity with four arms. Alongside the Vishnu statue was a statue of the Buddhist, Bodhisattva, from the same period.

The current king, King Sihanouk, lives in the center of the city in the Royal Palace. This public palace is wonderful. There are many interesting structures with characteristic Khmer style and the most outstanding one is the Silver Pagoda with silver floor tiles and two life-size Buddhas, one silver and one gold. Surrounding the Pagoda is a large enclosure with a 100-year-old mural of the Ramayana story running along all four walls. The Ramayana is an epic Indian poem of love lost, love challenged, and love regained.

Our next stop brought up the issue of traveling with kids of very different ages. My son, Adam, and I wanted to see the genocide museum, "Security Prison 21," a former high school where the Khmer Rouge terror regime tortured and killed many innocent civilians. While I did not want Hannah to see it, she did not want to be separated, so we all went together. This turned out to be a mistake. The documentation of the horrific atrocities was so graphic that neither Hannah nor I could stand it, so we retreated outside to wait for Adam and the guide. Hannah's mood was appropriately somber when I explained the situation in very general terms, wishing that I could oblige her pleas and promise that such horrors will never happen again.

As we were going to see the famous temples of Angkor in the town of Siem Reap, Hannah asked us "what exactly is it going to be like . . . what do the temples look like . . . how is the hotel." She was disconcerted when we told her that we did not know since we had not been there ourselves. I explained to her that if I took her to Disney World, I could tell her exactly what she would see, what she would do, what it would be like, and what the hotel looked like. I pointed out how lucky she was that we were taking her to places that even we, her parents, had not been to before and, therefore, there was a heightened sense of adventure.

Angkor was a terrific place to explore together. The 1,000-year-old temple of Angkor Wat is considered to express the quintessential character of the Khmer civilization. It is a beautiful sprawling temple consisting of multiple structures and intertwined galleries with balustrades in the shape of an undulating "naga," the mythical serpent. The temple is enclosed within a series of successively larger, nested, rectangular courtyards surrounded by a protective moat. A beautifully detailed bas-relief encircles the entire base of the temple and illustrates daily life, historic battles, battles between Hindu Gods and demons, and many disquieting visions of heaven and hell, so captivating that Adam and Hannah got some fresh ideas for their sibling torture techniques.

In the nearby ruins of Angkor Thom, there is the famous Bayon temple that has tall towers with gargantuan faces, presumed to be those of Buddha. Their bemused, enigmatic smile is the source of the moniker: "The smile of Angkor." When we got to the Ta Prohm Buddhist temple, Hannah begged to be in charge of the camera, realizing that this was truly special. This is one of the temples that has not been restored. Since the temples have been forgotten for centuries, they have been swallowed up and reclaimed by the jungle. The above-ground thick roots of the huge kapok and banyan trees surround the temple walls and give the appearance of a giant octopus insinuating its tentacles into every crevice, lifting and shifting stones, giving an awesome display of the architectural analogue of nature versus nurture. The man-made structures are inextricably intertwined with nature, totally interdependent, since removing one would cause collapse or degeneration of the other.

Siem Reap is on the edge of Cambodia's major lake, Tonle Sap, which swells to five times its normal size during rainy season. This creates a unique ecosystem of a "flooded forest" which is actually an ideal breeding ground for the fish and many bird species in this lake. The fish are of major importance to the livelihood of the Cambodian people. We hired a small motor boat to take us around the lake. The houses on the lake were very primitive, leaky houseboats where people slept in hammocks to keep dry. Other one-room houses teetering on the edge of the lake were simply lifted and moved up when the water level rose. There were entire villages made up of houses on very long stilts that usually cleared the water level when the lake rose . . . but not always.

Since the men were out fishing, we saw mainly women doing their daily chores: standing in the water, dressed, washing themselves and their hair, cooking food on small open fire stoves on their small wooden boats, leaning out of the boats to wash their cooking utensils, their clothes, their babies. In between were small canoe-size boats paddling in and out of the congested lake traffic, selling fruits, vegetables, and household goods. An elementary school consisting of two plain rooms of children sitting on the floor floated by. To this day, Hannah often muses what life would be like for her if she were born here.

My husband and I enjoy taking our children to different parts of the world for many reasons. First of all these trips are a true bonding experience for the family since we encounter the unknown as a unit. We like learning together about the varied cultural and historic diversity of people in the world. Second, we would like our children to be broad-minded citizens of the world and be aware of circumstances outside of their own privileged life in Boston. Possibly as a result of this attitude, our 21-year-old daughter, who is a junior in college, has spent three summers acting on her growing passion for global civic duty. One summer she volunteered in the social service arm of a microfinance bank which lends money to poor women in La Paz, Bolivia. The following summer she volunteered in The Cheshire Home of abandoned, handicapped adults and children in Delhi, India. Most recently she helped set up health surveys for the community workers in a small village in Uganda.

Our 17-year-old son has also developed a keen sense of the intricate issues involved in the gap between the developed and developing world. His schoolwork often reflects his interest in a deeper analysis of world problems as experienced by his travels. His recent summer job was tied to observations he made while traveling with us in tropical countries. He chose to work in a laboratory that does molecular research on malaria. Seven year old Hannah would still probably prefer to go to Disney World than to South East Asia, but she came with us happily and enjoyed it. She was delighted when we celebrated her seventh birthday in a colonial style hotel in Siem Reap, Cambodia. In fact, except for the day that she was born, she has always had her birthday in a country other than her own!

CAMBODIA OVERVIEW

- Cambodia: roughly the same size as Oklahoma
- Population: 10 million
- Capital: Phnom Penh (Population: 920,000)
- Ethnicity: 94% Khmer, 3% Chinese, 4% other
- Religious Affiliation: 88% Buddhist, 2% Moslem, 10% other
- Language: Khmer (official)
- Currency: Riel

PLANNING AND PREPARATION

Passports

A passport and visa are required. Tourists and business travelers may purchase a Cambodian visa, valid for one month, at the airports in Phnom Penh and Siem Reap. Both require a passport-sized photograph.

When to Go

Cambodia can be visited throughout the year. The climate is tropical and features three distinct seasons. The most pleasant season is the dry season from November to March. Temperatures are 68 to 82 degrees. During the hot season, March to June, temperatures range from 82 to 95 degrees. The rainy season lasts from May to early October.

Health Issues

A yellow fever vaccination certificate is required from travelers coming from infected areas, but not from the U.S. or Europe. Although other vaccinations are not officially required, it is recommended that travelers get vaccinated for cholera, typhoid, tetanus, and hepatitis A and B if they are going to the provinces. Malaria risk exists throughout the year in the whole country except in the Phnom Penh area and close around Tonle Sap. Malaria does, however, occur in the tourist area of Angkor Wat. Recommended prophylaxis is mefloquine; but in the western provinces, doxycycline.

Safety

Crime and banditry are persistent problems in many areas of the country. A number of tourists have been robbed at gunpoint in Phnom Penh. Most were robbed while riding on motorcycle taxis or cyclos (passenger-carrying bicycles) and generally after dark. Many rural parts of the country remain without effective policing and are subject to banditry. Land mines and unexploded ordnance can be found in rural areas throughout Cambodia. At no time should travelers walk in forested areas without a local guide.

What to Bring

Like its neighboring country Thailand, Cambodia is always warm and often hot throughout the year. Consequently, visitors should bring comfortable and cool clothing. Sun in the tropics can burn; bring sunscreen and a hat as well.

THINGS TO SEE AND DO

Activities for Kids

- Ask your children to list the differences between their home and their life and the homes and lives of the Cambodians living on the water at Tonle Sap.
- Have your kids observe the different items in each of Vishnu's four hands. Help them find the reason each item is held.
- Let your child make a photo collection (their own photos) of the temples at Angkor Wat and Angkor Thom. Show them how to shoot close-up details and distant panoramic scenes.

Phnom Penh

The Markets—Adults and children alike will enjoy the capital's markets. The four wings of the yellow Central Market are teeming with numerous stalls selling gold and silver jewelry, antique coins, clothing, clocks, flowers, food, fabrics, shoes, and luggage. For paintings and antiques, there is the Tuol Tom Poong Market, also known as the Russian Market. Bargaining is the order of the day at Cambodia's markets.

Royal Palace—In the heart of the city, quite near the Tonle Sap (river) is the Royal Palace. The grounds contain a number of buildings, including: the Throne Room, used for the coronation of kings, official receptions and traditional ceremonies; the Chan Chhaya Pavilion, a venue for dance performances; the king's official residence, the Khemarin; and the spectacular Silver Pagoda. If you choose to see only one building here, it should be the Silver Pagoda. Five thousand silver tiles each weighing about two pounds cover the entire floor. An emerald Buddha sits on a pedestal. In front stands a life-size Buddha made of solid gold. It is covered with diamonds and other precious stones.

Security Prison 21—The Tuol Sleng Museum has taken over this former Killing Fields prison. Most of the 17,000 prisoners held here during Cambodia's Khmer Rouge-generated genocide in the 1970s were ultimately executed and buried in mass graves. Many after being tortured. The Khmer Rouge keep thorough records of their atrocities, and these records, including photographs of thousands of victims, are on display. Parents should ensure that their children are developmentally ready to visit this museum. It is as disturbing as the Nazi death camps in Europe.

Siem Reap

The town of Siem Reap is the home of Angkor Wat and Angkor Thom, two of Cambodia's oldest and most spectacular complexes. Located 195 miles northwest of Phnom Penh, one can travel by bus (eight hours), by express river boat up the Tonle Sap (five hours), or quite cheaply by slow boat. Bring your own hammock and food, as this slow boat trip takes 36 hours.

Angkor Wat—Located four miles north of Siem Reap, Angkor Wat was built in the first half of the 12th century. (Wat is the Thai word for temple.) Angkor Wat was a funerary temple for King Suryavarman II and faces the west to conform to the symbolism between the setting sun and death. Photographers should note that the best light is in the afternoon. The enormous size and beauty of Angkor will likely overwhelm the visitor. Its height, over 600 feet, outstrips that of the Washington Monument. Angkor Wat, the largest monument of the Angkor group and the best preserved, is an architectural masterpiece. Its bas-reliefs are renowned. Be sure and take the kids to the Hall of Echoes, so named because of its unusual acoustics.

Angkor Thom—Angkor Thom, the last capital of the Khmer Empire, was a fortified city enclosing residences of priests, officials of the palace and military, as well as buildings for administering the kingdom. The city of Angkor Thom consists of a square, almost two miles long per side, that is defended by a wall 26 feet high around the city. A moat the width of football field surrounds the outer wall. Five entry towers and five long causeways offer access to the walled city. Each causeway is flanked by a row of 54 stone figures on each side—demons on the right and gods on the left—to make a total of 108 mythical beings guarding the city of Angkor Thom. In the exact center of the square city sits the Banyon Temple. Exploring this jungle-surrounded monument is a must.

Tonle Sap—South of Siem Reap, the Tonle Sap River widens into a lake. Driven by monsoon weather, this lake expands and shrinks markedly throughout the year. Inhabitants of the lake have adjusted their lives to the seasonal ebb and flow of the water. Tourists can book boat trips on the lake to visit local floating and stilt villages. Tours or individually arranged guides will show visitors such things as shrimp basket weaving, food production, and cast net fishing. One may also explore the flooded forest in wooden dugouts and a bird sanctuary on the Tonle Sap. Those wanting to spend the night can sleep aboard a floating house, in a house boat, or in a village pagoda. All options can be arranged by your guide. One tour organizer offering Tonle Sap boat trips is Terre Cambodge in Siem Reap. Tel: (855) 63 964.391. Website: www.terrecambodge.com/eng. Email: info@terrecambodge.com.

Hotels in Phnom Penh

Raffles Hotel Le Royal—Cost: Double room $140. Grand historic hotel established in 1929. Tel: (855) 23 981 888. Fax: (855) 23 981 168. www.raffles.com.

Royal Phnom Penh Hotel—Cost: Double room $85. Resort hotel with spa facilities located near the Mekong River. Tel: (855) 23 982 6735. Fax: (855) 23 982 661. www.royalphnompenhhotel.com.

Hotel in Siem Reap

Angkor Village Resort—Cost: Double room (high season) $82. Beautiful boutique hotel located 15 minutes from Angkor Wat. Tel: (855) 63 963 561. Fax: (855) 63 963 363. www.angkorvillage.com.

Restaurants in Phnom Penh

Le Louisiane Bar and Restaurant—#76 Street Sothearos. Tel: (855) 12 804 875. Southern French cuisine with a bar and pool.

Khmer Kitchen Restaurant—#41 Eo, Street 310. Tel: (855) 12 712 541. Authentic Khmer cuisine in a garden setting.

Restaurant in Siem Reap

Chao Say Restaurant—Opposite Old Market. Tel: (855) 63 964 381. Cambodian, Thai, and Chinese cuisine.

RESOURCES

Official website

www.embassy.org/cambodia/tourism/
Useful tourism website: www.tourismcambodia.com/

Books for Adults
Lonely Planet Cambodia by Nick Ray
Angkor: Celestial Temples of the Khmer by John Ortner, et al.
First They Killed My Father: A Daughter of Cambodia Remembers by Loung Ung

Books for Children
The Caged Birds of Phnom Penh by Frederick Lipp
Cambodia (Cultures of the World) by Sean Sheehan

Videos and DVDs
Exploring Thailand and Cambodia, directed by Sheryl Brakey

*Hannah Sachs rides a yak on the Tibetan
plateau—17,000 feet above sea level.*

CHAPTER 22

TIBET: PILGRIMAGES AND HOT POTS

BY SONIA EHRLICH SACHS

FAMILY TRAVEL TO TIBET

If grandma saw what we do with her grandchildren on some of our trips, she would file for custody of our offspring. Driving through Tibet in a small bus with our two teenage kids, Lisa and Adam, our six-year-old Hannah, along with another family with three children, we were enjoying the scenery until we started climbing a mountain range where the width of the road coincided with the width of the bus. As the bus was making its hairpin turns, we kept shifting to the uphill seats, not wanting to sit next to the edge of the cliff. When fear abated and our faces relaxed, we were rewarded by spectacular vistas of the Himalayas with snow-capped peaks, the tallest one of which was the less frequently ascended side of Mt. Everest.

At each stop of the bus, a small crowd of Tibetan children and adults seemed to come out of nowhere, offering trinkets and, what Hannah coveted the most, a ride on a colorfully attired yak. Walking alongside her yak, we tried to climb a gentle slope that would afford a better view of the mountains above and a lake below, but we quickly realized that the breathtaking views did just that—took our breath away! At this high altitude, the low oxygen concentration made us all pant even with minimal exertion, all except for the local kids, that is, who were running around unaffected.

Driving back to the capital city, Lhasa, we passed a few villages of flat-roofed houses surrounded by walls that invariably had the emblematic red, green, blue, white, and yellow prayer flags hoisted on sticks at each corner. We got to see the inside of some of these "houses" which were single room huts with a dirt floor, an open fire, a table, and a large wooden bed for the whole family. Hannah, who barely understood the concept of having to share a bathroom, was full of questions about the lifestyle of a family living on less than a dollar a day. The adults and children were clad in many layers of woolen sweaters with colorful scarves for the women. We saw many children who were not in school, having to help with chores, especially shepherding the cattle. As Hannah pointed out, some of the shepherds were younger than she was.

In Tibet, Buddhism is not just the main religion, but also the way of life. Until 1959, when the Chinese People's Liberation Army suppressed the monks' revolt for the independence of Tibet, a large plurality of Tibetan men was monks. The rest of the population, which consisted of very poor subsistence farmers, toiled the infertile land, eking out a meager sustenance for themselves and for the monks in the monasteries. During the Chinese Cultural Revolution, many monks were killed and thousands of ancient monasteries were partially or totally destroyed. The spiritual leader of the country, the Dalai Lama, escaped to India. For some time, Hannah thought that Chairman Mao was the Dalai Lama because Mao's picture is everywhere, whereas the Dalai Lama's image is prohibited and, therefore, never seen.

The famous Potala temple is as spectacular as we anticipated. Built into the Red Hill, it has reigned over Lhasa for over 400 years. Run by 10,000 monks, this has been the religious and administrative center of Tibet. It is a complex maze of hundreds of staterooms, offices, ceremonial rooms, prayer rooms, meditation rooms, and storage rooms. It also houses the schoolrooms and living quarters for the monks and the Dalai Lama. Additionally, there are libraries housing the thousands of manuscripts that the monks have to master.

My husband, kids, and I were pushed along by the throngs of pilgrims reciting prayers while filing from room to room. The rooms, dimly lit, were densely decorated with paintings, statues, relics, and heavily bejeweled tombs of past Dalai Lamas. At the numerous altars, the pilgrims spooned out rancid yak butter to keep the wick in the butter lamps burning, and they deposited money in the coffers. All the rooms were tended by monks sitting on the floor and chanting prayers for hours on end. Both monks and nuns wore a maroon toga-type robe, sandals, and a crew cut.

We were taken to a monastery set in the hills where a few nuns were living in solitary confinement in closed caves for the rest of their lives, praying for the possibility of reaching a higher level of reincarnation. At yet another monastery, the nuns were very cordial, laughing with the kids and trying to communicate in some tidbits of English. Hannah, being the youngest, was the center of attention. She was passed from lap to lap and fed candy. The nuns wanted the kids to take pictures of all of them together and then giggled uncontrollably when shown the images on our digital camera. In general, when the monks and nuns found out that we were American, they were particularly but furtively welcoming since they knew that Americans are supportive of the Dalai Lama and, in principle at least, are supportive of Tibet's independence movement.

Our kids were mesmerized by the scene we witnessed at a central Tibetan temple called the Jokhan temple that dates back to the 7th century. Tibetan pilgrims come to this holy site, many having walked for months from their home villages. Whirling their prayer wheels, which house the scroll of the written mantra, so that even the illiterate can "pray," the throng of pilgrims circumambulates the temple for hours. The younger men wear a leather apron and wooden clogs on their hands to lessen the pain of throwing themselves on the ground and sliding for several feet, only to get up, say a prayer, walk three steps, and prostrate themselves again, continuing this all the way around the temple for many hours a day, many days in a row. This procession is intermingled with a very colorful, lively market with merchants displaying their wares on the ground or on rudimentary tables.

Our kids don't particularly enjoy going to museums, but the new museum in Lhasa was so wonderful that even our six-year-old did not want to leave. She particularly liked the acoustic guide which was fun to operate and was set up so that you could choose which exhibit you wanted to have explained, at your own pace and in your choice of order. We watched her zigzag her way from one display to another, absorbed and attentive. The museum tells Tibetan history from Stone Age onward. The explanation of recent events is somewhat ideologically tainted by the Chinese hegemony over Tibet.

Our kids, as well as their gourmand parents, enjoyed the traditional Tibetan meals. Everyone's favorite meal was the hot pot served at a round table with large pots of boiling water in the center. Using chopsticks, one cooks his own choice of items such as meat, vegetables, mushrooms, and noodles and then dips them in spicy sauces. The kids were particularly happy that no "weird" animals were served.

The last day of our stay, as the kids stood at a mountain pass, looking out from a vista from the height of 17,000 feet, one of them commented on the richness of this poor society. Indeed, if richness is judged not by material possessions but by artistic beauty, culture, and warmth of hospitality, Tibet really is at the top

TIBET OVERVIEW

- Tibet: Larger than Texas, smaller than Alaska
- Population: 2.6 million
- Capital: Lhasa (Population: 360,000)
- Ethnicity: 93% Tibetan, 7% Han Chinese
- Religious Affiliation: Predominantly Buddhist
- Language: Mandarin Chinese (official), Tibetan
- Currency: Renminbi Yuan

PLANNING AND PREPARATION

Passports

Americans are required to have a valid passport, visa, and a special travel permit to enter Tibet. The visa and special permit can be obtained through the Chinese Embassy in the United States or other Chinese embassies and consulates throughout the world (see chapter on China). Travelers wishing to visit Tibet usually have two choices: join a tour group arranged by a Chinese travel agency, or create your own tour group, which could conceivably be your family, and hire a guide. The required permits and bureaucracy make it difficult to tour Tibet on an individual basis. If you decide to join a tour, the travel agency will arrange for the necessary visas and permits, and collect any fees. If you decide to create a group (of five or more), you will have to obtain the necessary documents on your own. The Chinese government requires U.S. citizens wishing to visit Tibet to apply for both a visa for the People's Republic of China and a permit from the Tourist Administration of the Tibetan Autonomous Region. For more information consult the Chinese National Tourist's association's web site: www.cnto.org/.

When to Go

Tibet is a dry country that experiences little rainfall. Despite its high altitude, it is also not as cold as you may think. Lhasa, the most visited city, is also known as "the Sunlight City." Temperatures can get higher than 80 degrees during the summer months, but usually dip down at night. In winter, Lhasa can be very cold. In northern Tibet, the weather is extremely cold for a longer period of time, with winter lasting from October through June. If your travels include northern Tibet, be prepared with serious cold weather gear.

Health Issues

Tibet is a fairly disease-free place compared to other countries. No inoculations are required and anitmalarial drugs are not recommended. However, because of Tibet's position high above sea level, altitude sickness can be a problem for some travelers. Symptoms include: difficulty breathing, headache, sore throat, and nausea; and they usually occur within the first few days of the trip. Lower your risk by drinking plenty of fluids, avoiding alcohol, and possibly taking Diamox. This prescription medication helps both preventatively and by treating the symptoms of altitude sickness. Discuss the use of Diamox with your health-care provider before you leave. For more information on health issues in Tibet consult the Center for Disease Control's web site: www.cdc.org.

Safety

Tibet is generally a safe country to visit. One should be alert in crowded situations for pickpockets. When walking in rural areas, be especially alert for unleashed dogs. Peasants often keep unrestrained (and sometimes aggressive) dogs as pets.

What to Bring

Because of Tibet's high altitude and thin air, temperature variations from day to night can be quite noticeable, even in the summer. If you plan to visit then, it would be wise to pack a wide brimmed hat, plenty of high SPF sunscreen, and a combination of light clothing for the day, and warmer clothing for the evenings. Pack warm hats, sweaters, and wind-resistant coats if you visit in winter.

THINGS TO SEE AND DO

Activities for the Kids

- Ride a yak, then have your child draw a comic strip about her experience.
- Eat a hot pot meal, sampling all of the dishes and sauces. If you feel particularly adventurous, ask the waiter what you just ate.
- Spend quiet time at the Potala Palace, listening to the monks chant.

Around Lhasa

Jokhan Temple—One of the most revered religious structures in Tibet. It bustles with worshippers and pilgrims. The quadrangle of surrounding streets known as "Barkhore" is part of the pilgrimage circuit. This area of the Old Town is both the spiritual heart of Lhasa and the main commercial district for Tibetans.

Potala Palace—This UNESCO World Heritage Site sits on The Red Hill overlooking Lhasa. Potala is actually composed of two palaces: the White Palace and Red Palace. The former is used for politics and the daily life of the Dalai Lama (although he lives in exile). The latter houses tombs of past Dalai Lamas and a multitude of rooms. The Grand Hall of the Red Palace consists of dozens of Buddhist halls, scripture halls, and mourning halls, connecting with each other by painted corridors and staircases. A great amount of ancient scriptures are stored in the Scripture Halls. All the halls are full of streamers elaborately embroidered with scriptures. Hundreds of butter lamps burn day and night. Most fascinating about the Potala Palace are the lifelike Buddhist statues of various sizes made of copper, gold, or silver. Some of them have a height of several feet, and some, only a few inches. There are over 200,000 statues in all.

Norbulingka Park—Located in the western part of the city, this park was a summer resort for Dalai Lamas. In the garden, colorful, exotic flowers shaded by towering trees and golden buildings around the lake add beauty to the surroundings.

Further Afield

Mt. Everest—The Tibetan name for Mt. Everest, "Quomolangma," means "The Third Goddess." Towering more than 29,000 feet in the middle section of the Himalaya, Quomolangma teems with snow-capped peaks around it, and glaciers at its foot. Deep caves and snaking ice rivers present a magnificent view around the Quomolangma. A visit here requires a multi-day guided trip.

Hotels in Lhasa

Hotel Lhasa—Cost: Double room $68–$138. The largest and most modern hotel in Tibet. Located next to the Norbulingka, the summer palace of the Dalai Lama and about 10 minutes by rickshaw to the ancient city. Comfortable guest rooms include color TV's and private bathrooms. 1 Minzu Rd, Lhasa. Tel: (86) 891 683 2221. Fax: (86) 891 683 5796.

Tibet Hotel—Cost: Double room $75. A four-star hotel designed in the traditional Tibetan style and run by the administration of Tibet Tourism Bureau. Near Potala Palace and Norbulingka. 64 middle Beijing Rd., Lhasa. Tel: (86) 891 683 4966. Fax: (86) 891 683 6787.

Shangbala Hotel—Cost: Double room $44. Located in downtown Lhasa, near Barkhore Bazaar. Simple hotel with clean comfortable accommodations. 1 Danjilin Rd., Lhasa. Tel: (86) 891 632 3888. Fax: (86) 891 632 3577.

Restaurants in Lhasa

Snowland Restaurant—Next to Jokhang Monastery. Great selection of food, including Yak steak, at very affordable prices.

Mad Yak—Tibetan buffet dinner, includes dance performances. Ask at your hotel for directions.

Food stalls—Near the Potala in Lhasa is "food stall heaven," with every Tibetan culinary delight that you could possibly want.... including pots of Tibetan butter tea.

Xue She Gong Restaurant—Tel: (86) 891 900 3803. This is the right place for those who would like to try typical Tibetan food. It lies west of Potala and is clean and stylish. Mashed yak meat, Yak blood sausage, Tibetan momos, and yogurt are served by Tibetan waitresses.

RESOURCES

Official Website
www.tibet-tour.com/

Books for Adults
Lonely Planet Tibet by Bradley Mayhew
The Tibet Guide Central and Western Tibet by Stephen Batchelor

Seven Year in Tibet by Heinrich Harrer, Dalai Lama
Doctor from Lhasa by T. Lobsang Rampa
The Art of Happiness: A Handbook for Living by Dalai Lama

Books for Children
Tibet: Through the Red Box by Peter Sis
Tintin in Tibet (Adventures of Tintin) by Herge
All the Way to Lhasa: A Tale from Tibet by Barbara Helen Berger

Videos and DVDs
Seven Years in Tibet
Heart of Tibet: An Intimate Portrait of the 14th Dalai Lama
Nova: Lost Treasures of Tibet

*Hannah Sachs and two gesticulating friends alongside
the Yangtze River in China.*

CHAPTER 23

CHINA: FROM THE FAR EAST TO THE FAR WEST

BY SONIA EHRLICH SACHS

FAMILY TRAVEL TO CHINA

The first time we went to China was August 1981, our last childless summer, when my husband, Jeff, was a young professor of economics and I was a resident in a hospital. At that time one could visit China only in a closely supervised officially sponsored tour. This is not the way we like to travel. Traveling with a group of tourists did not allow us flexibility in schedule or choice of activities. Our group of American tourists was not the most inquisitive type. Some preferred to sleep in; some preferred to go shopping whenever given the choice. (Shopping meant being bussed to a sterile, government store set up exclusively for tourists.)

The bigger problem at that time was that China was still a "closed" country. The Chinese people, all wearing the same drab Mao-style uniform, were reluctant to talk to foreigners for fear of government retribution. Our itinerary was meticulously choreographed and scripted by the government tourist bureau. To prevent any possibility of spontaneity, we had two guides. Jeff and I called them guide A and guide B. It was very transparent that this system was one of self-policing, of one checking on the other, making certain that neither one deviated from the party line. Having grown up in communist Czechoslovakia, I consider myself an expert in this type of censorship and how to get around it. Using a simple ruse of playing one guide against the other, Jeff and I did manage to escape the watchful eye of both and we visited a hospital across the street from our hotel. This escapade turned out to be an eye-opening experience.

I would not have recommended taking children to China at that time. There were no shops with packaged, western foods, no diapers or other amenities necessary for traveling with small children. All our meals were in large government dining halls where the food—even for a grateful omnivore like me—was awful. It consisted mostly of over-cooked chicken and cabbage with heavy, brown, starchy sauces. During one particularly memorable yet quite representative dinner, we were fed a chicken that was not thoroughly plucked and, in addition to that unappetizing fact, many of us found hair in our meal. We were not at all surprised when the chef, who came out to greet us at the end of the meal, was practically bald!

Once China became more open and tourist-friendly, we took our children with us and found the experience very rewarding. With the change of political regime, the Chinese became more interactive with us, but frank discussions about politics still continued to be restrained. As the private sector started to boom, we could buy the kids their favorite brand of crackers or even go to McDonalds when, after a couple of weeks of traveling in the hinterland of China, they wanted a respite from a diet of thrice daily Chinese food. Since it became normal to travel privately without any government restrictions, we could tailor our itinerary including sites for our children's preference, such as visiting the Panda sanctuary in Sichuan, where we saw one newborn panda in an incubator, the other napping next to his mother.

Our two blond-haired children always get a lot of attention in this country where there is no such pigment on a single one of the 1.3 billion heads. Even our seven-year-old, Hannah, a brunette with red highlights, attracted small crowds wherever we traveled in the Western Provinces. Adults came up to shake her hand and kids gave her hugs or just grabbed her hand and walked with her. In Nanning, the capital of Guangxi province, I took her to the zoo which featured such imponderables as a man putting his head and neck into the open jaws of a live alligator. As Hannah and I were taking pictures and staring incredulously at that sight, we noticed that there was a sizable crowd focusing their cameras not on the man-eating alligator, but on my own exotic mammal, Hannah. Again in front of an audience of smiling mothers and giggling children, Hannah fed the large orange carps which practically jumped out of the water, splashing and twisting furiously, often hoisting themselves above water on top of the backs of fellow carps, mouths wide open to catch the food.

Traveling in China is a wonderful way for our children to learn the complexity of the world that is hard to fathom from school, books, and other media. For instance, our teenagers were surprised to learn that China is not the homogeneous country of "Chinamen" stereotyped and even caricatured in the West. In fact, they learned to see how the country is a kaleidoscope of diversity. We learned first hand of the multiethnic composition of whatever province we visited, which some-times had only a small minority of the Han Chinese that we blithely assume are the sum total of the demography of this huge country.

In Tibet, part of China by forceful annexation, the Han Chinese are a small minority ruling over the Tibetan majority. When we went to the northwestern most province of Xinjiang, again, the Han Chinese are but a fraction of the population which is mostly Turkik people of Central Asia such as Uygurs, Kazakhs, Kirghiz, Uzbeks, Tartars, Mongols, Tadjiks, and Russians. In Yunan province in southwest China, there are the Naxi people with a subgroup, Mosuo, being a traditional matriarchy. All these groups have a slightly different physiognomy, language, customs, and history. And yet for most foreigners, China is all amalgamated into one homogenous group, which belies the subtlety of the myriad permuta-tions and the consequences of this multiethnic cauldron.

The kids learned this first hand by seeing the different type of clothing, hearing the different languages—all quite incomprehensible to us—eating different foods, and participating in different cultural events. They observed a wedding ceremony of the Tu people living in Xinghai province. We spent a day with a Tibetan family in their traditional house in the Tibetan plateau of the Yunnan province. Of course, we spent many days with the Han Chinese in Beijing, visiting them in their tiny, tidy apartments.

To our guide's surprise we asked to spend a day visiting the poorest section on the outskirts of Kunming where people migrate to escape the hopeless poverty of their home villages. Their upgraded situation is still quite bleak by our standards: four adults sharing a small tenement room with a communal water faucet and toilet in the hallway. We sat down with them to learn about their 12- to 16-hour work days, six days a week, hearing how much happier and more optimistic they are about their future than when they lived in their villages.

What better way for a child to learn geography than to actually walk or ride through it? We swam on the beautiful beaches of Hainan Island in the south. We climbed the ramparts of the Great Wall of China where the kids ran up and down the long stretches of the wall. Sitting on the steep steps with their dad, they discussed the likelihood of the legend that the Wall is the only man-made structure that can be seen from the moon using the naked eye. (Radar image yes, naked eye no.) Following the Silk Road to the part of China that is deep in Central Asia, we spent some time in the Taklamakan Desert (Someone told us the meaning is, "Once you go in, you do not come out.") The desert sand has swallowed up many towns along this Middle Aged trade route.

The sand dunes of the Taklamakan Desert are tall hills with beautiful curves and ledges with absolutely nothing else around except for the sand and the searing sun. We rode through parts of the desert on camels. The kids really liked this even though our son almost fell off as his camel rose from a sitting position by first straightening his hind legs—thereby nearly evicting the unsuspecting passenger out of the seat and over the head of the animal—only to be rescued when the front legs straightened. In our own version of a caravan, we strode through the desert with a guide who, much to our kids' delight, encouraged us to climb to the top of a gigantic dune, several hundred feet tall. Panting, scorched, and dehydrated once we reached the "summit," we had a breathtaking view of the other dunes. We all then chose different modes of the much-anticipated descent: some of us rolled down, some jumped down with giant leaps, some skidded down, and one even used a wooden sled. We all ended up at the bottom, on our bottoms, with sand in our pockets and in our hair, all the while frolicking and laughing hysterically.

We drove along the famous Yangtze river in a region where the river snakes through the Snow Mountains, famous for the Tiger Leaping Gorge. We got to appreciate the gorge intimately. We were stuck on a cliff for the whole day when a landslide obstructed the road, supplanting our worries about the hairpin turns along the edge of the steep precipice. A few days later we drove through the endless rice paddies of Sichuan province, known as the rice bowl of China. Still later we visited the famous jutting hill formations of Guilin while navigating on the Li River, seeing the scenes that inspired so many Chinese paintings. We now realize these paintings were no flights of fancy, but realistic pictorials of this unique region. We explored grottos with tremendous stalactites and stalagmites while learning about the geochemistry of their birth.

Throughout China we ate unimaginable inedibles like a plateful of tiny birds (in their entirety, just skinned), scorpions, insects, turtles, frogs, worms, and organ meats. In India, the streets are swarming with animals, from small ones like rats and cats, to big ones like donkeys, bulls, and the sacred cows which often cause traffic jams by sitting with impudence but impunity in the middle of intersections. The cows are not slaughtered even in times of famine. In contrast, in Chinese cities one does not see *any* animals at all, because in China anything that moves gets skewered, barbecued and served.

Our children did not appreciate this culinary bonanza and often, even during 15-course banquets, agreed only to eat rice with some rice on top of rice followed by a desert of rice. Breakfasts were particularly challenging with the congee, soy bean milk soup, greasy noodles, deep fried buns, and fermented tofu, which, I learned the hard way, is not to be eaten in big chunks. Seeing our displeasure at eating congee, one of our hosts explained that congee is eaten every morning as a digestive aid; one of our kids said they would prefer a bottle of Pepto Bismol. We were very proud of our picky-eater son who outdid himself by eating, for the cameras, of course, a bunch of fried silk worms.

Our seven-year-old Hannah, in a second grade social studies unit on China, asked the teacher if she could do a show-and-tell about her trip. Her father was her assistant while she explained what she saw and learned—and ate—in this far-away land. The enchanting adventures when East meets West continue for the next generation.

China Overview

- China: Slightly smaller the United States
- Population: 1.3 billion (most populous country in the world)
- Capital: Beijing (Population: 12.4 million)
- Ethnicity: 92% Han Chinese, 55 minority groups
- Religious Affiliation: 50% Atheist, 20% Confucian, 30% other (including Buddhist, Taoist, Christian, and Islam)
- Language: Mandarin Chinese (official)
- Currency: Renminbi Yuan

Planning and Preparation

Passports

Americans are required to have a valid passport and a visa to enter the People's Republic of China. Visas can be obtained through the Chinese Embassy and consulates in the U.S., or overseas through Chinese embassies and consulates, visa offices, and the consular department of the office of the Commissioner of the Ministry of Foreign Affairs of China. There are different types of visas depending upon your reason for traveling to China. A standard 30-day tourist visa cost $50. It would be wise to ensure that all of the necessary paperwork and documentation are in order before you leave, as even a slight discrepancy could cause you and your family frustrating delays. For detailed information on where and how to obtain a visa, visit the Chinese Embassy's website at: www.china-embassy.org/visa passport/english/lq.htm.

When to Go

China, as large as the United States, experiences regional climates much like the U.S. From skiing and ice festivals in the north to water sports and tropical beach resorts in the south, China is a year-round destination. Keep in mind the vast distances between places when planning your trip. Traveling along the popular Golden Route (Beijing, Xi'an, Shanghai, Guilin) is the rough equivalent of visiting Chicago, Washington D.C., Atlanta, and Miami, all in one trip. Weather wise, Shanghai's climate resembles that of U.S. southeastern coastal states, while Beijing's climate is more like Chicago's. The majority of China's rainfall happens between May and early October in the southern regions.

Health Issues

The recent outbreak of SARS (Severe Acute Respiratory Syndrome) has left many people wary of travel to China. The Center for Disease Control has issued two types of notices to travelers: advisories and alerts. A travel advisory recommends that nonessential travel be deferred; a travel alert does not advise against travel, but informs travelers of a health concern and provides advice about specific precautions. For the most up-to-date information on health issues and travel to China consult the following web sites: www.cdc.gov/travel/other/sarschina2.htm and www.who.int/country/en/.

During the peak of the SARS outbreak, a travel advisory was in effect for Beijing, while a travel alert was in effect for the rest of China. In general, do not drink the tap water in China and avoid ice cubes and fountain drinks. Drink only bottled or boiled water. It is not necessary to take an anti-malarial drug, as malaria is not prevalent in China.

Safety

As in most countries, pick pocketing and petty thievery can be a problem in the larger cities. Exercise caution with your valuables.

Violent crime is not a big problem in China, as compared to many Western countries. It is not legal for an ordinary citizen to own a gun. There have been very few incidences of crime against tourists, and hotels are generally safe. Occasionally, in the larger cities, you may notice a street scuffle between locals. This is usually caused by tensions related to long lines, overcrowding or a traffic incident. It is best to move along and not interfere.

What to Bring

Bring a pocket-size Mandarin phrase book. The Chinese people clearly appreciate visitors who attempt to say a few basic words in their (difficult-for-westerners) language. Thank you = *xie xie.*

THINGS TO SEE AND DO

Activities for Kids

- Hike the Great Wall near Beijing. Help your kids find the interesting facts about the Wall: length, when built, how did some sections go missing? (Answers: 3,950 miles long, built over the centuries, peasants who lived near the wall used its stones as building material for their houses.)
- Visit a silk factory in Suzhou. See all stages of production from the live silk worm to the cocoon to spinning silk thread to weaving a fabric. Let them pick out a silk souvenir to take home.
- Take them to a tea house in Shanghai (or elsewhere for that matter). Sample the sweet buns filled with red bean paste. They have an interesting taste (and they are *not* made from worms).

Deciding Where to Go

China is a large and geographically diverse country, much like the U.S. in size and diversity. Most visitors stay in the eastern portion of the country, often including Beijing, Shanghai, Guilin, and Xi'an in their itineraries. Much further west there are fascinating destinations, including Tibet and the Taklamakan Desert. Match the distances you plan to travel to the length of your visit. After all, you wouldn't try to see the entire U.S. on a two week vacation. Most visitors to China include Beijing in their travels. Here are a few suggestions for Beijing:

The Great Wall—The Great Wall is a symbol of the ancient Chinese civilization. Stretching 3,950 miles, it was built as a defensive structure. The Wall is listed in the UNESCO World Heritage List. The best preserved and most imposing section of the wall is at Badaling, 50 miles north of Beijing.

The Forbidden City—This is the largest and most well-preserved imperial residence in China, and it is the largest palace in the world. Located in the center of Beijing, The Forbidden City was built early 1400s and served as the imperial palace for the Ming and Qing dynasties. The word "forbidden" is quite literal, as the palace was heavily guarded and off-limits to ordinary people. It has 9,900 rooms and halls (don't try to see them all). A 170-foot-wide moat encircles the Forbidden City along with 32-foot-high walls. UNESCO has listed the Forbidden City in the World Heritage List.

The Temple of Heaven—This temple was built in 1420 during the Ming Dynasty, and is located in the southern part of the city. It was the place where emperors of the Ming and Qing would pray to heaven for good harvests. It is one of the most strictly protected and preserved cultural heritages of China. It is the largest temple complex in China with 12 million people visiting the temple every year.

The Summer Palace—Yet another grand imperial palace. It boasts a fabulous royal garden from the Qing Dynasty. The Summer Palace contains tens of thousands of precious cultural relics. The imperial garden covers an expanse of 17.3 acres, with more than 100 picturesque sites of interest. Do not miss the Marble Boat, permanently moored in Kunming Lake on the grounds of the Summer Palace. This large, wooden side-wheeler is painted white to make it appear as marble.

Beijing Zoo—The Beijing Zoo is the oldest zoo in China. The zoo's residents consist of more than 6,000 animals of over 500 species, including giant pandas—always popular with the kids—golden monkeys, and brown bears. The zoo also houses many animals from other parts of the world: hippopotami, zebras, giraffes, chimpanzees, lions, and antelopes from Africa; parrots from South America; birds and polar bears from the Arctic; bison from Europe; and apes from Asia.

Hotels in Beijing

Beijing Hotel—Cost: Double room $160–$350. One of the most historic hotels in Beijing, this century-old edifice has played host to many famous dignitaries including Chairman Mao and former President Richard Nixon. The hotel's unique design, a mix of early 1900's French art deco and contemporary Chinese architecture, makes it a stand-out in the city and popular with both the Chinese and foreign tourists. Located close to the shopping district at Fu Jing Street, Tain An Men Square, and the Forbidden City, the hotel has recently been renovated and offers modern, even luxurious, rooms and amenities. www.chinabeijinghotel.com/index.html. Number 33 East Chang An Avenue, Beijing. Tel: (86) 10-6513-7766. Fax: (86) 10-6513-7307.

Great Wall Sheraton—Cost: Double room $220. A modern five-star hotel with all the standard Sheraton amenities including a large heated indoor swimming pool that can be a life saver when traveling with children. It is located about five minutes from the Agricultural Exhibition Center and the China International Exhibition. Check for special discounted room rates throughout the year. www.sheratonbeijing.com. 10 North Dong San Huan Road, Chaoyang District, Beijing. Tel: (86) 10-6590-5566. Fax: (86) 10-6590-5878.

Friendship Hotel—Cost: Double room $70–$150. One of the largest garden-style hotels in Asia (meaning pristine gardens and elegant fountains are interwoven with traditional Chinese architecture), the Friendship offers a taste of serenity in the middle of a busy city. Facilities such as an outdoor swimming pool, bowling alley, and billiards room make it a good choice for families looking for a fun, but more authentic, Chinese experience. www.c-b-w.com/hotel/friendship/. 3 Bai Shi Qiao Road, Beijing. Tel: (86)10-6849-8888. Fax: 86-10-6849-8866.

Hotels in Nanning

Mingyuan Xindu Hotel—Cost: Double room $72–$90. Located beside People's Park, this recently built five-star hotel offers new, well-appointed rooms and recreational amenities like karaoke, bowling, billiards, and chess. It is also close to White Dragon Park, Exhibition Center, Diamond Plaza, Marketplace Building, and Yongjia Famous Shop Plaza. www.nn-myxd.com/index_en.htm. 38 Xin Min Road, Nanning. Tel: (86) 771-211-8668. Fax: (86) 771-283-0811.

Nanning Yong Jiang Hotel—Cost: Double room $30–$50. This high-rise hotel with clean, comfortable rooms is located near the Yong River and a few minutes away from the central city. 41 Jiang Bin Dong Road, Nanning. Tel: (86) 771-280-8123. Fax: (86) 771-280-0535.

Hotels in Guilin

Sheraton Guilin Hotel—Cost: Double room: $107–$137. Situated on the Li River, this hotel offers modern rooms, some with water views, plus such amenities as a swimming pool and fitness center. Close to Elephant Trunk Hill and Seven Star Park. www.starwood.com/sheraton. Bin Jiang Nan Road, Guilin. Tel: (86) 888-625-5144.

Golden Elephant—Cost: Double room $35–$63. This three-star hotel is smaller and less modern than the Sheraton, but has a more local feel. Located directly across from Elephant Trunk Hill, the rooms are clean and cozy. 36 Binjiang Road, Guilin. Tel: (86) 888-280-8888. Fax: (86) 888-280-9999.

Food

One of the best things about visiting China is the food. Although it may be a bit different from the Chinese food you are used to at home, it is usually quite good and varied enough to satisfy the palates of children and adults alike.

Restaurants in Beijing

Fangshan Restaurant—Beihai Gongyuan Park, 1 Wenjinjie. Tel: (86) 10-6401-1889. Located on the grounds of a former Imperial palace, this is one of the most upscale and popular restaurants in China. It serves a range of dishes from regions across China with a focus on Imperial cuisine (i.e. fancy food). Reservations are recommended.

Sichuan Restaurant—51 Xi Rongxian Hutong. Its classic Peking architecture and delicious Sichuan dishes, including a fabulous smoked duck, attract tourists in droves.

Makai Canting—33 Di'anmenwai Dajie. For those who like it hot, this restaurant serves a range of Hunan spicy-hot and sweet and sour (spicy-hot) dishes.

Restaurants in Nanning

The are a number of stalls in Nanning that specialize in dog hotpot (yes, your suspicions are correct), which most Westerners find "hard to swallow." More recognizable Chinese fare is available at a number of fast food joints in the southern end of the city.

Muslim Restaurant—Qingzhen Fandian. A great spot because of the menu, which is partially in English, and which features a variety of appetizing dishes.

Restaurants in Guilin

Chengdu Xiachi—Yiren Lu 7 Zhengyang Lu. Serves a variety of fresh noodle dishes and soups.

Coffee–Language 101—Mingdian Zhongshan Zhonglu. If you are craving a taste from home, head to this hip cafe that offers Chinese and Western dishes and drinks.

RESOURCES

Official Website

China National Tourist Office: www.cnto.org

Books for Adults

Baedeker's China by Baedeker's Guides
The Cambridge Illustrated History of China by Jacques Gernet
The Good Women of China: Hidden Voices by Xinran Xue
Dragon Bones by Lisa See

Books for Children

China's Son by Da Chen
Tikki Tikki Tembo by Arlene Mosel, Blair Lent
Kids Like Me in China by Yin Ying Fry, Amy Klatzkin, Bryan Boyd
Eyewitness: Ancient China by Arthur Lotterell, Alan Hills, Geoff Brighting

Videos and DVDs

Touring China
China: A Century of Revolution
Crouching Tiger, Hidden Dragon
From Mao to Mozart—Isaac Stern in China

Sonia and Hannah Sachs with Indian villagers in Andhra Pradesh.

CHAPTER 24

India: Crowded, Chaotic, and Charming

BY SONIA EHRLICH SACHS

Family Travel to India

When we decided to go to India—pre-kids—in 1978, we had never before been to a developing country (a euphemism for a poor country). My future husband, Jeff, and I, along with another couple, decided to travel around the sub-continent-sized nation. We had a premonition that this would be our last carefree summer when we were not yet held accountable to family or society since we were single and in graduate school. That trip to India made an indelible impression on all of us, and it determined the course of Jeff's professional life. As a budding economist, he switched from studying unemployment and exchange rates, to devoting the rest of his life to improving the living standards of poor people in many countries, including India. Now that we are all grown up and held responsible for our jobs and our families, we take our children on these trips to India and other developing countries, with an explicit hope to enhance their understanding of the complexity of the bigger world, and with a covert, complicit hope that the impact will help shape their professional aspirations.

I must admit that the first trip to India was a painfully startling jolt. I have never seen such profound poverty, on such a massive scale. I did not anticipate the ambivalence I would have appreciating the exquisite beauty of some of the Wonders of the World, such as the Taj Mahal, since I was not capable of compartmentalizing them away from the abject poverty surrounding and encroaching on them. You do not have to go far or for long to see *everything* since *everything* happens right there, on the streets, right in front of you.

For instance, walking down Chandni Chowk, a busy commercial street in Delhi, gives you the uncensored, unsubtle panoply of human activities, accentuating the vast and stark differences between the rich and the poor, without the veil of privacy that we can afford in well-to-do countries. You see bejeweled women in beautiful, silk saris haggling with shopkeepers, fending off dirty, emaciated women in filthy rags who are holding sickly, scrawny babies in their arms, begging. You walk past fancy restaurants and you are surrounded by small children, carrying even smaller children, motioning to their mouths asking you to give them something to eat. You see small groups of men wearing their "dhotis," a wrap-around-cloth worn around the waist, squatting and chewing beetle nut, occasionally jettisoning a red spittle. You see people squatting at the curb to defecate. You may have to wait till a cow decides to free up the grid-lock it created in the intersection, and once you reach the curb, you often have to step over people who sleep on the sidewalk. You frequently dodge small, grieving groups carrying makeshift gurneys with barely covered corpses.

India is one country I am glad we pre-experienced before taking our children. In addition to many vaccines necessary to travel safely, you also need a hefty inoculation against the discomfort of witnessing a society where most people spend the day simply trying to survive till the next. Once I got "used" to the idea, callused a bit in order to be able to function in this unfamiliar setting, I became a bit more discerning, a bit more relaxed, more able to learn about India's extraordinarily rich cultural and historical heritage. Then, I started appreciating what an extraordinary place India is and was able to bring our children there.

Even just walking through the markets became a memorable sensual feast and a pleasant activity for our children. They were spellbound by
the displays of familiar and unfamiliar goods of exotic colors and smells
and uses. I took many a photo of the kids standing next to the vendor
with his rows of burlap sacks with tall mounds of heaped-up spices of
multitude of shades and textures standing next to rows of baskets with
identifiable and unidentifiable nuts and roots and plants. Recognizing
meat only as clean slices in Styrofoam packets with cellophane wrap as
presented in our supermarkets, the kids were mesmerized by seeing
blood spattered butchers heaving cleavers to split open an animal's head,
separating bones and meat on wood blocks behind lines of hooks with
dangling heads of lamb, dripping fresh blood from the slaughter,
dangling intestines and some unrecognizable—and if recognized,
unmentionable—body parts. Stands of kitchen wares, shoes, clothing,
men's and women's underwear . . . all transactions taking place amidst
throngs of people in the unabashed atmosphere of an outdoor market.

The unfathomable juxtaposition of the sublime, supreme human
accomplishments, and the unsolved problem of allowing a dignified
daily existence for the masses is seen everywhere in India. Typical
scenario for me was the first time we drove up to the Taj Mahal, the
beggars, mostly crippled, surrounded our car, knocking on the windows, hoping for handouts; and the peddlers thrusting their hands
through the open car windows, dangling in front of our faces the trinkets they were hoping to sell. Our local driver closed the windows and
drove right through the crowd, pushing the people out of the way
with the hood of the car, reminding us yet again of the disdain of one
social class for the lower one. When we opened the car door to get
out, we were immediately surrounded by hawkers shoving each other,
and us, to get attention, pressing trinkets into our hands, forcing a
transaction. If you buy, hoping to stop the forceful, unrelenting sales
pitch, you invite even more hopefuls to pursue you. Once in the
enclosure of Taj Mahal, where the entrance ticket costs about ten days'
worth of "income" for these supplicants in front of the gates, we faced

a monument to human creativity that dazzles and transports with its ethereal, breathtaking beauty and soothing symmetry.

Our oldest daughter, Lisa, and son, Adam, were 12 and nine when we first took them to India. With them in tow we attracted even bigger crowds. These two kids have blond hair and fair skin so people, especially women, came up and touched their skin and stroked their hair and hugged them. At first the kids complained and clung to us, but eventually they started to tolerate it and ultimately they worked the crowds with the finesse of a politician, smiling, shaking hands and generally delighting the delighted. We once stopped our car on a dirt road in a very remote village and immediately a crowd of excited, barefoot children swarmed around our children, and suddenly we saw a bunch of them looking at themselves and at our children in the reflection off the car. Our children were shocked by the realization that the car, the villager's own mirror image rarely if ever seen, and our Caucasian appearance, were all extremely exotic for these village children.

Our children decided on their own to use up all their pocket money on charity, handing it out especially to children and to crippled people. They encountered one of their first moral dilemmas when a book that we were reading stated that out of desperation some poor families maim their own children to make them more "effective" beggars. Our children debated with each other and with us the conflict they felt while wanting to give help but realizing that handouts don't help and that actually they could be abetting the unimaginable. Seven years later, Lisa chose to return to India on her own spending the summer working in Delhi, in the Cheshire Home for the utterly destitute, severely handicapped, and abandoned children and adults.

On all our trips we read books along the way about different aspects of the country's history, culture, economy, fiction, and art. We attend plays, concerts, and museums, with sometimes more, sometimes less protest from the kids. We get age-appropriate books for the kids on some of these themes, because we believe that reading, seeing, and discussing ideas together as a family helps broaden their world view. Our daughter, Hannah, traveled with us on an extensive trip through most of Southern

India when she was just five years old (turning five in an overnight train to Kerala). She was reading a book that had clever ways of simplifying big concepts for little people. It had a small plastic bag with uncooked rice showing the young reader the meager amount of food an average child in India would consume in a day. She was particularly absorbed by an activity with a pinwheel in the center of a colorful pie diagram that represented all children in the world, poor and rich. She was to spin the arrow and see the high odds she had to beat to be born into the tiny wedge of the pie representing children not born into poverty.

There were more mundane lessons for us to review with our children. They learned the advantages and disadvantages of Indian privies, which consist of a hole in the floor flanked by two metal plates in the shape of one's feet. Since often there was no toilet paper, we explained to the kids the unspoken but universally observed tradition of respecting the division of tasks between the left and right hand which was followed by the kids' discussion of how to be sure the person shaking your hand or giving you food was not a lefty. We always carry liquid soap with alcohol and none of our kids ever became ill.

When traveling we meet interesting people, local professionals, academics, politicians, and government officials, who show us around, invite us to their homes and explain subtleties of the society and its politics, giving us a more intimate inspection, more finely nuanced by the experiences of people involved in trying to shape the future of India. As our children get older, they become more astute listeners and even interlocutors in these discussions, amassing bit by bit an ever-widening base of understanding.

We have been going to India for the last 24 years. India, like China, is richer now than it was when we first saw it. The desperation of people's lives has been reduced, but can still be seen in rural areas. Diseases such as polio and small pox, which have destroyed millions of lives, have essentially been eradicated. India is still a spectacle of the wide gap between the rich and poor, but it is also a spectacle of change and of progress and it is certainly one of the great, enduring, and colorful civilizations in all of world history. The experiences learned in

India are so vivid and so remarkable that our children have carried the images with them as they have grown.

INDIA OVERVIEW

- India: Four times larger than Texas
- Population: 1.04 billion, second most populous country in world
- Capital: New Delhi (Population: 7.2 million, including Delhi)
- Ethnicity: 72% Indo-Aryan, 25% Dravidian, 3% other
- Religious Affiliation: 83% Hindu, 11% Moslem, 6% other (Christian, Sikh, Buddhist)
- Language: Hindi and English (both official), many local languages
- Currency: Rupee

PLANNING AND PREPARATION

Passports

American citizens require a passport and visa to enter and exit India. Visitors must obtain visas at an Indian Embassy or Consulate abroad prior to entering the country. There are no provisions for visas upon arrival.

When to Go

India is a vast country with a climate that varies from tropical monsoon in the south to temperate in the north. In general, India has three main seasons: The cool season runs from October to February; the hot season from March to June; and the rainy monsoon season, which starts in the middle of June and continues into September. Delhi, a common starting point for visitors to India, has moderate rainfall, about 25 inches a year. Temperature in Delhi during the colder months ranges from 50 to 77 degrees; during the hot season, 75 to 104 degrees.

Health Issues

Adequate to excellent medical care is available in the major population centers, but is usually very limited or unavailable in rural areas. Vaccination for yellow fever is required if arriving from an infected area. Malaria risk exists throughout the year. Recommended prophy-laxis: chloroquine plus proguanil.

Safety

India has a low incidence of violent crime and a generally welcoming population; the vast majority of visits to India are trouble free. Some petty crime and scam artists have been reported. There have been occasional terrorist bombing incidents in various parts of India, but mainly in Jammu and Kashmir where there exists an Islamic separatist movement. Travelers are advised to avoid this far northern region of the country.

What to Bring

Bring an ability to be compassionate towards India's poor, while not becoming overwhelmed by the poverty. First-time visitors usually report that the crushing poverty and the numbers of people begging on the streets is something they never experienced before.

THINGS TO SEE AND DO

Activities for Kids

- Take the kids to the spectacular Taj Mahal. Beforehand prepare them for the stark contrast of wealth (the Taj Mahal) and poverty (beggars around the site). Afterwards, discuss how people live under conditions of extreme poverty.
- Explore any of Delhi's markets. Seek out the meat section and observe a butcher at work. Point out the edible parts of an ani-mal that westerners normally don't eat.
- Take your children to Delhi's massive 350-year-old Red Fort. Let them explore the palace inside. Ask them to write a story about the Mughal emperor who lived there.

Where to Visit

India is so large and so diverse that the traveler must narrow his focus before departing. One would not advise a foreigner to "see the

U.S." Instead, the first time visitor to the U.S. would be told to see the Rocky Mountains or the California coast or New England. Similarly, regional or theme focus in India is the best way to begin one's enjoyment of this massive country. A few suggestions to get you started:

Delhi—The ideal place to start your exploration of northern India. The capital of India and a city of fascinating contrasts, Delhi's monuments and structures take you through the centuries past seven older cities that existed here. Agra and its Taj Mahal are 120 miles to the southeast.

Maharashtra—This western state is blessed with a rich heritage of ancient monuments and exquisite architectural marvels representing different phases of development in the art and architectural style of India. Here one finds rock-cut architectural cave temples at Ajanta and Ellora. The magnificent group of rock-cut shrines of Ellora represents three different faiths: Buddhist, Brahmanical, and Jaina.

Hyderabad—This southern locale is home to Charminar, a splendid piece of architecture standing in the heart of the city. This magnificent monument is the unique symbol of Hyderabad. Charminar is often called as "The Arc de triomphe of the East. Four intricately carved minarets reach a height of 157 feet. This monument is located amidst the colorful shops of Lad Bazaar.

Rajastan—A trip to this desert state is most rewarding. Here, the pink city of Jaipur is surrounded by palaces, many of which are also hotels. You could stay in one of these and, for a royal experience, wander off on elephant-back to view the Amber Fort—majestically located on a hill. A well-known shopping and handicrafts paradise, Jaipur's signature building is its multi-layered palace with delicately filigreed red sandstone, the Hawa Mahal, popularly known as "The Palace of Winds." Off the beaten track, visitors can discover the beauty of the desert on a camel safari. They can wander past colorful villages in the desert and sleep under a brilliant starlit sky.

Palace-on-Wheels (Train travel extraordinaire)—One way to cover the ground between Delhi and Rajasthan is by train. Book your family on a weeklong trip on the Palace-on-Wheels and experience a luxurious treatment that the Maharajas once experienced. There are four coupes with wall-to-wall carpeting in each coach of the Palace-On-Wheels train, a lounge car with a well-stocked bar, and two restaurant cars providing Indian, Continental, or rich Rajasthani cuisine. (See Cultural Heritage Travel Tours at www.indianmonumentsportal.com.)

Hotels in Delhi

Oberoi Maidens Hotel—Cost: Double room $62. Historic turn of the century hotel with gardens, in the heart of old Delhi. Tel: (91) 11 2397 5464. Fax: (91) 11 2398 0771. www.oberoihotels.com.

The Manor Hotel—Cost: Double room $190. Secluded designer hotel conveniently located in New Delhi. Tel.: (91) 11 692 5151. Fax: (91) 11 692 2299. www.themanordelhi.com.

Hotel in Agra

Amar Vilas Palace—Cost: Double room $320. Luxury hotel just 600 meters from the Taj Mahal. Tel: (91) 562 223 1515. Fax: (91) 562 223 1516. www.oberoihotels.com.

Restaurants in Delhi

Amarvathi—18/2, Arya Samaj Road, W.E.A., Karol Bagh 110005. Tel: (91) 562 571 5116. Southern Indian cuisine in central Delhi.

Asmeet's Saanjaha Chulha—2880 Hardhian Singh Rd., Opp Gaffar Mkt., Karol Bagh 110005. Tel: (91) 562 572 3233. Specializes in Mughlai and North Indian food.

Restaurants in Agra

Sheela—East Gate, Taj Ganj. Many Indian vegetarian dishes with garden seating.

Dasaprakash—Meher Theatre Complex, 1 Gwalior Rd. Excellent south Indian cuisine and an extensive ice cream menu.

RESOURCES

Official Website
www.tourisminindia.com/

Books for Adults
Fodor's Exploring India by Fodors
A Passage to India by E.M. Forster

Books for Children
The Ninth Jewel of the Mughal Crown: The Birbal Tales from the Oral Traditions of India by James Moseley
Shiva's Fire by Suzanne Fisher Staples

Videos and DVDs
Lagaan: Once Upon a Time in India
Monsoon Wedding

Alison and Will Nichols at Ephesus.

CHAPTER 25

Ephesus and Cappadocia, Turkey: Historical Havens

Family Travel to Ephesus and Cappadocia, Turkey

My family took a glorious march through history in Turkey, trekking through the last 2,500 years. We began our ancient wanderings in Cappadocia, a surreal landscape of erosion-shaped cones, then moved to the underground city of Derinkuyu, and finally to Ephesus, the most elaborate city in the Roman world. With each visit we garnered a sense of history and a notion of what life was like in these long-ago eras.

Our historical jaunt started in Cappadocia, an extraordinary scene of thousands of cones formed millions of years ago by volcanic activity and erosion. Ten million years ago, three volcanoes erupted and spewed their lava over the area. The lava cooled and formed tuff, a soft and porous stone. Eventually, the tuff fell prey to wind and water erosion, which sculpted the element into bizarre conical towers. These kooky structures lured an array of cultures such as the Hittites, Persians, Romans, Byzantines, and Ottomans, who made hide-outs, churches, monasteries, and homes from the 4th century to the 1950s.

Our kids, Alison and Will, were startled as they observed the vast expanse of these shapes. For as far as the eye could see they viewed cones that looked like massive stone teepees and lofty gray pinnacles. Nature had even precariously balanced huge boulders on top of some of these structures. "Those look like Dairy Queen vanilla ice cream cones," Will said as he viewed cones that resembled dripping pale rocks.

Parking our car, we maneuvered a winding path where masses of cones stood before us. Most had an arched opening for a doorway. Those that were nestled on the hills had carved steps. This site was a collection of homes and churches. The frescoed churches had detailed paintings of Jesus and other biblical characters on the ceilings, some of which had been carved in arched designs. Other cones were dwellings, which contained kitchens, storage rooms, and even horse stables.

We examined rock formations, known as "fairy chimneys," on the outskirts of Urgup, where we stayed. As we examined these conical shapes, we read and pointed out to Alison and Will that they had been sculpted by wind and flood water flowing down the slopes of the valleys. The strong water ruptured the hard rocks and sculpted the erodable material. These fairy chimneys were formed by the porous tufa and volcanic ash. Many of these conical-shaped fairy chimneys had a boulder balanced on top, formed by a more resistant rock called "lahar" or "ignimbrite." We had absorbed nature's classroom!

We exited this area and drove to the nearby town of Chapuchin for a late lunch at an outdoor café. Walking through the town, we stepped into a carpet shop, where the owner's grandmother sat on a low stool, weaving a carpet on a large loom. She motioned for Alison to come over, then patted the stool, instructing her to sit down. Alison complied, and the grandmother took her hands to the loom and instructed her in the art of weaving. They weaved together for 45 minutes, as Alison glanced over her shoulder with a huge smile. As the weaving curtailed, we felt compelled to buy something, so we purchased a brightly colored camelbag. We said our good-byes to these gracious people and went on our way.

That evening, we drove back to Urgup to catch the setting sun as it shown its searing magnificent hues on the cones.

In the Cappadocia region, there are 150–200 subterranean settlements. Some of these communities housed up to 30,000 residents and were primarily used as shelters from danger. Hundreds of rooms in these underground cities were linked to each other with low and narrow passages and labyrinth-like tunnels; a plan to restrict the movements of enemies. One settlement even drilled vertical holes into the tunnels so the residents could pour hot oil on their foes who had breached the underground village's defenses. There were also communication holes between some rooms.

As we descended into our underground destination, Derinkuyu, Alison said, "This is scary, Mom." I couldn't have agreed more as we entered the dark labyrinthine crevice. Derinkuyu has 18–20 floors, however, eight are open for visitors, and that was more than enough, as I counted over 300 steps to tour the many rooms. The first room we viewed was a horse stable with a room used for religious ceremonies not too far away. This underground city, which housed 10,000, contained living rooms and kitchens with cooking niches and storage spaces carved into the wall. Even these ancient people needed libation, so they carved a winery which included a pressing room and a canal carved out of stone for the flow of grape juice. We observed living spaces, a ventilation pipe (carved out of stone, of course), and a church with a cruciform layout. The room that the kids identified with the most was a large school room where the students sat on dirt mounds. There was also a whipping post, which Will tried out as he assumed a spread eagle pose. Derinkuyu had captured our nightmares and our dreams.

Our next ancient jaunt was to Ephesus, a city started in 356 BC. We checked into Hotel Kalehan, located in the charming town of Selcuk. This hotel caters to families with its tranquil gardens, a swimming pool, and a superb restaurant. Selcuk is a walking town with a massive outdoor market and an excellent collection of restaurants serving typical Turkish fare.

Ephesus is a startling place, especially for children. Here they will hike along trails and view the remains of this ancient city which was the most elegant of the Roman Empire. They will view one of the Seven Wonders of the ancient world—Artemesium, an Ionic temple in honor of Artemis the fertility goddess. Ephesus, in the 2nd century

BC, was the fourth largest city in the Roman Empire, and in addition to Artemesium, was also home to a gymnasium and a hub for the fine arts, sciences, and philosophers, and one last thing—it offered a medical school. One of the best-preserved structures is the Library of Celsus, a two story structure with eight massive columns, and statues poised in niches symbolizing wisdom, knowledge, destiny, and virtue. We climbed the seats of the theater which sat 24,000 and still provides a stage for entertainment. In fact, that evening whirling dervishes were performing. We even imagined, as we exited Ephesus, walking in the very footsteps of Julius Caesar, who also trekked through this city.

Our trip through historic Turkey had given us a sense of history and provided us with knowledge about nature, culture, and the arts.

TURKEY OVERVIEW

- Turkey: Slightly larger than Texas
- Population: 67 million
- Capital: Ankara (Population: 3 million)
- Ethnicity: 86% Turkish, 11% Kurdish, 2% Arab, 1% other
- Religious Affiliation: 99% Muslim (mostly Sunni), 1% Christian and Jewish
- Official language: Turkish
- Currency: Turkish Lira

PLANNING AND PREPARATION

Passports

In addition to a valid passport, U.S. citizens are also required to obtain a visa, which can be obtained at the Turkish Consulate, or at the border.

When to Go

In the spring and fall temperatures are most pleasant. Summer months are hot, but not humid. In the winter, temperatures can drop considerably and are cold enough for snow; prices are at their lowest in winter.

Health Issues

Check with your travel clinic for advice about vaccinations against diphtheria, hepatitis A, tetanus, and polio. These immunizations are not required but could be recommended. Families that go to the coasts of the Marmara or the Black Sea should consider anti-malaria pills. Do not drink tap water. Bottled water is recommended.

Hospitals vary greatly in Turkey, except private medical facilities in Istanbul and Ankara, which have modern equipment, however these facilities may be unable to treat serious medical conditions.

Safety

Street crime is low in Turkey, however, families should exercise the same cautions they take in the U.S. and keep valuables out of sight. Security is stable in Turkey, however there have been infrequent incidents of internal terrorism, not directed towards Americans. These incidents have occurred in parts of Southeastern Turkey, and the Turkish government is committed to eliminating this internal issue.

What to Bring

Bring comfortable clothing and shoes for hiking around. I advised my daughter not to wear the clothes she wears at home, such as the bare midriff and other revealing styles. Bring lots of film as it may be difficult to find it in small towns.

THINGS TO SEE AND DO

Activities for Kids

- Inform your children of the process by which the cone-shaped tuffs of Cappadocia were sculpted.
- Encourage your children to draw the wide array of conical shapes in Cappadocia.

- Buy an Ephesus guide that shows all the sites. Have your children pick their favorite ruin or the one that interests them most. Have them read about it, examine the ruins, and if there is ongoing archeology activity at the site, have you kids observe the process.

Cappadocia

Urgup—This town offers a wide array of hotels for visiting Cappadocia. This charming town offers a broad range of restaurants and stores. Visit the Zelve Open Air Museum which was home to one of the largest communities in this region. Zelve, sculpted into pink tufa, housed monks, Greeks, and Turks. Open daily 8:00 A.M.–5:30 P.M. Admission: $3.

Cappadocia Balloon Tour—This spectacular tour starts 5:30 A.M. and lasts about 3 to 4 hours. The balloon flight takes lasts 1 ½ hours, and upon landing customers are served a champagne breakfast. This flight is spectacular for camera bugs. The basket can carry eight people. Be sure to bring a light jacket. Cost: Contact the agency. Includes breakfast, transfers, flight certificate, and champagne. Contact: Rocktown Travel Agency, Neveshir. Tel: 90-384-212-82-75. Fax: 90-384-212-82-74. Email: info@rocktowntours.com.

Underground Cities—Be sure to take the family down under. There are several of these cities open to tourists, including Kaymakli, Derinkuyu, Ozkonak, Acigol, Mazi, and Tatlarin. There is a minimal charge to visit each city.

Ephesus

Selcuk—This charming town is located within walking distance of Ephesus. It houses a number of historical sites of its own, including the Virgin Mary's House, a small stone house of typical Roman architecture. There is also a 4th century AD church that has been added. An intriguing attraction is the "Water of Mary," where visitors can drink from this curative spout.

Sirince—This beautiful village, lying 10 miles east of Selcuk, is known for lacemaking and fine wine. Lacemakers display their work outside their homes and in shops on the winding pathways. A range of stores sells wonderful artistic items as well as wine.

Hotels

Cappadocia Area

Perissia Hotel—Cost: Double rooms $45–$75. Located on the eastern edge of the town of Urgup in the heart of the historical sites. Tennis court, gymnasium, and large outdoor pool. Kayseri CD, Urgup. www.PerissiaHotels.com. Tel: (90) 384-341-29-30. Fax: (90) 384-341-45-24.

Best Western Cappadocia Ataman Hotel—The core of the hotel is an old house carved out of rock 200 years ago and further extended to become a large estate in the 1950s. Since 1985, it has been restored as a hotel. The hotel has a research library with books on Cappadocia. Uzundere Cad. No 37, Goreme-Nevsehir. Tel: (90) 384-271-23-10. Fax (90) 384-271-23-13. Email for room rates: info@atamanhotel.com.

AllStar Surban Hotel—Cost: Double room $39–55. Hand-carved stone rooms give the atmosphere of a cave house. The hotel is located beside an old district overlooking the town of Urgup, only a short walk from the town center. Yunak Mah, Urgup. Tel: (90) 212-513-6301. Fax: (90) 212-513-6398.

Ephesus Area

Hotel Kalehan—Cost: Double room $56. Located in the town of Selcuk, just two miles from the ancient ruins of Ephesus. Outdoor pool in pleasant garden. www.kalehan.com. Tel: (90) 232 892 6154. Fax: (90) 232 892 2169. Email: ergirh@superonline.

AllStar Merry Hotel—Cost: Double room $60. Large, multi-story, four star hotel with private beach on the Aegean Sea. Alacabey Mevkii Kusadasi, Aydin. Tel: (90) 212-513-6301. Fax: (90) 212-513-6398.

Restaurants in Cappadocia Area

Rose Kebab House—Urgup. Cheap, small, clean and friendly place. Try the apple tea and chicken kebab.

Ataman Restaurant—Uzundere Cad No. 37, Goreme Nevsehir. In the hotel of the same name. Set in the midst of Cappadocia's "fairy chimneys." Serves international cuisine.

Restaurants in Ephesus Area

Kalenin Prensi—35920 Selcuk (Ephesus). Tel: (90) 232 892 20 87. Offers several dishes on its "Antique Menu," from recipes used in the Roman period 2,200 years ago, in Ephesus region. Sample the stewed veal.

RESOURCES

Official Website

www.turkey.org
The Turkish Newspaper, *Daily News*, is published daily in Turkey.

Books for Adults

Lonely Planet Turkey by Pat Yale
Kingdom of Snow: Roman Rule and Greek Culture in Cappadocia by Raymond Van Dam

Books for Children

Exploring Turkey by Amy Chaple, Audrey Boobar

Videos and DVDs

Turkey: Enchanted Land of Cappadocia

A doorway in Doha, Qatar.
Inset: Amalia, Mary, and Antonio Sandoval.

CHAPTER 26

QATAR: DUNES, WATER, AND SOUKS

BY MARY NICHOLS SANDOVAL

FAMILY TRAVEL TO QATAR

Now, with the world situation as it is, everyone has heard of Qatar. Al Jazeera, the Qatari broadcasting system that has been dubbed "the CNN of the Arabic world," has been in the news frequently since September 11. There is an enormous U.S. air base in Qatar and the U.S. Central Command moved headquarters' units to the country to oversee operations during the war with Iraq. No doubt, choosing Qatar as a family destination would be unwise at the moment, but the world situation was quite different pre-9/11 when we visited Qatar with our children. We would happily return when the tension in the Middle East dies down.

I heard the kids arguing, "But you can't EVER have a "q" that's not followed by a "u"!" "Yes you can! Just look at the map! Where's the "u"? Q-a-t-a-r, no "u"." "It's got to be a mistake. Sometimes even books have mistakes. My teacher said..." "Ask mom, she'll tell you."

I had to explain that "Qatar" was just a phonetic approximation of an Arabic word that has a sound we don't have in English, and that was the closest spelling possible. We also had to look closely at the page in the atlas because Qatar is not a large country. We would never have thought of spending a family holiday there had it not been for friends stationed in Saudi Arabia who had visited with their children and loved it.

Still a conservative and traditional Moslem country, Qatar is more open to tourism than other countries of the Arabian Gulf (don't call it the Persian Gulf while on the Arabian peninsula) and family tourism is welcome, in a limited way. We did our background research and decided to bring bathing suits and scuba diving equipment along with rather conservative clothing for walking around the souks. Women are allowed to drive in Qatar and alcoholic beverages are sometimes offered in large hotels, but not always. Pork products are not available. Tampons are sometimes available and sometimes not, so take a supply if necessary.

The month of Ramadan, which falls each year according to the lunar calendar and rotates throughout our months on the Gregorian calendar, is strictly observed. Thus, during Ramadan, restaurants and snack bars are not open on the streets and in shopping centers until after sunset. If your family can be respectful of the local culture and eat and drink only in the privacy of your hotel room, then you will have no problem should you travel during the month of Ramadan. The weather in the summer months is *extremely* hot (upwards of 110 degrees). The best months to visit Qatar are October to April.

We flew to Doha, the capital city, through London on Qatar Airways. The children had their noses pressed against the windows before landing. "There's nothing but sand down there. Mom!! I can't even see a town. It's all desert. What a boring vacation!" However, it turned out to be anything but boring!

It took a while to get through customs in Doha, mainly because of a fashion magazine our daughter had bought in the London airport. We had to wait while the customs' official went through the magazine, page by page, and calmly tore out the pages with pictures of men and women who weren't fully dressed. Unless you have unlimited time to spend in the customs line, leave any magazines on the aircraft before deplaning in Doha. Be sure that your passports and visas are strictly in order, too. We had no problems, but saw others from our flight who weren't allowed through customs because of bureaucratic problems with their documents.

Our family stayed at the Doha Sheraton Hotel, located at the end of a beautiful sea walk. The hotel has its own private "beach," which is really a paved entrance into the sea, several pools, a gym, restaurants—which offer thematic food nights and open-air barbecues—and snack bars spread throughout the gardens. Many expatriates living in Doha go to the hotel often for meetings and cultural activities, so there were plenty of other children to make friends with. The children could probably have happily spent their entire holiday in the hotel. All of us had an afternoon of fun walking (the parents) and skating (the children) all the way down the corniche and back. The lovely seaside walkway begins just outside the Doha Sheraton and stretches for several miles along the coast. Families, joggers, cyclists and skaters share the space.

Our first cultural outing was a visit to the "souk" or market area. Though not architecturally or historically interesting, once inside you get that same feeling you get in Istanbul or Fez of stepping back in time. The exotic mixtures of sights, sounds and smells create an atmosphere that overwhelms the senses. Doha has many Pakistani and Indian inhabitants. The red hennaed beards of the older Pakistanis and the brightly colored blouse and trouser outfits of the women mingling with the more sedate black and white robes of the Qatari women and men was set against the multi-colored merchandise of the market stalls. Add to this, the ever-present aromas of the spice market and the sound of hundreds of voices which fall still as the call to prayer from the central mosque drifts out over the souk. This assault on the senses made an impression that won't be forgotten.

While walking through toy shops in the souk, our daughter said, "Look, someone has colored all over the boxes of toys!" Upon closer observation, we realized that the boxes with Barbie dolls had indeed been altered. Someone had taken a black marker and covered up the pictures of Barbie's legs, arms, and midriff on all of the boxes. My daughter and I both grabbed a box at the same time. We just had to know what had happened to the Barbie inside! There she was though, in all her splendor, in a tiny pink bikini. We had to laugh. The government policy of protecting the population from improper images was carried out with zeal.

Our daughter was fascinated by all of the gaudy hair baubles, lacy socks, velveteen purses, sequined shoes, and other accessories for endless hours of dressing-up pleasure. The same things are available elsewhere, but it was the "ambiance" that heightened their value in her eyes, I'm sure. Our son was interested in the stalls with electronic devices, cameras, recording equipment, etc. My husband had a sport jacket made in a little tailor shop and I spent my time between the spice market, the gold market, and shoe shops. (If you are interested in investing in gold jewelry, gold is sold by the gram and the design of the piece doesn't figure into the price, so prices tend to be lower than in Europe or the United States.)

Most of Doha is modern and non-descript, but there are several architectural features worth noticing. One is the wind tower, which is a natural air conditioning system developed in the desert before the advent of modern technology. Many homes and buildings have a tall chimney-like structure which catches the wind, draws it down inside the tower, and channels it into the home or building where it feels somewhat cooler than outside. The children especially enjoyed a drive through the city looking for the wind towers. There is a beautiful one in the center of old Doha, many that are only decorative spread throughout the newer residential neighborhoods, and some interesting modern adaptations on government buildings and especially on the Doha University campus.

We have found, while traveling with the kids, that we can usually maintain their interest, at least for a while, with "assignments," like looking for wind towers. Three other architectural features we looked for were the plaster jalousies, intricately designed window screens developed in ancient times to let in air and light while providing privacy inside the home; ornately carved heavy wooden doors, prevalent throughout the city; and enormous outdoor sculptures, located in every roundabout in the city.

Doha is a center for many sports activities and you could plan your trip at a specific time of year to coincide with your favorite sport: The Doha Open tennis tournament with top notch players (we saw Pete Sampras while we were there), the Doha Badminton Open, the Doha Golf Open, the Desert Classic Horse Race, Asian Soccer tournaments, scuba diving, deep sea fishing, and camel races. We boycotted the latter since we learned that jockeys in some Arabian Gulf countries are children who have been kidnapped or purchased from very poor families in Bangladesh and Pakistan, been given only subsistence diets so that they won't gain weight, and been abandoned when they become adolescents and were too big to ride the camels. We certainly hope this is not the case in Qatar, which is a moderately open and "westward" looking country.

There is an amusement park in Doha. There are also mini-golf courses, shopping malls, bowling alleys, and skating rinks, but even with children in tow these activities aren't as interesting as the natural wonders available. Forget the roller coaster when you can ride on the "Singing Dune." A short drive from the capital, in the desert, are sand dunes which are wonderful to hike, though a bit difficult to climb. The children could have done that for hours and hours, but the culminating point of the dune trip was the visit to the "Singing Dune," the largest in the area. After an arduous climb to the top, there are many ways to go down: on your feet, on your bottom, on a flat surface like a piece of cardboard, or on a waxed board similar to a snowboard (which someone lent our son). The kids tried them all. The best thing about the ride down is that the dune "sings" to you, an eerie, haunting sort of melody that fluctuates as you descend and seems to come from the very heart of the dune, in the center of the vastness of the desert and brilliance of the cloudless sky. We know it's only a natural phenomenon caused by air currents and your body compressing the sand, but scientific explanations have no place as you slide down the dune.

We were in Doha during our Christmas holiday and were lucky to visit the Singing Dune twice. The second time, invited by a group of expatriates, we went caroling on a deep winter's night (dress warmly—

evening lows fall to 40 degrees.) and listened to our voices echo off of the dune which had been decorated with hundreds of little paper lanterns with candles inside. I'm not sure which of the two trips was most memorable, but we have not forgotten either.

No excursion to an Arabian desert is complete without seeing a real camel caravan and camping out in a Bedouin tent after eating a whole roast lamb for dinner. We traveled to the Inland Sea, a brilliant body of turquoise water south of Doha, shared by Qatar and Saudi Arabia, in a caravan of jeeps with local drivers which traveled, literally, over the dunes. That was a bit too "extreme" for me and I would have preferred the dirt road, but the rest of the family was in the majority. Our jeep got stuck in the sand numerous times, which I'm sure was meant to be part of the adventure, and we all had to get out to push and twice even had to tie our jeep to another to be pulled out. At least we didn't tip over! I'm a tiny bit frightened of heights and some of the dunes were very high, so this part of the excursion was not my favorite, but the children were ecstatic.

Our camp site was located on a rise overlooking the desert and the sea. The rest of the family went swimming in the Inland Sea (though the winter temperatures—70 degrees during the day—were too cool for me) and came back with plastic buckets overflowing with clams which we gave to friends we had made in Doha. Night falls quickly in the Arabian desert and the temperature falls as well, but our tents had been pitched by our drivers and the lamb was already roasting in a pit in the sand when the family came back from the sea. The absolute blackness, save the millions of stars, and the absolute silence are two things I have only found in deserts. The next morning there were dunes to climb and from the top of one, our son flew a large kite which actually lifted him up in the air and carried him for several yards.

The present Emir of Qatar, Sheik Hamad, has vowed to make Qatar a tourist paradise for the 21st century, so it should become easier to get there and to travel in the country. Our visit was certainly unforgettable and perfect for a family—even one with a somewhat unadventurous mom!

QATAR OVERVIEW

- Qatar: Slightly smaller than Connecticut
- Population: 700,000
- Capital: Doha (Population: 300,000)
- Ethnicity: 40% Arab, 18% Pakistani, 18% Indian, 10% Iranian, 14 % other
- Religious Affiliation: Moslem
- Language: Arabic (official), English commonly used as second language
- Currency: Qatari Riyal

PLANNING AND PREPARATION

Passports

Passports and visas are required. U.S. citizens may obtain a tourist or business visa at the airport in Doha upon arrival. These visas are valid for 14 days and may be extended for an additional 14 days. However, U.S. citizens will be able to clear Qatari immigration more quickly and be granted a longer stay in the country by obtaining visas prior to arrival.

When to Go

Summers in Qatar are extremely hot. Although the weather is more pleasant in the spring and winter, sandstorms are common during this time of year. The best time to visit is November or late February to early March, to avoid the unbearable heat and sandstorms.

Health Issues

Qatar is a fairly healthy place. There are no endemic diseases. No immunizations are required. Basic modern medical care and medicines are available in the government-run Hamad General Hospital and the privately run American Hospital in Doha. Tap water, though biologically safe, is not particularly pleasant since it is desalinated, and most minerals have been removed.

Safety

Crime is rare and generally not a problem for travelers in Qatar. However, Americans in Qatar should exercise a high level of security awareness. The Department of State remains concerned about the possibility of terrorist attacks against United States citizens.

What to Bring

Bring your snorkeling equipment. There are ample opportunities to enjoy the sport at several spots in Qatar's warm waters.

THINGS TO SEE AND DO

Activities for Kids

- Take your kids to have their hands hennaed. Ask your hotel to find a henna artist to perform this traditional body artwork. Henna is a natural vegetable dye used to create beautiful "tattoos" that fade within seven to ten days.
- Take your kids to the Singing Dune and after they slide down, have them hypothesize about what makes the dunes "sing."
- Walk through the souk and discuss with your kids the differences and similarities between this type of shopping area and their local mall.

Doha

Palm Tree Island—Take a boat ride on a traditional dhow to Palm Tree Island. The dhow jetty is close to Doha Sheraton Hotel. The Island has children and family amenities, a restaurant, a café, and water sports facilities.

Khor Al-Udaid—Located south of Doha, this nature site is difficult to reach due to coverage of the area with many sand dunes. It can only be reached using four-wheel-drive vehicles. Sand dunes embrace the sea, and there are wonderful dune climbing and swimming opportunities. You can ask your hotel to arrange an overnight camp in the desert for you.

Snorkeling trip—Have your hotel organize a snorkeling trip for your family. The best place for experiencing marine life is out from the east and northeast of Qatar, on reefs some distance from shore. In addition to snorkeling to admire shallow-water fish, one may also encounter some of the Gulf's marine mammals, including humpback and bottlenose dolphins and, if you are very lucky, dugongs. This shy marine mammal, a sea cow, feeds on bottom grasses.

Walk the souks—Of course no visit to Doha would be complete without a visit to the souks. Even if not purchasing, you and your kids will enjoy the exotic sights, sounds, and smells of the marketplace. They can pick their favorite item to observe: spices, traditional clothing, modern electronics, local produce, and fish.

Hotels in Doha

Doha Sheraton Hotel—Cost: Double room $147. Modern hotel overlooking the Arabian Gulf. Tel: (974) 485 4444.

Movenpick Hotel Doha—Cost: Double room $102. Located on the seafront esplanade near the National Museum. Tel: (974) 429-1111. Fax: (974) 429-1100.

Restaurants in Doha

Most of the fashionable restaurants are located inside the hotels and clubs. A large number of good restaurants that suit every taste and budget are also available either on Al Sadd road or on Al Mirghab road, parallel to Al Sadd road. They include Arabian and Asian fast food and take away restaurants and cafes.

Shebestan Palace—Al Sadd Street. Tel: (974) 442-5999. Syrian restaurant known for its traditional snacks and meals. They also offer Persian delicacies.

Chingari—Doha Corniche. Tel: (974) 431-1818. Resembles three ships directly overlooking the corniche. Offers a wide range of Western, Eastern, and seafood cuisines.

Kababji—Serves a variety of grilled, fried, and charcoal oven dishes. Arabic Cuisine is also on offer at Kababji.

RESOURCES

Official Website
www.qatartourism.gov.qa

Books for Adults
Qatar compiled by Stacey International
Lonely Planet Bahrain, Kuwait, and Qatar by Paul Greenway and Paul Robison

Books for Children
Qatar by Lisa McCoy

STRADDLING TWO CONTINENTS

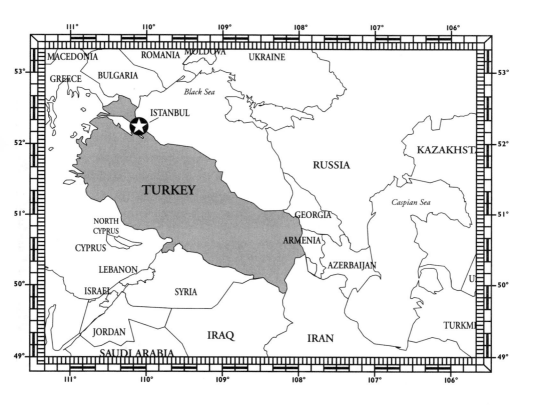

Jennifer, Bill, Will, and Alison Nichols shop for carpets in Istanbul.

CHAPTER 27

ISTANBUL, TURKEY: EUROPE/ASIA'S MOST INTRIGUING CITY

FAMILY TRAVEL TO INSTANBUL, TURKEY

My kids can't stop talking Turkey. After all, spending a week in Istanbul, the heart and soul of Turkey, exposed Alison and Will to startling historical sites, astonishing culture, and gracious people . . . so talking without reserve about this captivating city seemed natural.

Turkey is bordered by the Black Sea to the north, the Aegean to the west, the Mediterranean, Syria, and Iraq to the south, and Iran to the east. This country combines western-style economics and liberalism within an Islamic backdrop.

Istanbul, one of the world's most magnificent cities, was originally called Byzantium, then later, Constantinople. Once the most powerful city in the world, it claims 3,000 years of civilization layered one upon the other and boasts such tradition-searing cultures as the Ottomans, Romans, and Greeks. Today, Istanbul is an international crossroads, straddling both Europe and Asia.

There is so much for families to see and do in this city of 12 million. We went through our guidebook and picked the things we wanted to visit, from shopping in the Grand Bazaar to viewing magnificent architectural sites.

We based ourselves in the oldest section of the city, Eminonu, the heart of Istanbul's architectural masterpieces—the Topkapi Palace, the Blue Mosque, the Hagia Sophia—and home to the Kapali Carsi, or Covered Bazaar. Our hotel, Konuk Evi, was at the apex of all these lures, and less than a fifteen-minute walk from each. Konuk Evi occupies a four-story, renovated Ottoman mansion and is elegantly furnished in the style of the period. Each room features elaborate wrought iron beds, elegant draping curtains and a bevy of large windows that look onto the vibrant life on the streets.

Our first day was a whirlwind of activity, as we decided to shop till we almost dropped, first in the sprawling Covered Bazaar, and then in the nearby Egyptian Spice Bazaar or Misir Carsisi.

The Covered Bazaar, Istanbul's 450-year-old market, has over 4,000 tiny shops and 20,000 employees. It sells everything from jewelry to luggage, pottery, leatherwear, antiques, belly dancing garb, and of course carpets . . . Turkey's claim to fame. And all the items are negotiable—in fact, it is expected that you bargain. This labyrinth of old and new treasures is a shopper's paradise. Alison and Will asked to shop on their own, so we gave in to their teen independence, and agreed meet in one hour outside a jewelry store. The kids were on time, looking at their watches as we approached them. My husband and I had gotten lost!

Continuing our jaunt through the market, we were amused by the merchants—all male—who humorously hassled the customers. "Come look at my rubbish," one shopkeeper called out as we passed his jewelry shop. As Alison poised to snap a photo, yet another said, "Take a picture of me, I'm famous." Rug dealers were the most persistent. As we strolled the rug section, shop owners sat on ottomans sipping tea, and immediately latched on to us with a relentless barrage of comments. "Please tell me sir, when are you going to spend your money?" And when we ignored them, they called out, "Don't break my heart. You don't like us?" or "Don't come in my shop, I'm not inviting you . . . you broke my heart. I'm still your friend, even as we can't agree." "Where are you from?" many inquired.

"America . . . Boston."

"Ah, Larry Bird," several replied.

Finally lured into a carpet shop, we decided we had to purchase one, and only one carpet. The owner, whose name was Nail Can (that really was his name!), scurried us up the stairs, served us apple tea, and proceeded to unroll at least a hundred carpets. "This is a *kilim* . . . this a *cicim* . . . here's a *sumak* . . . " Our heads spun as he explained each carpet type and the associated technique.

"Please, Mom, can I have a carpet for my room?" the kids begged. We broke down—big time—and ended up falling in love with five pieces.

Bargaining for a Turkish carpet is an art, and an essential. After pointing to our five favorites, Nail Can sat down and performed some serious calculating, or so it seemed.

"Here's my final price," he said, "I can let you have them for $1,930."

"That's too much," we countered. "Half is all we can afford."

"No," he said.

Silence.

"I can let you have them for $1,700."

After ten minutes of negotiation, we proposed our final price. "Okay, $1,350, that's it."

"You're a hard bargainer, sir. I'm still your friend, even if we can't agree."

No comment.

"Okay, you can have them."

Within eight minutes, our carpets were rolled up tightly and shoved into a large pull suitcase. We had heard about customers buying carpets, having the store send them, and not receiving them, or opening the package to find totally different wares. So out of the market we went, pulling our carpet bag behind us and ready for more bargaining at the Egyptian Spice Market.

This market dates back to the early 17th century and stocks heaps of spices, nuts, herbs, and other food. We paused for fresh squeezed orange juice and a sampling of nuts, then continued winding our way through the alleyways and finally arrived outside the market where there are other stalls selling clothing, toys, and fruit. The kids were lured by the live baby animals—puppies and chicks.

Istanbul continued to lure us, so we hopped in a cab to take us to the Kumkapi section of town, on the coast of the Sea of Marmara, where scores of fish restaurants line the shore and the adjacent streets. The area was full of wafting smells of food, the chatter of diners, live music, displays of fish, and, of course, the bantering merchants. "Why did you already spend your money? I could have given you better." And "This restaurant is terrible... that's why there are so many people here."

After feasting on seafood delight at an open-air restaurant on the shores of Marmara, we walked through a fish market, where the merchants pulled the kids aside and then handed them their products—huge dead fish. "Take a picture!" they said, and the kids sidled up with the fish and the fishmen and we snapped, snapped, snapped.

Rising early on our second day, we walked five minutes to Topkapi Palace. This Ottoman architectural gem sprawls over 173 acres and regally perches on a promontory that rises above the Bosporus and the Sea of Marmara, granting spectacular views of Europe and Asia. Built by Sultan Mehmet II in the mid-1400s, subsequent sultans also occupied Topkapi.

Following our guidebook's advice, we bought tickets to the popular harem as soon as we entered the grounds. While waiting for our harem tour, we toured room after room of treasures, including Ottoman costumes from 1450–1901, weapons, armor, cookware, jewelry, and paintings. "You guys have to see this," Alison called out as we rushed over to look. It was the arm and skull of St. John the Baptist, encased in gold jewel boxes. We also saw the fifth largest diamond in the world called "kacikci," and the footprint of Muhammad. Caution: Don't photograph inside the palace. One visitor snapped Mohammed's footprint, and immediately, a woman rushed up to him, grabbed his camera, and by the time we left, had still not given it back.

Finally, it was time for the harem tour, and it was well worth the wait. "Harem," Arabic for forbidden, housed the sultan's wives, concubines, and children, all protected by black slave eunuchs. Room after room of regal architecture dazzled us—all were decorated with well-preserved mosaics.

After lunching near our hotel, we walked through a park observing Turkish women modestly dressed and wearing black head scarves, arm-in-arm with friends decked out in tight jeans and t-shirts. Lining the park benches were an Italian soccer team in their uniforms. As Alison walked by, one guy said, "You're American, aren't you?" She nodded, then the entire team broke out in song, serenading her with an odd rendition of our National Anthem. As we left the park, we could tell she was embarrassed, but overriding that was extreme flattery.

The next morning we had a religious extravaganza as we visited two famous places of worship: the Ayasofya or Church of the Divine Wisdom and the Blue Mosque. Ayasofya was constructed by the Emperor Justinian in 537 AD, and was the dominant church in Christendom for a thousand years. This architectural masterpiece was turned into a mosque during Ottoman times and is now a museum. It remains today a hallmark of Istanbul.

Next, we headed to the Blue Mosque; the only mosque in Turkey with six minarets and 260 windows. The blue in its name is not from the searing light that filters in, but from 21,000 blue and white tiles that blanket the interior walls. This astonishing religious monument welcomes all faiths for a visit—if they are dressed properly. We weren't. Our Bermuda-shorts-wearing males were made to swath themselves in wrap-around skirts, and Alison and I wrapped our heads in scarves, leaving our shoes at the door. But it was worth it. We silently observed barefooted men, kneeling down with their heads to the ground and gathered in the enormous prayer room, facing Mecca. "Where do the women and kids worship?" Will whispered. We found them. They were in small rooms at the back of the mosque.

We got back into our American garb, and walked to a section with old Ottoman houses lining the streets. We lunched at the Ottoman Palace, an atmospheric restaurant that had a woman making bread and typical Turkish cuisine. Potato pancakes, yogurt soup, and mezze filled us up. The kids, still with thoughts of the Blue Mosque in their minds, asked our friendly waiter if he worshipped every time he heard the call to prayer five times a day.

"I go to the mosque on Friday, then otherwise, I pray in here," he replied as he patted his heart. We visited several mosques in Turkey, and Alison and Will came to appreciate this religion with practices so different from their own.

As we walked to the hotel, we passed by several restaurants that had low cushioned seating and elaborate smoke pipes, with ceramic bases, and tubes coming out for smoking. We had seen them in Morocco, as well. I could tell what the kids were thinking. "No, they don't use them to smoke pot, they are water pipes, used to smoke flavored tobacco," I said.

Continuing our jaunt through Istanbul, the next day we went under the ground to view the palatial Sistern Basilica, a 6th-century underground reservoir supported by 336 columns. This calming, mystical structure is so quiet that you can hear a drop of water fall on the vast water that blankets the ground. Two stone-carved Medusas add flair, with one upside down to cast a right-side-up reflection in the water.

Our next activity was totally random. Since Alison reads all Agatha Christie mysteries, we heard of the hotel where this author wrote many of her books, including *Murder on the Orient Express*. So we hailed a cab and went to Hotel Perla Palas where we had tea and cookies served in elegant silver dishes. We toured the lobby and the dining room so we could soak up some of the writing aura that embraced this famous author.

We reluctantly departed Istanbul the next day. This captivating city had lured us with its historical treasures, dramatic architecture, and startling sights. The kids can't stop talking Turkey—nor can we.

TURKEY OVERVIEW

- Turkey: Slightly larger than Texas
- Population: 67 million
- Capital: Ankara (Population: 3 million)
- Ethnicity: 86% Turkish, 11% Kurdish, 2% Arab, 1% other
- Religious Affiliation: 99% Muslim (mostly Sunni), 1% Christian and Jewish
- Official language: Turkish
- Currency: Turkish Lira

PLANNING AND PREPARATION

Passports

In addition to a valid passport, U.S. citizens are also required to have a visa, which can be obtained at the Turkish Consulate, or at the border.

When to Go

In the spring and fall temperatures are most pleasant. Summer months are hot, but not humid. In the winter, temperatures can drop considerably and are cold enough for snow; prices are at their lowest in winter.

Health Issues

Check with your travel clinic for advice about vaccinations against diphtheria, hepatitis A, tetanus, and polio. These immunizations are not required but could be recommended. Families that go to the coasts of the Marmara or the Black Sea should consider anti-malaria pills. Do not drink tap water. Bottled water is recommended.

Hospitals vary greatly in Turkey, except private medical facilities in Istanbul and Ankara, which have modern equipment, however these facilities may be unable to treat serious medical conditions.

Safety

Street crime is low in Turkey, however, families should exercise the same cautions they take in the U.S. and keep valuables out of sight. Security is stable in Turkey, however there have been infrequent incidents of internal terrorism, not directed towards Americans. These incidents have occurred in parts of Southeastern Turkey, and the Turkish government is committed to eliminating this internal issue.

What to Bring

Bring comfortable clothing and shoes for hiking around. I advised my daughter not to wear the clothes she wears at home, such as the bare midriff and other revealing styles.

THINGS TO SEE AND DO

Activities for Kids

- As you visit the Grand Bazaar, have your children find small items that are typically Turkish. If they want to purchase them, depending on your children's ages, have them bargain for them. This is expected. Start at half the asking price, then after some haggling, come to an agreement. Make sure they do it politely.
- A minaret is a tall slender tower attached to a mosque. Most mosques have two to five, although the Blue Mosque has six. The minaret's balcony houses the "muezzin," or crier, who calls the faithful to prayer five times each day. There are a variety of shapes of minarets—round, square, and multi-sided. Encourage your children to draw the many different minarets they observe.
- As you visit a mosque, encourage your children to explain the differences between their religion and Islam.

The Grand Bazaar and Egyptian Spice Market—Open daily, except Sunday, from 8:30 A.M. until 7:00 P.M.

Topkapi Palace—Open daily, except Tuesday, from 8:30 A.M. until 4:30 P.M. Admission $4.

Hagia Sophia—Open daily, except Monday, from 9:30 A.M. to 4:30 P.M. Admission $5.

Blue Mosque—This famous mosque and other mosques are open all the time. Entry is free. If not dressed properly, one may borrow proper attire at the door of most mosques.

Bosporus Cruise—There are several options for this cruise, from inexpensive ferries to boats that provide dinner. On this trip, families will observe palaces, lavish summer homes and embassies as well as other intriguing sights. Most ferry boats leave from Eminonu dock number three for the four- to five-hour round trip. Cost: $3. The dinner boats leave from Bebek, north of Istanbul. The fare is between $30 and $50.

Hotels

Konuk Evi—Rates: $90–$160. Situated in a four-story Ottoman mansion, this elegant hotel is at the center of many sites. Tel: (90) 212 513 36 60. Fax: (90) 212 513 36 69. To make reservations: ayapans@escortnet.com.

Yesil Ev—Rates: $150–$200. Also located in an Ottoman mansion, this hotel is situated between the Blue Mosque and the Hagia Sophia. Tel: (90) 212 5176785. Reservations: yesilevhotel@superonline.com.

Restaurants

Daruzziyafe Sifahane Cad—No. 6 Suleymaniye. Tel: (90) 212 511 84 14. The oldest restaurant in Turkey. Ottoman cuisine is served in an authentic and peaceful atmosphere.

Pandelli Spice Market—Entrance no. 1, Eminonu. Tel: (90) 212 522 55 34. One of the best traditional restaurants of Istanbul. Pandelli restaurant serves traditional Ottoman Cuisine in the Spice Market.

Kor Agop Ordekli Bakkal Sok—No. 7, Kumkapi. Tel: (90) 212 517 23 34. Live traditional music, fish, grills, and starters.

RESOURCES

Official Website

www.discoverturkey.com

Books for Adults

Let's Go Turkey by Allison Melia
Eyewitness Travel Guide to Istanbul by Deni Brown
Istanbul: The Imperial City by John Freely

Ancient Turkey: A Traveller's History by Seton Lloyd
A Fez of the Heart: Travels Around Turkey in Search of a Hat by Jeremy Seal

Books for Children
Exploring Turkey by Amy Chaple
Daily Life in Ancient and Modern Istanbul by Robert Bator
Letters Home from Turkey by Lisa Halvorsen
Turkey: Enchantment of the World by Tamra Orr
Welcome to Turkey by Vimala Alexander

Videos and DVDs
Eastern Cities: Prague, Budapest and Istanbul

TEENS TRAVELING
ABROAD

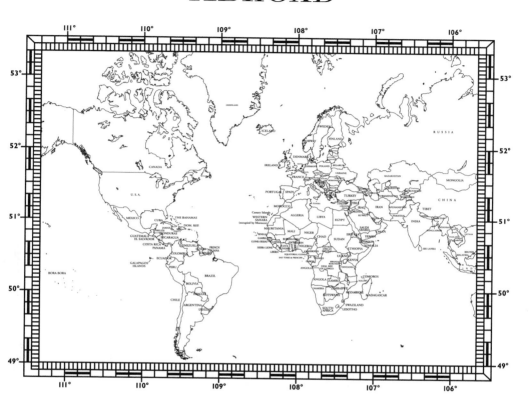

Alison Nichols at home with her Turkish family in Gunduzlu, Turkey.

CHAPTER 28

TEEN TRIPS
AROUND THE WORLD

SELECTING THE RIGHT TRIP

Our two children attended the typical range of summer camps as they progressed through elementary and middle school. In early elementary they joined local and school-based summer programs. In their later elementary years, nearby day camps that offered adventure activities and a two-night campout were the norm. By middle school, they each had found a multi-week overnight camp to attend in the mountains of Vermont with several close friends. Expecting our older child, our daughter, to sign up for the Vermont camp again after 8th grade, we were quite surprised when she requested a trip to Spain in place of her summer camp in Vermont.

While we had already traveled abroad quite extensively with our kids, we had never contemplated sending a 14 year old alone to a foreign country. But we were open minded and as we researched options we discovered numerous well-supervised programs that could provide us peace of mind and provide our daughter a superb growth experience.

Teens can choose from three basic categories of "abroad" programs: language study, community service, and adventure/culture.

Sometimes these categories are blended, for example some teen trips begin with a community service project and end with a mountain trek or whitewater rafting. All three types of trips sometimes include a homestay where the student spends a week or more living with a host family—often communicating in the local language.

Trip organizers cater to students from 14 to 18 years old, generally graduates of 8th through 11th grades. Typically they group students by age level: ages 14 and 15 together and ages 16 to 18 together. Duration of trips is usually four to five weeks, late June to early August. Prices for summer programs abroad range from $1,000 to $2,000 per week. Community Service programs generally price out at the lower end of the range. The more expensive programs often, but not always, include airfare in their tuition.

After our daughter, then 14, returned from her summer language program in Spain with glowing enthusiasm and much improved Spanish-speaking skills, we were sold on the concept. She has, in subsequent summers, been to Ireland on a community service program, back to Spain for more language study, and to Turkey where she lived in a small village with a traditional Turkish family and where she and her trip participants built a new volleyball court at the local school. She even convinced her younger brother to follow her footsteps to Spain when he turned 14, and he is scheduled to return to Spain to continue language study in his 15th summer.

If your teenager is interested in a language program overseas, have him read the **Language Trips for Teens** in the words of our 14-year-old son about his summer language study in Spain.

If instead, he or she is interested in Community Service travel, then skip several pages to **Community Service for Teens** by our 17-year-old daughter. Her report describes the program in Turkey in which she participated.

Language Trips for Teens

by Will Nichols

I saw the group of 15 kids who stood together on the far side of the terminal in JFK Airport. I was nervous as I cautiously approached them, hoping that I would fit in with these strangers since I would be spending the next five weeks with them. As I got closer, I noticed that they too looked anxious, and occasionally chatted with one another, but I could tell that they felt the same way I did. We were gathering here for the same reason: to spend five weeks in Spain, learn about Spanish culture, study the language, but most of all, to have fun adjusting to a foreign country and an unfamiliar atmosphere.

I introduced myself to the other three boys first, and then to the girls, some of whom were still standing with their parents. I then met the group leaders, a male and a female, both just out of college. I began to bond with other group members, especially with a boy who happened to live near my hometown. We discovered that we both played basketball and football, and after about an hour, I felt as though I had known him for years.

As our group boarded the plane to fly to Madrid, I felt excited, but nervous to leave my home country for five weeks. However, apprehension faded as I spent time with this group, and it had disappeared by the time we landed in Madrid. Upon arriving, we were exhausted after more than 12 hours of non-stop travel. We found the hotel with ease and promptly everyone was asleep.

Early the next morning, we boarded the train to Luarca, a small fishing town in northern Spain. During the six-hour train ride, our group continued to bond and become closer. We shared details about our personal lives, families, friends, and hometowns. The topographically diverse and beautiful Spanish countryside flew by as we headed north. Luarca was too small to support a train station, so we got off in the nearby city of Oviedo, and from there we continued on a bus to Luarca. As we entered the village, I immediately noticed the small-town beauty and the grassy rolling hills. Many fishing boats were crowded around the dock, and seafood restaurants lined the streets.

We stayed in Luarca for nearly a week, socializing with the locals and tasting northern Spanish culture. We embarked on a canoe trip one day, went to the beach another, and later hiked up a mountain for a picnic lunch. Trying to fit in with the local teenagers, we danced at the local discotheque and eventually found our groove. Our group leaders organized language exercises in the mornings, which were always informative and often very fun. For example, during a scavenger hunt throughout the town, one item we needed to find was a hair from a man's beard. This involved asking a stranger in Spanish for his hair. This was quite humorous and rather embarrassing . . . but he did comply.

After six days in Luarca, we left for a tiny spot, called Cordiñones de Valdeon, in the Picos de Europa— the mountains of northern Spain. Here, we slept in a very clean, comfortable, family-run hostel, mostly attracting young hikers and backpackers. It was situated between towering and breathtaking peaks. Each morning we rose early, at least by teenage standards, and hiked as a group to a beautiful location high in the mountains, where we would eat a picnic lunch. On these journeys, I shot countless photographs of the incredible peaks that poked through the clouds. Each night, the hotel proprietors prepared delicious homemade dinners for us in their large communal dining room. After dinner, I sat out on the hostel's patio and enjoyed the view and admired the sunset over the Picos de Europa.

A 10-hour bus ride from Cordiñones took us to Cuenca, a city to the east of Madrid, where we were to stay with a Spanish family for a week. My Spanish "mother," Ada, came racing around the corner of the bus station in a small, dilapidated yellow Peugeot that had to be at least 30 years old. I nervously greeted her, threw my luggage in the trunk, and hopped into the old jalopy. We arrived at her fourth floor apartment, and Ada immediately offered me a mouth-watering meal of home-cooked chicken and French fries. She then gave me a brief description of Cuenca: the history, hangouts, nightlife, restaurants, and the Old Town. Ada then called up a teenage boy she knew, and he and a friend picked me up in a two-seater blasting the latest Spanish hits. I squeezed into the back and off we went, first to listen to music in a run-down complex that housed practice rooms for amateur bands, and then to the cliff that overlooked the old section of Cuenca.

Each night in Cuenca, I would meet up with my American friends and some new Spanish friends, and we would all stroll over to "La Calle," a street where many discos and clubs were located. We would dance and attempt to blend into the Spanish culture. Although we never really blended, we did manage to meet and befriend some young Spaniards. That in itself was very rewarding.

During the day in Cuenca, I would socialize at the local swimming pool, the hangout spot for every self-respecting teenager, until the early afternoon. I would then explore a section of the city, or take advantage of some special event. For instance, a medieval fair was held in the Old Town on one occasion. With two friends, I ventured to it and immersed myself in old Moorish arts and crafts, the traditional swords and daggers of the region, and the intense smell of roasting pig and other "Medieval" foods. I paid 10 Euros to be hennaed (temporary tattoo) by a man dressed as a 16th century Moorish peasant.

Every day in Cuenca, I experienced something new and exciting. This home stay portion of the program was my favorite part, and I was reluctant to leave the city I had fallen in love with after just a week. Hugs and goodbyes were exchanged between my American companions and their Spanish "families" as we boarded the bus for our next destination.

Another 10-hour bus trip took us to Spain's capital city, Madrid. Upon arriving, we visited the Plaza Mayor in the heart of the city. Buildings there were once used as a home for the government; they now function as high-end apartments, and the plaza is lined with countless souvenir shops and *tapas* bars. We visited Madrid's Palacio Real, as well as the Prado and the Reina-Sofia museums. Although art museums and ancient history are not always appealing to teenagers, we were able to practice our Spanish there and I enjoyed seeing these sights.

From Madrid, we took the train to Granada, the heart of southern Spain—a region once ruled by Moors from Morocco. Consequently, Granada has a lot of North African influences, apparent all over the city. We walked to the Albacín, Granada's Moorish neighborhood, where we explored the Arabian Market that stretches for blocks in all directions. Virtually everything in the market was a North African product, from the engraved Arabic plaques to the Islam-inspired art. After spending the entire morning in the market, we lunched at an authentic Moroccan restaurant.

Granada is renowned for its Flamenco dancers, and we found a small Flamenco joint one night. We all crowded into the one-room performance area, and as the show began, I let myself become totally immersed in the spellbinding rhythm as the dancers passionately stomped their feet. I loved watching the graceful dancers twirl and move, and I was mesmerized throughout the show.

Our last night in Granada, we rented a two-hour time slot in a traditional Arabic bath house. We entered the steam-filled room, with mosaic-covered walls, and relaxed first in a hot pool, and then in a cold one. I continued this cycle for a while, until my turn came for a massage from a professional masseur. Afterwards, I felt more relaxed than I had ever felt before, as I suspect was the purpose of the bath house.

We awoke early the next morning for our next destination: A nauseatingly long and winding road carried us up through the Sierra Nevada mountain range to a small village called Capileira. Capileira attracts many hikers and mountaineers, as it lies only one hour away from Spain's tallest peak, the Mulhacen, over 11,000 feet high. We stayed in a charming pension with the traditional whitewashed walls of southern Spain and a breathtaking view of the valley below. One morning, the more adventurous group members woke at 5:00 A.M. to hike up to the top of the Mulhacen. We took a sleepy one hour bus ride to the base of the mountain, where we met our guide, a comical guy named Fernando who amused us with his interpretations of the English language. The 12-mile hike took us about five hours to the top, and a little less than that back down. From the summit, we could see North Africa across the Mediterranean Sea. Exhausted, we descended and returned to the pension for a relaxing swim in the pool.

From Capileira, we proceeded further south to a small beach town on the Costa Blanca called San José. Mainly a tourist town, San José is home to beautiful white-sand beaches and warm azure-blue waters. Many Italian immigrants had settled in the town years ago, and consequently, San José boasted numerous excellent Italian restaurants, to go along with the countless seafood places that lined the beach.

This was our final destination in Spain, and with only three days left before we split up and went home, we decided to make the best of our remaining time together. This meant relaxing on the beach, swimming, exploring, shopping, and taking in the sights and smells of Spain's southern coast. We reminisced about everything we had experienced during the trip. We admitted to mixed feelings about leaving the country we had all grown accustomed to over the preceding five weeks.

As I laid on the beach the day prior to returning home, I mused over how I had grown over the past five weeks. Not only had my Spanish language skills improved, but I had become noticeably more confident and independent as well. It was satisfying to see the coalescing of 15 young people as they worked together in a foreign country and relied on each other for support. By the end, I felt a sense of trust and oneness with the group. As I stared out across the intense indigo of the Mediterranean, I envisioned returning home and plopping down in my favorite armchair, resuming my normal and familiar routines. But then a strange notion entered my head: Spain, this foreign place I had come to love, would suit me just as well.

COMMUNITY SERVICE FOR TEENS

by Alison McDonell Nichols

Dinner was set, and I was hungry. I sat cross-legged on the ground and waited until everyone had joined me before reaching for the food: fresh-baked bread, stuffed tomatoes and peppers, yogurt with cucumbers, and green beans. And plenty of hot, sugary tea. We were about to dig in when we heard the *muezzin*, the call to prayer, emanating from a nearby mosque. The room suddenly went silent as everyone lowered their heads respectfully. As soon as it was over, the women begin to talk and joke as my host mother poured the tea.

It was the summer of 2002, and I was in Gunduzlu, Turkey, a small, traditional village five hours southeast of Istanbul. My 11 group members and I were a novelty in the village, as we were the first foreigners to visit. Night after night, the village women came to the house in which I was staying to welcome me and find out what

Americans were really like. After almost two weeks here, I felt comfortable laughing with these women, even though they spoke no English, and I spoke little Turkish. Now I could even laugh at the memory of myself arriving in the village two weeks previously, nervous and not knowing what to expect. I had climbed out of the rickety bus and into a different world. The few people on the main road (a wide, dusty street) stared at me curiously. My new "family" was waiting to meet me. The two daughters, 18 and 21, wore colorful headscarves, while their mother wore a long black skirt and black shawl, with a black headscarf. Her 12-year-old son hung back shyly. They smiled warmly at me, but I began to panic when I determined that they spoke no English. Doubts began to fly through my head. They were so different from me—would they even like me? How would I communicate with them? Would I be able to adjust to their way of life? How would I be expected to dress? In my halting Turkish, I introduced myself and tried to sound more confident than I felt.

The days flew by, and between working with my group to build a volleyball court at a local school and adapting to my host family's lifestyle, I was very busy. I prepared food with my host mother and sisters, kneading dough that would later be baked in the clay oven outside the house, visited the mosque and learned how they pray, and milked cows at a neighbor's house. I began to feel at home, and the things that had seemed so strange to me upon my arrival now became more natural. I could even understand some Turkish.

Much too soon, I found myself packing my bags. On the evening that I was due to leave, many new friends came over to bid me goodbye. As I hugged one after another, tearfully promising to write and thanking them for being so kind, I realized something: these people were little different from my family and friends back in America.

Although they spoke a different language, observed a different religion, and led a totally different lifestyle, they shared the same hopes and fears as families from my culture. My host mother worried that her oldest daughter's boyfriend wasn't right for her. My host father wanted his children to get a better education. His daughters gossiped with their friends about boys, school, strict parents, other friends . . . the same things that I talked about with my friends back home. I never would have guessed this two weeks earlier, marveling at the "strangeness" of everything. Some things would always remain different: hearing the call to prayer five times a day, or the fact that only men could go to the tiny cafes lining the main street. But I now could see deeper than those surface disparities. I could see that families all over the world have more in common than in contrast.

I have always enjoyed traveling for the opportunity it gives me to explore new cultures. However, I now realize that travel should not only expose us to the aspects of the culture that are dissimilar to our own, but also make us realize how much we have in common with people all over the world.

RESOURCES

An excellent resource to help parents and children find the appropriate summer program to match a child's interest is Student Camp & Trip Advisors (SCATA). This no-fee organization (over 700 camps and summer programs fund SCATA) is based in a Boston suburb. SCATA will ask you to fill out a questionnaire regarding your child's summer interests, then they will respond with several programs that should be of interest to you and your child. They will send brochures, applications, and program descriptions. Families contact the program providers directly—and mention that SCATA referred them.

Student Camp and Trip Advisors
181 Wells Ave.
Newton Centre, MA 02459
(800) 542-1233
www.campadvisors.com/

Our children had especially good experiences with the following summer programs:

Putney Student Travel—This program offers language, community service, and adventure travel for teenagers. Destinations are worldwide, including some in the U.S. The company has been providing summer programs for over 50 years.

Putney Student Travel
345 Hickory Ridge Road
Putney, Vermont 05346
Tel: (802) 387-5000 Fax: (802) 387-4276
www.goputney.com/index.html

Global Works—They have been in business since 1988. All Global Works programs provide community service and adventure activities, some programs also offer other features such as homestays and language learning. Global Works boasts of a 5-to-1 student-to-staff ratio.

Global Works, Inc.
RD2, Box 173 A
Huntingdon, PA 16652 U.S.A
Tel: (814) 667-2411 Fax (814) 667-3853
www.globalworksinc.com/index.htm

Academic Study Associates—ASA offers intensive language instruction at three locations in France, five in Spain and one in China. Students either live on the campus of a university or participate in a homestay program. ASA has been providing excellent language programs for 20 years.

ASA Programs
10 New King Street
White Plains, NY 10604
Tel: (800) 752-2250 Fax: (800) 686-7740
www.asaprograms.com/flash/index.html

Experiment in International Living—This program is the granddaddy of them all, having been in business over 70 years. They currently offer travel to 26 countries for a wide range of activities, including community service, language study, travel, peace studies, ecology, the arts, and outdoor adventure.

Experiment in International Living
P.O. Box 676
Brattleboro, Vermont 05302-0676
Tel: (800) 345-2929 Fax: (802) 258-3428
www.experiment.org/

Rassias—They offer a limited but highly effective menu of language programs. Spanish at three sites in Spain and French at two sites in France make up the options. Classes are taught in the Rassias Method, an intensive training technique developed at Dartmouth College in the late 1960s. Homestay and in-country travel are included.
Rassias Programs
P.O. Box 5456
Hanover, NH 03755
Tel: (603) 643-3007 Fax: (603) 643-4249
www.rassias.com/

Bill and Jennifer Nichols on board a ketch off the Galapagos Islands.

ABOUT THE AUTHORS

JENNIFER MCDONELL NICHOLS and her husband, Bill, believe in global family travel. In fact, once their children were born they gave each one a three-month respite, then bundled them up to travel across continents and oceans. Now teenagers, these two children have journeyed to 27 countries on five continents, and have participated in safaris, animal treks, sports adventures, historical trips, eco-tourism, camping, cruises, hiking, farm holidays, visits to indigenous cultures, and just relaxing. These traveling children provided their parents with broad-based experiences of the rigors, challenges, and joys of traveling with children.

Jennifer M. Nichols published travel articles on global family adventures in the *Los Angeles Times, Boston Globe, Denver Post, Kansas City Star*, and *Diversion Magazine*. She traveled to 55 countries and lived in Europe and Central America, and her two teenagers traveled to 27 countries on five continents.

Bill Nichols has been the travel partner and writing collaborator of Jennifer M. Nichols for the past 31 years. As a child he traveled domestically with his family, but after marrying Jennifer, he began his global explorations. He has now visited 58 countries. When he's not globetrotting, Bill works as a marketing strategy consultant. He lives in Newton Centre, Massachusetts.

About the contributors

Cindy McDonell Mitchell lives in Chicago and has traveled the world with her son and husband. Ms. Mitchell, Chicago Parks Commissioner, also heads the Chicago-Casablanca, Morocco sister city program.

Sonia Ehrlich Sachs has journeyed the world with her husband and three children; in fact, her eight-year-old daughter must hold the world travel record for her age—she has been to 40 countries. Ms. Ehrlich Sachs, a pediatrician, lives in New York City.

Mary Nichols Sandoval has lived in Iran, Saudi Arabia, and Qatar with her husband and two children, and has traveled that part of the world extensively. Currently living in Madrid, Spain, Ms. Sandoval is a teacher at the International School of Madrid.

Kerry McDonell Halasz is a professional photographer living with her husband and three children in Alpharetta, Georgia. She is relatively new to exotic travel, but once she started she did it in style by staying in a medieval Tuscan castle, riding camel-back in the Sahara, and participating in a dinosaur dig in Niger.

BOOKS AVAILABLE
FROM SANTA MONICA PRESS

Blues for Bird
by Martin Gray
288 pages $16.95

The Book of Good Habits
*Simple and Creative Ways
to Enrich Your Life*
by Dirk Mathison
224 pages $9.95

The Butt Hello
*and other ways my cats
drive me crazy*
by Ted Meyer
96 pages $9.95

Café Nation
*Coffee Folklore, Magick,
and Divination*
by Sandra Mizumoto Posey
224 pages $9.95

Cats Around the World
by Ted Meyer
96 pages $9.95

**Discovering the History
of Your House**
and Your Neighborhood
by Betsy J. Green
288 pages $14.95

Dogme Uncut
*Lars von Trier, Thomas Vinterberg and
the Gang That Took on Hollywood*
by Jack Stevenson
312 pages $16.95

Exploring Our Lives
*A Writing Handbook for
Senior Adults*
by Francis E. Kazemek
288 pages $14.95

Exotic Travel Destinations for Families
by Jennifer M. Nichols and Bill Nichols
360 pages $16.95

Footsteps in the Fog
Alfred Hitchcock's San Francisco
by Jeff Kraft and
Aaron Leventhal
240 pages $24.95

**Free Stuff & Good Deals for Folks
over 50, 2nd Ed.**
by Linda Bowman
240 pages $12.95

**How to Find Your Family Roots
and Write Your Family History**
by William Latham and
Cindy Higgins
288 pages $14.95

How to Speak Shakespeare
by Cal Pritner and
Louis Colaianni
144 pages $16.95

**How to Win Lotteries, Sweepstakes,
and Contests in the 21st Century**
by Steve "America's Sweepstakes King"
Ledoux
224 pages $14.95

**Jackson Pollock: Memories Arrested
in Space**
by Martin Gray
224 pages $14.95

James Dean Died Here
*The Locations of America's Pop Culture
Landmarks*
by Chris Epting
312 pages $16.95

The Keystone Kid
Tales of Early Hollywood
by Coy Watson, Jr.
312 pages $24.95

Letter Writing Made Easy!
*Featuring Sample Letters for Hundreds
of Common Occasions*
by Margaret McCarthy
224 pages $12.95

**Letter Writing Made Easy!
Volume 2**
*Featuring More Sample Letters for
Hundreds of Common Occasions*
by Margaret McCarthy
224 pages $12.95

Nancy Shavick's Tarot Universe
by Nancy Shavick
336 pages $15.95

Offbeat Food
*Adventures in an
Omnivorous World*
by Alan Ridenour
240 pages $19.95

Offbeat Marijuana
*The Life and Times of the
World's Grooviest Plant*
by Saul Rubin
240 pages $19.95

Offbeat Museums
*The Collections and Curators of
America's Most Unusual Museums*
by Saul Rubin
240 pages $19.95

Past Imperfect
*How Tracing Your Family Medical
History Can Save Your Life*
by Carol Daus
240 pages $12.95

A Prayer for Burma
by Kenneth Wong
216 pages $14.95

Quack!
*Tales of Medical Fraud from
the Museum of Questionable Medical
Devices*
by Bob McCoy
240 pages $19.95

Redneck Haiku
by Mary K. Witte
112 pages $9.95

The Seven Sacred Rites of Menarche
*The Spiritual Journey of the
Adolescent Girl*
by Kristi Meisenbach Boylan
160 pages $11.95

**The Seven Sacred Rites
of Menopause**
*The Spiritual Journey to
the Wise-Woman Years*
by Kristi Meisenbach Boylan
144 pages $11.95

Silent Echoes
*Discovering Early Hollywood Through
the Films of Buster Keaton*
by John Bengtson
240 pages $24.95

Tiki Road Trip
*A Guide to Tiki Culture in
North America*
by James Teitelbaum
288 pages $16.95

What's Buggin' You?
*Michael Bohdan's Guide to
Home Pest Control*
by Michael Bohdan
256 pages $12.95

ORDER FORM 1-800-784-9553

	Quantity	Amount
Blues for Bird (epic poem about Charlie Parker) ($16.95)	_____	_____
The Book of Good Habits ($9.95)	_____	_____
The Butt Hello . . . and Other Ways My Cats Drive Me Crazy ($9.95)	_____	_____
Café Nation: Coffee Folklore, Magick and Divination ($9.95)	_____	_____
Cats Around the World ($9.95)	_____	_____
Discovering the History of Your House. . . ($14.95)	_____	_____
Dogme Uncut ($16.95)	_____	_____
Exotic Travel Destinations for Families ($16.95)	_____	_____
Exploring Our Lives: A Writing Handbook for Senior Adults ($14.95)	_____	_____
Footsteps in the Fog: Alfred Hitchcock's San Francisco ($24.95)	_____	_____
Free Stuff & Good Deals for Folks over 50, 2nd Ed. ($12.95)	_____	_____
How to Find Your Family Roots . . . ($14.95)	_____	_____
How to Speak Shakespeare ($16.95)	_____	_____
How to Win Lotteries, Sweepstakes, and Contests . . . ($14.95)	_____	_____
Jackson Pollock: Memories Arrested in Space ($14.95)	_____	_____
James Dean Died Here: America's Pop Culture Landmarks ($16.95)	_____	_____
The Keystone Kid: Tales of Early Hollywood ($24.95)	_____	_____
Letter Writing Made Easy! ($12.95)	_____	_____
Letter Writing Made Easy! Volume 2 ($12.95)	_____	_____
Nancy Shavick's Tarot Universe ($15.95)	_____	_____
Offbeat Food ($19.95)	_____	_____
Offbeat Marijuana ($19.95)	_____	_____
Offbeat Museums ($19.95)	_____	_____
Past Imperfect: Tracing Your Family Medical History ($12.95)	_____	_____
A Prayer for Burma ($14.95)	_____	_____
Quack! Tales of Medical Fraud ($19.95)	_____	_____
Redneck Haiku ($9.95)	_____	_____
The Seven Sacred Rites of Menarche ($11.95)	_____	_____
The Seven Sacred Rites of Menopause ($11.95)	_____	_____
Silent Echoes: Early Hollywood Through Buster Keaton ($24.95)	_____	_____
Tiki Road Trip ($16.95)	_____	_____
What's Buggin' You?: A Guide to Home Pest Control ($12.95)	_____	_____

Shipping & Handling:	Subtotal _____
1 book **$3.00**	CA residents add 8.25% sales tax _____
Each additional book is **$ .50**	Shipping and Handling (see left) _____
	TOTAL _____

Name _____

Address _____

City _____ State _____ Zip _____

❏ Visa ❏ MasterCard   Card No.: _____

Exp. Date _____ Signature _____

❏ Enclosed is my check or money order payable to:

Santa Monica Press LLC
P.O. Box 1076
Santa Monica, CA 90406
www.santamonicapress.com 1-800-784-9553